The Business
of Higher Education

The Business of Higher Education

Volume 3: Marketing and Consumer Interests

JOHN C. KNAPP AND DAVID J. SIEGEL, EDITORS

PRAEGER PERSPECTIVES

PRAEGER
An Imprint of ABC-CLIO, LLC

A B C ❖ C L I O

Santa Barbara, California • Denver, Colorado • Oxford, England

Copyright 2009 by John C. Knapp and David J. Siegel

All rights reserved. No part of this publication may be reproduced, stored in a retrieval system, or transmitted, in any form or by any means, electronic, mechanical, photocopying, recording, or otherwise, except for the inclusion of brief quotations in a review, without prior permission in writing from the publisher.

Library of Congress Cataloging-in-Publication Data

The business of higher education / John C. Knapp and David J. Siegel, editors.
   v. cm. — (Praeger perspectives)
  Includes bibliographical references and index.
  ISBN 978-0-313-35350-5 (set: alk. paper) ISBN 978-0-313-35351-2 (set ebook) v. 1. Leadership and culture ISBN 978-0-313-35352-9 (v. 1: alk. paper) ISBN 978-0-313-35353-6 (v. 1 ebook) — v. 2. Management and fiscal strategies ISBN 978-0-313-35354-3 (v. 2: alk. paper) ISBN 978-0-313-35355-0 (v. 2 ebook) — v. 3. Marketing and consumer interests. ISBN 978-0-313-35356-7 (v. 3 alk. paper) ISBN 978-0-313-35357-4 (v. 3 ebook)
  1. Education, Higher—United States—Finance. 2. Universities and colleges—United States—Finance. I. Knapp, John C. II. Siegel, David J., 1966–
  LB2342.B88 2009
  378.1′060973—dc22   2009027997

13 12 11 10 09   1 2 3 4 5

This book is also available on the World Wide Web as an eBook.
Visit www.abc-clio.com for details.

ABC-CLIO, LLC
130 Cremona Drive, P.O. Box 1911
Santa Barbara, California 93116-1911

This book is printed on acid-free paper ∞
Manufactured in the United States of America

Chapter 2 is excerpted from "CASE Principles of Practice for Communications and Marketing Professionals at Educational Institutions," adopted by the CASE Board of Trustees in July 2004. Copyright © Council for Advancement and Support of Education. Used with permission. Web site: http://www.case.org/Content/AboutCASE/Display.cfm?CONTAINERRID=127&CONTENTITEMID=4384&CRUMB=3.

Chapter 11 is reprinted with permission from Education Sector Reports, September 2006. © Copyright 2006 Education Sector. All rights reserved. 1201 Connecticut Ave., N.W., Suite 850, Washington, D.C. 20036. http://www.educationsector.org.

Contents

Foreword by E. Gordon Gee — *vii*

General Introduction — *xi*

Introduction to Volume 3 by John C. Knapp and David J. Siegel — *xv*

Chapter 1	University Leadership in an Era of Hyperaccountability *John C. Knapp*	1
Chapter 2	Universities and the Business Practice of Marketing *Curtis Carlson*	21
Chapter 3	Marketing the Academy: Benefits and Barriers *Larry D. Lauer*	47
Chapter 4	Seeing Is Believing *Malcolm Grear*	57
Chapter 5	Coping with Crises: Special Challenges for Universities *Andrew Westmoreland*	77
Chapter 6	The Escalation of Consumerism in Higher Education *Michael S. Harris*	89

Chapter 7	Academic Customer Service *Neal A. Raisman*	107
Chapter 8	The Pre-College Quagmire *Rachel Toor*	127
Chapter 9	The Importance of Business and Economic Models in Understanding the Historical Provision of Student Aid *Fred Galloway*	153
Chapter 10	The Business of Intercollegiate Athletics *J. Douglas Toma*	179
Chapter 11	College Rankings Reformed: The Case for a New Order in Higher Education *Kevin Carey*	217
About the Editors and Contributors		*255*
Index		*267*

Foreword

Today, higher education faces a simple choice: reinvention or extinction. I write this with a mixture of caution and optimism. The economic meltdown that has swept the globe has brought colleges and universities to the edge of chaos. Budgets are up. Endowments are down. Too many students and too many families are stranded in debt. These are, by any calculation, difficult times. But they are also times of tremendous opportunity. Financial pressures are bringing to the surface issues that we have kept under the carpet for far too long. Our communities are counting more than ever on the promise of postsecondary education. By abandoning bunker mentality and pushing forward, this can be the moment when we transform our institutions and reimagine higher education in America.

Change, of course, will not come easy. In fact, it would be hard to imagine a more formidable challenge. The modern university is a juggernaut, with little material resemblance to our ancient roots or nineteenth-century pedigree. At my own institution—The Ohio State University—the sheer complexity of a campus with 60,000 students and 40,000 faculty and staff is mind-boggling, and that is before factoring in development officers, athletics departments, and research facilities that generate more revenue than most small businesses. In their wildest dreams, neither Aristotle nor James Morrill could have imagined schools the size of cities, complete with multibillion dollar budgets, high-rises, and medical centers.

How do we manage, let alone revolutionize, these vast and sprawling institutions? How do we make them intellectually agile, responsive to the needs of students, and free from Kafkaesque bureaucracies? How do we help the university achieve its pride of place in the American project, as both our economic engine and the center of our civic life?

These are the core questions taken up in *The Business of Higher Education*. And, I am pleased to report, the contributors' answers are both honest and robust. Drawing from a multiplicity of perspectives within the academy, the scholars and administrators in these volumes have carved out the critical debates facing higher education today. Even more important, they have framed the debates without taking refuge in that famous false binary: the Ivory Tower versus the corporate university. After nearly 30 years of leading universities, I have yet to meet the oft-demonized bureaucrat who wants to turn the classroom into an assembly line, nor the faculty member whose raison d'être is to indoctrinate students and then secede from society. Simplification is a natural response to an overwhelming challenge, but the stakes are simply too high for us to continue invoking scarecrows and bogeymen.

Our metaphors do matter, however, which is why the intellectual haggling that occurs in the chapters that follow is so important. And with all due respect to the editors, I have to take sides on one issue: "business" is too clumsy a word to capture our character or our sublime purpose. Teaching that profoundly changes lives and research that expands the boundaries of the knowable universe cannot be reduced to dollars and cents. Further, to allow science to flourish and to allow our students to cultivate an appreciation for reason, we must preserve the sanctity of a sphere beyond the influence of commerce and beyond the vicissitudes of politics. How we choose to discuss higher education will indelibly shape it, and equating knowledge with a product, and students with consumers, is neither the best way to envision ourselves, nor an effective way to articulate our unique mission to others.

But just because higher education is not a business does not mean that we should not thrive and compete, or that we should not cultivate and hire the best leadership available. The ideal of the university—whether expressed by Newman or Dewey—is precisely that: an ideal. Historians will never find a university that was not reliant on some measure of business, governmental, or philanthropic support, and the 21st-century university must forge productive relationships with all three. Competing for federal research dollars, encouraging innovative partnerships with industry, and building the community coalitions that can make a difference in people's lives require that we maintain state-of-the-art facilities, invest wisely, and manage with superhuman efficiency. It also means that we must harness the tools of marketing, branding, and public relations to champion our achievements. Just as we respect and trust our astrophysicists' ability to chart new planets, or our English professors' knowledge of narrative, so we must rely on the expertise of those who can best steer our course in the economic arena.

Achieving our economic potential while maintaining academic integrity is a monumental task. But it is Herculean, not Sisyphean. Accountability does not mean servility to accountants. Nor does academic freedom mean willful irrelevance. Success will be the tightrope balance between ideals and expediency. We must move swiftly to achieve lasting partnerships with industry, but we must never sacrifice our higher calling to the bottom line. Likewise, we must learn to teach beyond the classroom walls, but we must never forget that departments and disciplines, not politicians and legislators, are the true judges of academic merit.

These challenges will never be resolved in the abstract; they will take root only in the realm of practice. To realign our institutions, we need a mission that demands a refocusing of our strength. Sustainability—the demand for new thinking about the environment and energy—presents one prime opportunity. At Ohio State, we are already beginning to use sustainability to reimagine our academic structures, bringing together departments and faculty that for too long have been connected only by a heating plant. Moving beyond "interdisciplinarity" and toward true transinstitutional partnership, these new connections between fields of study, between students, between industries, and even between universities are the first step toward realizing a renewed purpose for higher education, one that shares the fruits of our expertise, assures our relevancy, and gives external partners reasons to invest in us.

Change is a chain reaction, and by casting out old dogmas, we necessarily must reinvent our practices, including our centuries-old promotion and tenure model. This is not an argument for eliminating academic freedom; it is an effort to save it. If we wish to encourage innovative faculty collaboration and new forms of scholarship, academic publishing cannot remain our only metric of merit. Contrary to Marx's axiom, it may finally be time to acknowledge that not all of us are cut out to be teachers by day, department leaders in the afternoon, and world-class researchers at night. Let us stop punishing those who excel in *merely* one of these areas and begin thinking creatively about how to reward everyone for their vital contributions to the university community. And let us use this as an opportunity to fully appreciate the contributions of teachers throughout higher education, especially our embattled and undervalued community college colleagues, who are at the frontlines of higher education.

This will certainly be the most contentious of our conversations. And, as the essays in these volumes indicate, consensus will not come easy. But employment is the most critical question facing us, and where faculty, administration, and staff will find agreement is this: true inequity lies in opacity. We must acknowledge a long-overdue moral imperative to be transparent with our teachers, particularly the graduate students who work in the trenches of undergraduate education. Because of the tightening of the job market and changes in the faculty-mentor role, graduate assistantships—most notably in the humanities—have not been true apprenticeships for a generation. As many contributors to this book have noted, we have an obligation to cease such nostalgic talk and be straight with our students and adjuncts about the opportunities and realities of University employment. Only then can we make the adjustments necessary to recruit and retain the best and brightest teachers and thinkers and scientists, too many of whom we are currently losing to the private sector.

The challenges ahead of us are daunting. But the resources at our disposal are unparalleled. Higher education in America is the envy of the world, and at its heart is our thoroughly democratic *ethos,* which says that debate is always more valuable than consensus, and that from furious disagreement eventually comes wisdom and resolve. On campuses across this country, some of the most brilliant minds on the planet walk among us, and the time is now to apply their intellect to saving the institutions that we all hold so dear. We cannot wait for eureka moments, nor can we wait for gradual evolution. In our faculty meetings, hiring committees, conferences, and edited collections, we must begin in earnest to implement the changes we know are necessary for the Academy to emerge from this financial crisis as the rightful centerpiece of American intellectual, cultural, and economic life. The contributors to this volume have made a noble start; it is time for the rest of us to follow through.

E. Gordon Gee
Columbus, Ohio, March 2009

General Introduction

Anyone in and around higher education in recent years cannot have failed to notice the steadily rising hue and cry for academic institutions to operate more like business organizations. Perhaps it is unsurprising that an enterprise as massive, complex, and resource-intensive as higher education should find itself the subject of public demands to make it behave like other massive, complex, and resource-intensive enterprises, namely, large corporations. After all, like corporations, colleges and universities are increasingly viewed as engines of economic growth and prosperity, as key actors in a sprawling global economy. We in higher education may have differentiated ourselves from business in the past, but societal forces and even our own ambitions have thrust us into a closer relationship and resemblance, prompting one exasperated college president to ask, "Are we in the business of *higher education* or are we in the higher education *business?*"

Of course, this development has not gone uncontested. Many still view the academy as a distinctive institution, one endowed with a special purpose that is simply not subject to the dictates of economic rationalism. In a pluralistic society, as Edward Shils noted, various institutions and occupations must reflect legitimately different societal aims. It would be a mistake to judge any one of them by the standards of the others. Academic institutions, according to this logic, should operate like academic institutions.

There is arguably no issue on the horizon that forces us to explain ourselves—to ourselves, to our stakeholders, and to the general public—more than the push to be like business, because on one level, the "corporatization" of the academy stands as a threat to our very nature. By engaging the issue, then, we seize an opportunity to narrate ourselves to the world and make a compelling case for our survival as a valuable and relevant institutional form—a form that has proven resilient and vital since the Middle Ages. Whether business models and business thinking help to advance our cause in the 21st century is an open question, one that animates *The Business of Higher Education*.

This three-volume set explores mounting pressures for colleges and universities to change, and it considers the costs and benefits to our institutions and to society when academe embraces business models of cost-efficiency, marketing, employment, and customer service. Thought leaders from various quarters of higher education and business have contributed original essays on a range of topics related to this central theme. Indeed, one of the unique features of *The Business of Higher Education* is that it offers contrasting perspectives—by those within the academy and outside of it—on whether and how higher education and the public interest are ultimately helped or harmed by the application of business methods to essential academic functions. The multiplicity of voices and styles, we believe, fairly captures the complexity of this topic. In these pages, our objective is to model and advance a critical dialogue on the future of higher education in an era of increased public accountability and engagement with all sectors.

Readers may wonder straightaway what is meant by the particular phrasing of *the business of higher education*. We think it best to let the contributors speak to that question, open as the phrasing is to multiple interpretations. Briefly, though, we note that the title—the central organizing principle, as it were—can be read as pertaining simultaneously to the role or *mission* of higher education and the *manner* in which it goes about fulfilling that role or mission. That the phrasing also (and perhaps primarily) suggests an interaction between two arenas that are commonly held to be in opposition—higher education and business—is very much to the point of the dialogue that follows.

As far as this project is concerned, we do not start with a philosophical or ideological orientation with regard to the subject matter it addresses. Our hope is to illuminate key tensions the academy is experiencing as a citadel of learning, a publicly engaged institution, and an increasingly bureaucratic structure. The wide berth we gave to authors is commensurate with our own thinking on the matter, which can be described as ambivalent, conflicted, and (perhaps more positively) open to the merits of strong arguments.

These volumes do not aim to settle an argument. In fact, we observe that the argument has yet to specify its terms. What *is* the business model, for example, that higher education is being asked to emulate or adopt? Should we pattern our culture, strategy, and operations after those of AIG, Apple, or American Airlines? The injunction to become more businesslike does not by itself offer much guidance. It often seems a more convenient than helpful way to talk about how to solve whatever is perceived to be wrong with higher education.

ORGANIZATION OF THE SET

If we wanted to see or experience the business of higher education, where might we look for it? The organization of the book set points to (1) leadership and culture (the subject of volume 1), (2) management and fiscal strategies (the subject of volume 2), and (3) marketing and consumer interests (the subject of volume 3). These three themes may be visualized as concentric circles, with leadership and culture occupying the innermost core (to represent the character, values, and principles that define the academy), surrounded most immediately by management and fiscal strategies (that enable colleges and universities to better serve their purposes), followed by marketing and consumer interests (indicating the stakeholders for whom value is created and delivered, as well as the ways in which we interact with them). We suggest that the circles have dotted lines to indicate permeability; each of these areas constitutes and is constituted by the others. The general progression of the three volumes, then, goes from core values to enabling strategies to external constituencies.

AUDIENCE

Given the broad nature of the topic, the intended readership is wide-ranging. It includes academic leaders, business leaders, those charged with spanning the boundaries between the two sectors, parents, policymakers, scholars, and students.

From the beginning, our idea was to contribute new ideas and perspectives to the ongoing conversation. We invite readers to join the dialogue by arguing back to the contributors, by writing up their own thoughts, or by engaging colleagues in conversation about the contents of this set. The essays themselves are a testament to the virtues of unhurried contemplation and disciplined thinking about complex issues, exemplary of how the difficult and contentious dialogue about higher education's future must be conducted. Readers will find little in the way of the rash accusations that are so often hurled by critics of—or apologists for—higher education, who often appear to be more concerned with winning points for their arguments than with illuminating blind spots. In short, we hope readers will use the model provided by our contributors to extend and enrich public dialogue.

ACKNOWLEDGMENTS

For the editors, this project has been a rare opportunity to collaborate with an extraordinary group of thinkers, each of whom brings deep expertise and experience to this important conversation. We extend to them our gratitude for their superb contributions to these volumes. They have added much to our own appreciation and understanding of the multi-faceted business of higher education. We also appreciate the guidance provided by Jeff Olson, our able editor and advisor at Praeger Publishers.

On a more personal note, we are mindful that projects such as this, which invariably consume time beyond the normal work day, are not without a cost to our families. David would like to thank Jeanie, Jacob, and Nicholas, whose entreaties to "take a little break" or "speed things up" are always perfectly timed. John is grateful, as always, to Kelly, Amanda, Tracy, Charlie, Mary and Ronnie for their encouragement and remarkable patience. We both are very fortunate indeed.

John C. Knapp
Birmingham, Alabama

David J. Siegel
Greenville, North Carolina

Introduction to Volume 3: Marketing and Consumer Interests

John C. Knapp and David J. Siegel

Volume 3 of the *The Business of Higher Education* addresses marketing and consumer interests. In this volume, the discussion turns to considerations of how higher education relates to a broad spectrum of external constituencies.

Universities are confronted with demands for greater accountability in every area, from academic performance to financial management to athletics. In the first chapter, John Knapp argues that we are in an era of *hyperaccountability* that requires a proactive, strategic approach to stakeholder relationships, rather than the defensiveness of university leaders resistant to change. He reviews a wide range of issues where higher education is now subjected to relentless scrutiny and questioning.

Given the realities of the external environment—including intense competition among colleges and universities—the question on most campuses these days is not whether to engage in the business practice of marketing, argues Curt Carlson in chapter 2, but how to do it more effectively so that institutions stand out in a crowded marketplace. It is now generally accepted that marketing, communications, public relations, advertising, and branding are crucial to institutional success, and faculty members and administrators exhibit much less self-consciousness about such efforts than they did 25 years ago. Carlson draws on his personal experiences to illustrate how marketing and other external relations disciplines have moved from the periphery of the academy to center stage, where they are now firmly ensconced as strategic management functions.

Marketing the academy has become a hot topic all over the world, observes Larry Lauer in chapter 3. It has become so in the United States because of increasingly intense competition for students, money, and reputation. It has become a hot topic worldwide because of changes in government funding, new global networking possibilities of the Internet, the general economic shift toward Asia, and the effects of all of this on university fund-raising, alumni cultivation, student recruiting, and overall strategic planning. Lauer advises an integrated process in order to more effectively market colleges and universities.

An organization's visual presentation is one of the most influential means of revealing and communicating its identity, character, and purpose, suggests legendary designer Malcolm Grear, whose full-service studio has many higher education clients. Visual presentation is the scope of graphic design, and Grear contends in chapter 4 that when it is done well, it can actually enhance the performance of a corporation or university—both internally and externally—by activating pride in and emotional attachment to the organization. Grear describes the process his firm follows with clients, from the initial information-gathering interview to the production of graphic identifiers or visual symbols that will represent the client to the public.

Unlike strategic marketing and branding, in which messages tend to be crafted and communicated under conditions of relative calm, campus crises thrust institutions into the public spotlight without much warning. The mass killings at Virginia Tech in 2007 and other recent campus incidents have focused renewed attention on the importance of crisis communication plans and processes. In chapter 5, Andrew Westmoreland, President of Samford University, relates the details of a campus incident that forced him to activate an emergency management process. He analyzes his team's response to the incident, shares some of the lessons learned, and offers a comparison of crisis management expectations in the higher education and business communities.

Michael Harris suggests in chapter 6 that, although the trend is not a new one, the escalation of student consumerism in recent years challenges higher education in a variety of ways. From luxurious amenities to prioritizing student convenience, colleges and universities seek to attract and placate the demands of students and their parents. Out of necessity, both real and perceived, institutions are responding to consumerism; yet how well do we understand the implications of these reactions? Harris's chapter examines how these issues influence campus culture as well as students' curricular and co-curricular pursuits. Finally, Harris calls for the consideration of mission in institutional decision-making in regard to student consumerism.

The growing emphasis on customer service in higher education is a natural outgrowth of mounting concerns about student retention and revenue generation, according to Neal Raisman in chapter 7. Raisman chronicles the evolution of the concept of academic customer service as an institutional focus and research topic. At its base, academic customer service has to do with fulfilling the expectations of students and providing services that will allow them to achieve financial, emotional, and affective returns on their educational investment. Raisman describes the challenges institutions face in developing an ethic of customer service, and he offers several guiding principles to assist in the process.

One highly visible indicator of consumer interest in—and demand for—higher education is the industry that has grown up to support the college-going aspirations of students (and their parents) through enrichment programs, test preparation, private tutoring, and expensive college counseling. In chapter 8, Rachel Toor, a former admissions officer and college counselor, gives an insider's perspective on this evolving and diversified field, where "the itch to make a buck is getting scratched from all sorts of different places" and "new ventures are popping up like morels after a fire." Toor describes the landscape of the pre-college industry and challenges us to consider what it says about how we view higher education.

In chapter 9, Fred Galloway offers an historical look at the provision of student financial aid from federal, state, and institutional perspectives. Galloway uses these three different perspectives to construct a theoretical framework to help explain decision patterns in aid provision. Noting that "financial aid funding patterns and policies seem to oscillate between the poles of need-based and non-need-based aid," his analysis of three distinct time periods in the provision of student aid helps to surface an apparent natural decision-making order with respect to the government and institutions. He considers the consequences of his findings.

Doug Toma observes in chapter 10 that "the business of intercollegiate athletics occurs very much in two worlds, one revenue-generating where the athletic department can separate itself (including financially but also culturally in many ways) from the rest of the university, and the other subsidized in the same way most units are, including academic ones." Toma details the different revenue pictures of these two worlds, and several in between, and concludes that many aspects of intercollegiate athletics are more aligned with professionalism and commercialism than with higher education. While corporate sponsorships, opulent facilities, and outsized salaries for coaches have been fixtures of college sports for a long time, Toma believes that the increasing conspicuousness of them is what differentiates today's situation from earlier ones.

Easily among the most controversial developments in higher education over the last quarter-century has been the proliferation of rankings reports, none more (in)famous than the annual list of "Best Colleges" published by *U.S. News & World Report*. In an essay reprinted here with permission from *Education Sector,* Kevin Carey argues in chapter 11 that these rankings "have become the nation's *de facto* higher education accountability system—evaluating colleges and universities on a common scale and creating strong incentives for institutions to do things that raise their ratings." Instead of relying on them and their flawed representation of institutional quality, Carey advocates a new rankings system that would more accurately reflect the complexity of the higher education enterprise. He outlines the benefits that would flow to students, to institutions, and to society as a result of the change.

CHAPTER 1

University Leadership in an Era of Hyperaccountability

John C. Knapp

Higher education today faces unprecedented scrutiny by an array of interests whose demands for greater accountability touch every area of university life, from academic programs and fiscal management to athletics and fund-raising. We have entered an era of *hyperaccountability* where universities must reconsider many time-honored assumptions about institutional priorities and the nature of effective leadership.

Ivy-covered walls, once symbolic of the academy's insulation from external interference, have steadily given way to mounting pressure over the last 50 years. Accountability initiatives came to the fore in the United States after Sputnik in 1957, became pervasive after *A Nation at Risk* in 1983, and expanded through the 1990s to encompass not just quality but institutional effectiveness, productivity, and cost efficiency.[1] Today the trend is accelerating, prompting an increasingly rancorous debate among policymakers, university administrators, faculty members, and other stakeholders. Many leaders in the educational community argue that excessive external accountability threatens the freedom and autonomy that have permitted universities to flourish as centers of learning and thought leadership. Critics counter that it is only reasonable to expect universities to prove they are efficient and effective stewards of the substantial resources supplied by governments, parents, donors, grant-makers, and others. While much of the debate occurs in the public policy arena, university leaders face increasingly assertive stakeholders from many sectors of society.

In this climate of hyperaccountability, every part of the university seems subject to relentless examination and questioning. Not long ago, I facilitated a leadership development seminar for the presidents of 32 state institutions, all of whom agreed that this phenomenon constituted the major stress factor in their daily work. Whether at two-year colleges or major research universities, these leaders described pressures from government officials, donors, athletic boosters, parents, and faculty—interests that often conflict with each other. The presidents agreed that this broadening range of demands is a major reason for the declining length of presidential tenure in recent years.

Former Yale University President Bart Giamatti famously likened the university presidency to a "mid-nineteenth century ecclesiastical position on top of a late twentieth century corporation."[2] This description may be even more apt in the early 21st century, as leaders atop corporations are themselves struggling to respond to a chorus of cries for greater accountability and transparency. Those who lead universities may, in fact, have something to learn from their counterparts in other sectors, especially business, where the peril and promise of hyperaccountabilty are beginning to be understood and addressed in more sophisticated ways.

THE ACCOUNTABILITY LANDSCAPE

American higher education, long considered the best system in the world, is criticized for failing to keep pace with some competitors on a "flattening" planet.[3] Federal and state officials demand more data on outcomes, access, and fiscal efficiency, even as governmental budgets for higher education tighten. Parents and donors write checks to universities expecting more and more benefits in return. Accrediting agencies seek increasingly elaborate measurements of performance, and activist groups, blue-ribbon commissions, and study panels are intent on reforming higher education by extracting and analyzing a torrent of data.

Some college administrators were understandably surprised in 2006 when the final report of the U.S. Secretary of Education's Commission on the Future of Higher Education (hereafter, the Spellings Commission) lamented "a remarkable absence of accountability mechanisms to ensure that colleges succeed in educating students." The commission concluded that "students, parents, and policymakers are often left scratching their heads over the answers to basic questions, from the true cost of private colleges (where most students don't pay the official sticker price) to which institutions do a better job than others not only of graduating students but of teaching them what they need to learn."[4]

In testimony before the commission, an expert from the Rockefeller Institute of Government emphasized the lack of a coherent, nationally agreed-upon accountability system, describing the information now available as "usually too detailed for state policymakers and too general for potential clients . . . a grab bag of available indicators with no sense of state priorities or a public agenda."[5] This sentiment is echoed by Kevin Carey of Education Sector, who contends that the current accountability system is "no such thing," as higher education is "stuck in a seemingly endless cycle of attack and defense, of accountability conversations that founder on basic differences of definition." He adds that university leaders are understandably resistant to new demands, but cautions that their "endless fight against such accountability" is self-defeating.[6]

One member of the Spellings Commission even suggests that colleges fear measurement because it might produce unfavorable comparisons with other schools or uncover "things they don't want the public to know."

> Yet if colleges resist calls for accountability and transparency too much, they may pay a high price: the loss of institutional autonomy. The public and its political representatives are getting fed up. When that anger passes some threshold, the politicians will probably act, and colleges won't like the imposed solutions—and for good reason, because those solutions may meddle too much in institutions' affairs. Indeed, if you thought the Spellings Commission was rough on colleges, you haven't seen anything yet.[7]

Meanwhile, wary university leaders object that the commission and its supporters are pursuing a flawed ideal of consistent reporting, which Colorado College President Dick Celeste describes as an attempt to "paint all of American higher education with a single brush . . . [that] fails to recognize the distinctive contributions made by different types of colleges and universities. As a consequence, Commission members failed to offer solutions that resist a one-size-fits-all character." Their efforts, he fears, could "do more damage to higher education in the United States than the problems they are intended to address."[8]

U.S. Senator Lamar Alexander, a former Secretary of Education, also voices misgivings about a "system of accountability to tell colleges how to accept transfer students, how to measure what students are learning, and how colleges should accredit themselves. I believe excellence in American higher education comes from institutional autonomy, markets, competition, choice for students, federalism and limited federal regulation."[9]

Yet because few doubt that heightened accountability is inevitable, most of today's debate is about how much, to whom, at what cost, and for what ends. While it is beyond the scope of this chapter to enumerate all of the demands of university stakeholders, a brief summary of key categories may illustrate the complexity of the trend.

Federal and State Government

If university leaders are displeased about governmental intrusion, they may have themselves to blame. Peter Ewell, a longtime authority on university accountability, shows that educators unwittingly invited today's situation through their own lobbying efforts as far back as the early 1980s, when Reagan-era policies shifted more responsibility to the states. "For years, higher education's leaders had argued before legislatures that investments in colleges and universities would pay off in an array of public benefits—ranging from workplace revitalization to quality of life—and this was an argument public officials found very appealing. At the same time, it was a perceived 'bargain' that they would later hold us to."[10] This deal with policymakers led inevitably to expectations of endless data. Indeed, the 2008 reauthorization of the U.S. Higher Education Act effectively doubled the reporting task for colleges, requiring more information on such areas as financial aid and graduation rates.[11] Though the act does not contain penalties for poor performance, it does extract more data for lawmakers and others interested in the net cost of tuition and performance of federal financial aid recipients. In some respects, the federal government has begun to reassert control over higher education.

At the state level, where public funding is declining as a percentage of public universities' operating budgets (now less than 20% in many states), accountability pressures are also growing. It is now common for states to require reports on enrollment statistics, affordability, graduation rates, resource allocation, and economic impact, similar to the reporting criteria used by the National Center for Public Policy and Higher Education in *Measuring Up: The State-by-State Report Card for Higher Education,* a project that publishes comparative data on six performance indicators: preparation, participation, affordability, completion, benefits, and learning. Updated every two years, the online report is formatted to allow users to compare state-by-state performance of public and private institutions.[12]

Texas is an example of a state that has ratcheted up accountability and performance standards.[13] *Closing the Gaps by 2015* is the Texas Higher Education Coordinating Board's plan to close educational gaps within the state and in comparison to other states. Adopted in 2000 and updated periodically, it addresses student participation, student success, excellence, and research, prescribing strategies for improvement and performance measurement in each of these areas.[14] (The University of Texas System's response to the plan is a report with 69 performance measures.) The state's emphasis on accountability was underscored in 2004 when Governor Rick Perry issued an executive order calling for every public college and university to "create a comprehensive system of accountability" to provide citizens and public officials with information to assess the effectiveness and quality of individual institutions. The order declares that "the public has the right to demand complete accountability for its investment" and that institutions must "clearly define the need for additional state funding."[15] These developments continue the work that began with the landmark *Texas Charter of Higher Education* in 1987, which set goals, roles, and responsibilities for universities and became a model for many other states. The charter addresses access, diversity, and funding, and declares that Texans are "entitled" to efficient, effective, capable, and creative university leaders.[16]

Three other states provide noteworthy examples of the accountability measures being put into place across the nation:

- *New Mexico.* In 1999, the legislature enacted the *Policy for Accountable Post-Secondary Education* with goals of affordability, access, cross-sector collaboration, and efficient use of resources. More recently, the Commission on Higher Education has followed up with *First Principles for Linking Funding to Goals and Performance*.[17]
- *Connecticut.* State law mandates an annual report, *Higher Education Counts: Accountability Measures for the New Millennium,* to provide legislators and the public with data on student preparation for professions, connections to K-12 schools, affordability, minority participation, economic impact, and social impact.[18]
- *Virginia.* In 2001, a state law proposed by the State Council on Higher Education in Virginia began requiring colleges and universities to publish Reports of Institutional Effectiveness. The reports address goals including access, affordability, academic offerings, standards, student success, economic development, research, and cooperation with K-12 schools.[19]

Accrediting Agencies

Federal and state governments rely heavily on the work of private accreditation associations, to which colleges and universities are accountable for quality standards. The U.S. Department of Education is required by law to publish a list of recognized accrediting agencies deemed qualified to render reliable and authoritative opinions on the quality of education provided by the institutions they evaluate. These nongovernmental agencies, the first of which were chartered in the 1890s, operate independently and employ a uniquely American approach based on peer review by volunteers. Even so, governmental requirements influence the accreditation agenda, as when agencies began seeking data on learning outcomes in response to 1989 changes in rules for federal student aid eligibility. Some observers perceive a gradual shift from voluntary standards to government-prescribed regulation.

For many years accreditation involved a self-study and peer review once a decade. Upon completion, administrators put the matter aside for several years until the cycle was repeated. "Those days are past," says John W. Bardo, chancellor of Western Carolina University. "Now presidents and chancellors can expect to have their institutions under nearly continuous scrutiny by regional accrediting bodies." He predicts that the numbers of reports and measurements will only increase, straining staff and budget resources as year-round work and interaction with external agencies causes cultural change within institutions.[20] "It also should be expected that the accrediting bodies will increasingly be pressured to require institutions to collect assessment data on a much more regular cycle, perhaps even annually."[21]

Students and Parents

Former Secretary of Education Spellings criticized the accreditation process for being secretive and confusing, a concern shared by students and parents who are bearing a larger share of educational costs amidst alarming tuition increases that seem to add little value in the classroom. A study by the Delta Project on Postsecondary Education Costs, Productivity, and Accountability shows that average tuition at public research institutions jumped an average of 27 percent between 2002 and 2006, while per-student "education and related" spending grew by just 1 percent. Figures for other public colleges and universities were similar. By contrast, growth in per-student spending at private institutions actually outpaced tuition increases.[22]

For policymakers and prospective students alike, these tuition increases heighten concerns about access. A report by Public Agenda and the National Center for Public Policy and Higher Education describes growing public frustration: "At a moment when college is more frequently perceived as absolutely essential, more Americans think that a college education is out of reach for many." Their research finds that 8 in 10 Americans believe college tuition is increasing faster than the cost of health care.[23]

At the same time, many who do manage to fund a college education have become sophisticated and informed purchasers who expect considerably more for their money. As some universities respond with value-added amenities like health spas, upscale dorms, and gourmet dining, a fundamental change in the student–university relationship is emerging. Parents and students increasingly see themselves as customers and educators as vendors. Community college administrator Peter Katopes worries that this represents a movement away from traditional academic values and toward a "business model, which prizes 'customer satisfaction' or 'efficiency' above all else." He argues that this may be entirely appropriate for businesses, which operate primarily for the pursuit of profit, but is antithetical to the raison d'être of higher education and may actually undermine its mission.

> Driven by the desire to satisfy external agencies regarding "accountability," many colleges for some 30 years have effectively altered the relationship between student and institution by defining students as "consumers" who are asked to evaluate instruction in much the same way banks ask their depositors to rate their services . . . this practice runs the risk of turning faculty members into supplicants for student approval and creates a dangerous imbalance in the power relationship between faculty and students, one which might have a deleterious impact on the very thing—teaching—which it is supposed to improve.[24]

On many campuses, students' "helicopter parents" are a persistent source of pressure on many instructors and administrators. Before enrolling, they want to know standardized test scores, percentages of graduates accepted to professional schools, student involvement in various activities, student–teacher ratios, employment and income of graduates, demographics of the student body, rankings by various publications, grade-point averages, and even salaries of faculty. Once enrolled, they keep tabs on their students' progress and activities, not hesitating to interfere when their expectations are not fully met.

Alumni and Donors

In another instance where universities may get what they unwittingly ask for, benefactors increasingly expect to influence how their donations are used. Perhaps this should be expected after years of university fund-raising propositions promising value in return for generosity, usually in the form of naming opportunities for the programs, facilities, or positions being funded. As universities condition their supporters to see themselves as purchasers, rather than benefactors, it is little wonder that many expect to be treated as owners. Some professional advisors to philanthropists even argue that university boards should view themselves as agents of donors, much as corporate boards are agents of shareholders, despite the fact that donors retain no ownership interest in their gifts once their checks are cashed.

Roughly half of university donors surveyed by Goldman Sachs believe donors should have either "the most influence" or "a great deal of influence" in how endowment funds are invested, and 75 percent agree, "University endowments should only invest in funds that disclose which companies they invest in, because endowment donors deserve to know how their donations are being invested."[25] Yet two-thirds of institutions with endowments exceeding $100 million report that only senior administrators and trustees know such information.[26] At many universities, donors, alumni, students, faculty, and special interest groups—sometimes in collaboration with each other—are encouraging transparency and urging socially responsible investment policies. An organizing group called Responsible Endowments Coalition reports that it supports campaigns of this type at 69 institutions, both public and private.[27]

To be sure, colleges and universities owe a large measure of accountability to financial contributors and should make every effort to honor donor intent within the parameters of original agreements. Both parties' expectations should be reasonable, feasible, and clearly articulated, especially in light of recent court cases where donors claimed their intent was disregarded. High-profile lawsuits by disgruntled contributors to institutions like Princeton University, Randolph College, and Tulane University have fed the distrust of donors and led some to insist on greater involvement and accountability.

News Media and New Media

The news media, bloggers, social media, and Internet sites where universities are ranked, critiqued, and discussed—influencing politicians, students, parents, donors, and other stakeholders—fuel hyperaccountability. Best known among these information sources in the United States is *U.S. News & World Report*'s annual ranking of colleges and universities, which has become the standard yardstick for gauging reputations in a variety of academic, geographic, and institutional categories. College rankings of many types have proven profitable for publishers of magazines, newspapers, and college guides, and additional ratings are offered by a host of Web sites and bloggers worldwide. The Princeton Review, producer of print and online publications, ranks schools on academics, extracurricular activities, political leanings, social environment, and even parties. In 2008 *Forbes* magazine challenged *U.S. News & World Report* by launching its own rankings of "America's Best Colleges" with assistance from the Center for College

Affordability and Productivity. Leaders in academia are ambivalent about rankings, criticizing them as superficial and misleading, but extolling their importance when their own institutions are treated favorably.

Beyond rankings, the information environment for higher education comprises seemingly endless points of accountability. Students evaluate faculty on Web sites like RateMyProfessors.com; individual weblogs question everything from coaches' game-day decisions to the content of controversial courses; 24/7 news organizations publish information in real time at any hour of the day; and social media sites spread rumors with lightning speed through networks of students, faculty, and alumni.

Other Interests

Across the accountability landscape are many other stakeholders seeking to influence university policies and practices. Some key interests include:

- *Employment*. An annual study for the Association of American Colleges and Universities (AAC&U) reveals that employers are less than satisfied with the real-world preparedness of college graduates.[28] More than 60 percent of executives surveyed believe too few have the skills to compete in the global economy. They recognize the importance of higher education, but do not regard recent graduates as "very well prepared" in any of 12 categories of skill and knowledge. Very few rate transcripts as useful in informing hiring decisions, and many recommend that universities assess students' abilities to apply and integrate their learning in more practical ways. AAC&U concludes that "despite the development over the past three decades of a veritable 'assessment movement,' too many institutions and programs are still unable to answer legitimate questions about what their students are learning in college. Both the aims and the outcomes of college have remained unclear."[29]

- *Sustainability*. Campus sustainability has emerged as a critical interest of many students, faculty, environmental organizations, and education news media. A prominent example is College Sustainability Report, an online organization that publishes a "Green Report Card" on 300 colleges with large endowments. It gathers information and assigns letter grades in the areas of administration, climate change and energy, food and recycling, green building, student involvement, transportation, endowment transparency, investment priorities, and shareholder engagement.[30]

- *Diversity.* In the more than 50 years since the federal government intervened to force the University of Alabama to register African American students, issues of race and gender have remained near the top of the accountability agenda. The 1964 Civil Rights Act prohibited discrimination on the basis of race, color, or national origin at colleges receiving federal funds. By the 1970s, federal oversight of college desegregation was increasing and Congress passed the Equal Opportunity in Education Act (often referred to as "Title IX") to prohibit discrimination on the basis of sex. Since then, lawsuits have kept these matters in the news and on the desks of university attorneys and administrators. A 1992 case led the U.S. Supreme Court to raise the bar for states to remove vestiges of discrimination, and plaintiffs in the late 1990s challenged the University of Michigan's affirmative action policy, alleging that it unlawfully gave preference to minority applicants. Today, a host of organizations monitor diversity issues, publishing data on enrollment, hiring, faculty salaries and promotions, financial aid, contracting, and so on. The Association of American Colleges and Universities, which maintains a Web site on diversity, publishes reports including *A Measure of Equity: Women's Progress in Higher Education,* an overview of data on women's access to college and status as faculty members, administrators, and presidents.[31]

- *Athletics.* The scholastic performance of student athletes has always been an issue, both within universities and in the public arena. A 2009 study of 77 institutions finds a widening classroom performance gap between athletes and other students. The Andrew W. Mellon Foundation's College Sports Project, one of several organizations examining graduation rates, grade-point averages, class ranks, and other indicators of student athletes' performance, conducted the five-year longitudinal study of Division III schools of the National Collegiate Athletic Association (NCAA).[32] The accountability of intercollegiate athletics is also an internal challenge for many universities, especially where large sports programs have become more answerable to boosters and athletics boards than to academic administrators.

The latest academic frontier is the measurement of learning outcomes, a strong emphasis of the Spellings Commission and, more recently, of the various accrediting agencies. This presents considerable difficulty because learning goals vary widely from discipline to discipline and from course to course, and few assessment methods are considered reliable. The National Commission on Accountability in Higher Education (NCAHE) describes this responsibility as a particular challenge for faculties, who must "lead the way in devising more coherent programs of general education, more effective and efficient teaching techniques, and useful, authentic assessments of student learning." At many institutions this will require new reward systems to encourage and recognize faculty for work that falls outside typical tenure and promotion criteria. Even deans and presidents may not be sufficiently rewarded for their involvement in this work. "Increasingly institutional leadership has been measured in terms of fund-raising and other external responsibilities. These are essential functions, but better accountability for performance requires more vigorous attention to internal priorities."[33]

Faculty members have traditionally been insulated from many of the accountability pressures discussed in this chapter, but this is changing as new priority is given to learning outcomes, assessment of student performance, and relevance of course content to the marketplace for graduates. With more intra- and inter university comparisons of departments and programs, it will be in the self-interest of faculty members to take more ownership of academic accountability, from designing metrics to determining appropriate learning outcomes and assessments. Their traditional "check-the-boxes" approach to accreditation reviews may not suffice in a world where comparative assessment data are easily accessible to all stakeholders. Western Carolina's Bardo agrees that the buy-in of faculty is essential and encourages universities to foster a "culture of evidence" in "all aspects of institutional functioning," especially teaching.[34]

To facilitate public access to such data, NCAHE calls for a new system of accountability to "put more emphasis on successful student learning and high quality research, decrease the role of superficial comparisons and rankings, increase productivity, and provide parents, students, concerned citizens and policymakers the answer to reasonable questions regarding costs, what students are learning, and graduation rates."[35] A recent effort of this sort is the new *Voluntary System of Accountability* developed through a collaboration of the National Association of State Universities and Land-Grant Colleges and the American Association of State Colleges and Universities. The system's College Portrait feature provides online access to data on academic performance, student success, and other factors at public institutions.[36]

LEADERSHIP FOR ACCOUNTABILITY: A STAKEHOLDER-FOCUSED APPROACH

It is no coincidence that the escalation of accountability pressures parallels a well-documented decline of public trust in institutions in virtually all sectors of society.[37] If we understand trust as a bet that the future actions of others will produce good outcomes, it is apparent that fewer people are willing to risk wagers on institutions without verification that their expectations are being met. Hyperaccountability in higher education may be understood as a symptom of this broader erosion of trust. Public Agenda reports that "studies show rising anxiety and skepticism . . . a chipping away of public support for higher education and a growing suspicion about how well colleges and universities use the money they have."[38]

There was a time not long ago when good leaders assumed that trust could be taken for granted most of the time. If questions were raised about their performance, they expected to get the benefit of the doubt and a fair chance to respond. This is not a safe assumption for today's leaders, the best of whom understand that they must work intentionally and continuously to maintain the trust of a multitude of stakeholders. They know that trust is difficult to gain and all too quickly lost.

Many social scientists attribute the trust deficit to relentless communication driven by the exponential growth of the World Wide Web. Vastly more information about institutions is available now than even a decade ago. Though this has many potential benefits in disseminating messages, sharing knowledge, and engaging constituents, it also can undermine stakeholder relationships with incorrect, misleading, and conflicting information. This has a corrosive effect on institutional credibility, as leaders are daunted by the impossibility of monitoring the flow of information or responding to every voice demanding to be heard.

Stakeholder relationships are further strained by the severe economic downturn that began in 2008. Families are more worried than ever about college costs; universities are cutting expenses and eliminating programs and positions; endowments are earning less; state budgets are being reduced. "In post-crash America, there will be more intense demands for scrutiny and accountability as to the effectiveness of academe at fulfilling its public mission," predicts William M. Sullivan, senior scholar at the Carnegie Foundation for the Advancement of Teaching.[39] University leaders, who now must work harder to justify the freedom and relative autonomy their institutions still enjoy, will be aided substantially by adopting a much more strategic approach to stakeholder relationships.

What is a stakeholder-focused strategy for university leadership? First, it is a *pragmatic* way to manage the pressures of hyperaccountability by moving out of a reactive posture and gaining better control of the university's own agenda. Second, it provides a *unifying* vision that brings the many fragments of accountability together as components of an overall strategy. Third, it is an *ethical* approach that takes seriously the interests of all who have a legitimate stake in the university's activities.

The Lessons of Corporate Accountability

Here is an area where higher education may have much to learn from the corporate sector where many large businesses have adopted stakeholder-focused strategies to cope with the onslaught of hyperaccountability. From shareholders to activists to employees, key corporate constituencies are beginning to expect more transparency, reporting of data, and responsiveness to concerns. Governments, as well, are increasing reporting requirements through legislation like the Sarbanes-Oxley Act, which regulates financial reporting of publicly traded companies in the United States. Stakeholder strategies contrast favorably with traditionally reactive approaches to managing issues. "The impetus behind stakeholder management was to try and build a framework that was responsive to the concerns of managers who were being buffeted by unprecedented levels of environmental turbulence and change. Traditional strategy frameworks were neither helping managers develop new strategic directions nor were they helping them understand how to create new opportunities in the midst of so much change."[40]

Initially conceived as a play on the word stockholder, the intent of stakeholder management was to widen the strategic scope of business to consider the interests of any group or individual who is affected by or can affect an organization's work. Akin to systems theory, this approach views organizations as open systems that function interdependently with larger networks of interconnected stakeholders. Thus, strategies are designed to optimize these connections for mutual benefit, helping organizations strengthen relationships and trust with previously disaffected or even adversarial groups. Identifying a group as a legitimate stakeholder ensures that its interests are addressed when corporate plans are formulated. Accountability becomes a key component of *actively* managed relationships with defined objectives, rather than a reactive or compliance-based function.

Strategic stakeholder management has yielded impressive developments in corporate accountability, such as the Global Reporting Initiative (GRI), a multistakeholder network that collaborates to advance sustainability reporting in 55 countries. Some 1,500 companies, including many leading brand names, have adopted the GRI guidelines, which are now the *de facto* global standard for such reporting. Stakeholder representatives are from 55 countries.[41] Many major companies now proactively issue reports on social and environmental performance, in addition to their traditional annual reports, and make data available online to meet the informational needs of key constituencies. The stakeholder approach has also led to strategic partnerships and collaborative projects with groups whose demands for accountability previously were resisted. Corporations find that proactive reporting and stakeholder engagement lessens accountability pressures, preserves more autonomy, enhances reputations, boosts performance, and forestalls government intervention.

Stakeholder Accountability as University Leadership Strategy

The convergence of rising hyperaccountability and the declining of trust signals a need for fresh leadership strategies in higher education. As many as 15 years ago, Peter Ewell saw that self-regulation was already in jeopardy because public confidence was being undermined by higher education's failures to meet expectations of good stewardship. He cited "growing evidence that the rules of the accountability game have changed, as well as the ground on which it must be played."[42] He argued that the future of self-regulation rests on two pillars: effective assessment of outcomes and results, and a renewed commitment to time-honored academic values. "Following this premise, the essential future task for self-regulation is to help render what we actually do in our institutions consistent with what we historically have said we believed in."[43] Among these beliefs is that higher education is a public good, a conviction that undergirds voluntary accountability, equal access, community service, cross-sector engagement, and professionalism. A stakeholder-focused leadership strategy is entirely congruent with these values, but will require new emphases on proactive transparency and strategic integration of accountability across the university enterprise.

Proactive transparency. Unlike businesses, where overall success is measured by a financial bottom line, universities are evaluated on multiple factors that vary widely based on obligations to stakeholders. This fact, coupled with the public responsibilities of state and private universities, makes transparency even more crucial in higher education. "To be sure, transparency involves trade-offs—sacrificing a little institutional autonomy to meet the public's legitimate need for information," writes Vedder. "But colleges must move aggressively to meet this imperative—or face the consequences of increased, and perhaps costly and inefficient, regulatory mandates."[44] Proactive transparency means erring on the side of more disclosure, more communication, and more information in *anticipation* of stakeholders' questions and needs.

Today's stakeholders seek their own information when they need it; when this fails they intensify pressure to get it. They are also quick to turn to other sources, including Web resources like College Portrait, state education departments, online media archives, activist groups, or employees' blogs, some of which are neither reliable nor favorable. Proactive transparency initiates engagement with stakeholders to understand their needs better and to invite their input, helping university leaders identify emerging issues in time to avert future problems. Some institutions now make savvy use of social media and weblogs to facilitate stakeholder participation. The Center for Studies in Higher Education at the University of California, Berkeley, advises that an effective accountability strategy "requires communication, negotiation, compromise and transparency," but this effort saves time and resources over the long term, building credibility and bolstering the effectiveness of all university communications.[45]

Moving from reluctance or defensiveness to a posture of proactive engagement, the university may position itself as an expert and leader on important issues where it has heretofore been questioned. This coheres with the vision of the "engaged institution" advanced by the Kellogg Commission on the Future of State and Land Grant Universities, which proposes redesigning teaching, research, and service to be "more sympathetically and productively involved" with stakeholders.[46]

Strategic integration. Stakeholder accountability should be managed within a single strategic framework to reduce the usual fragmentation resulting from *ad hoc* responses to the fluctuating expectations and demands of the environment. R. Edward Freeman, a leading proponent of corporate stakeholder theory, stresses that stakeholder considerations must be "integrated into the very purpose" of the institution in a "coherent and strategic fashion," and describes a process whereby management "imaginatively plans how its actions might affect stakeholders and thus help to *create* the future environment. Stakeholder management is used to enrich management's understanding of the strategic options they can create."[47]

Strategic planning at most universities is closely tied to accreditation, as documentation of the planning process itself is required by reviewers. As accreditation evolves from an episodic event to a year-round, labor-intensive concern of faculty and administrators, strategic plan objectives gain greater influence in setting institutional priorities. Yet these objectives seldom speak to institutional accountability beyond the important, but limited, interests of students and accrediting bodies. When broader accountability objectives are incorporated into the strategic plan, they will become part of the assessment process—that is, information will be gathered, shared, and discussed, measurement methods will be developed, and everyone will become more conversant with the legitimate expectations of stakeholders. By better integrating accountability and strategy, universities may gain more control over how and where curricular and institutional policies are influenced by others.

Social trends researcher Daniel Yankelovich has begun advising large organizations to create "strategic dialogue" units to monitor and develop responses to stakeholders and changes in the external environment. "These would be among the most creative and thoughtful people irrespective of what [departments] or what functions they represent."[48] In a university setting, such a group could comprise faculty and administrators with expertise in academic assessment, governmental affairs, media relations, athletics, admissions, and other functions responsible for accountability to stakeholders. It would not make policy, but would foster reflection and propose strategies for consideration. The active participation of the president would be essential to mobilize the institution in developing and implementing action steps.

CONCLUSION

The phenomenon of hyperaccountability threatens to undermine the mission of higher education and the effectiveness of university leaders. Where most discussions of accountability have been limited to governmental and accreditation requirements, today's universities operate in environments defined by a more complex and increasingly demanding constellation of stakeholders. The task of university leadership in the early 21st century is made ever more challenging by a climate of incessant scrutiny and declining public trust. The stakes are high: "Public trust is the single most important asset of higher education in this nation. Without it the inextricable link between the public and its institutions will find decreased support from public funds; donors will not give, policymakers will become more adversarial, and resources and institutional autonomy will be replaced by increased governmental intervention."[49]

We must accept that hyperaccountability is here to stay and will only intensify in the future. Higher education's response must be a new kind of leadership—not from yet another blue-ribbon panel or commission, but from the trustees, presidents, administrators, and faculties of every institution. Universities can continue to flourish as the foundational institutions of our society while maintaining appropriate autonomy and self-governance, but we must lean into the challenge by embracing proactive transparency and strategically aligning stakeholder accountability with our time-honored institutional missions.

NOTES

1. National Commission on Accountability in Higher Education, *Accountability for Better Results: A National Imperative for Higher Education* (Denver: State Higher Education Executive Officers, 2005), 11. See also William I. Sauser and Ralph S. Foster Jr., "Comprehensive University

Extension in the 21st Century," in *Managing Institutions of Higher Education into the 21st Century: Issues and Implications,* ed. Ronald R. Sims and Serbrenia J. Sims (Westport, CT: Greenwood, 1991), 172.

2. A. Bartlett Giamatti, *A Free and Ordered Space* (New York: W. W. Norton, 1988), 17.

3. Organization for Economic Cooperation and Development, *Learning for Tomorrow's World* (Paris: OECD, 2004), 339–371. http://www.oecd.org/dataoecd/58/57/33918098.pdf. In 2004, OECD ranked the United States college graduation rate behind Denmark, Norway, Germany, Japan, Poland, Switzerland, Finland, Greece, Hungary, Italy, Czech Republic, Belgium, Iceland, and Ireland.

4. U.S. Secretary of Education's Commission on the Future of Higher Education, *A Test of Leadership: Charting the Future of U.S. Higher Education* (Washington, DC: United States Department of Education, 2006), vii. http://www.ed.gov/about/bdscomm/list/hiedfuture/reports/pre-pub-report.pdf.

5. Joseph Burke, *Accountability Reporting: With So Much Effort, Why So Little Effect?* Testimony to the National Commission on Accountability in Higher Education, 2004, 2. http://www.sheeo.org/account/comm/testim/Burke%20testimony.pdf.

6. Kevin Carey, "Truth without Action: The Myth of Higher-Education Accountability," *Change,* September/October (2007): 24.

7. Richard K. Vedder, "Colleges Should Go Beyond the Rhetoric of Accountability," *Chronicle of Higher Education* 54, no. 42 (2008): A 64.

8. Dick Celeste, "Spellings Commission Report Fails to Recognize Distinctive Contributions of Colleges and Universities," President's Blog, posted December 2006, http://www.coloradocollege.edu/welcome/presidentsoffice/blog/index.php/2006/12/06/spellings-commission-report-fails-to-recognize-distinctive-contributions-of-colleges-and-universities.

9. "Statement of Senator Lamar Alexander: Accountability in Higher Education," American Council on Education, May 24, 2007, http://www.acenet.edu.

10. Peter T. Ewell, "Accountability and the Future of Self-Regulation," *Change,* November/December (1994): 25.

11. Kelly Field, "Congress Shows Colleges They're Not off the Hook on Accountability," *Chronicle of Higher Education* 55, no. 2 (2008): A 32.

12. National Center for Public Policy and Higher Education, *Measuring Up: The National Report Card on Higher Education,* http://measuringup.highereducation.org/default.cfm.

13. *Accountability for Better Results: A National Imperative for Higher Education,* 20. Other notable accountability systems have been established

in states including Arizona, Connecticut, Iowa, Kentucky, North Carolina, North Dakota, South Dakota, and Wisconsin.

14. Texas Higher Education Coordinating Board, *Closing the Gaps*, 2000, http://www.thecb.state.tx.us.

15. Governor of the State of Texas, "Executive Order RP 31, relating to accountability of higher education systems and institutions," January 22, 2004, http://www.thecb.state.tx.us.

16. Texas Higher Education Governing Board, "Texas Charter for Higher Education," http: www.thecb.state.tx.us.

17. New Mexico Commission on Higher Education, "First Principles for Linking Funding to Goals and Performance," http://hed.state.nm.us/cms/kunde/rts/hedstatenmus/docs/36806432–06–09–2006–10–17–46.pdf.

18. Board of Governors for Higher Education, Connecticut Department of Higher Education, "Higher Education Counts: Accountability Measures for The New Millennium," 2005, http://www.eric.ed.gov/ERICDocs/data/ericdocs2sql/content_storage_01/0000019b/80/19/4f/ce.pdf.

19. State Council for Higher Education in Virginia, "Institutional Performance Standards," 2005, http://www.schev.edu/Reportstats/InstitutionalPerformanceStandards.pdf.

20. John W. Bardo, "The Impact of the Changing Climate for Accreditation on the Individual College or University: Five Trends and Their Implications," *New Directions for Higher Education* 145 (2009): 47.

21. Ibid., 50.

22. Jane V. Wellman, et al., *Trends in College Spending: Where Does the Money Come From? Where Does It Go?* (Washington, DC: Delta Project on Postsecondary Education Costs, Productivity and Accountability, 2009), 17–19. http://www.deltacostproject.org/resources/pdf/trends_in_spending-report.pdf.

23. *Squeeze Play 2009: The Public's View on College Costs Today* (Washington, DC: Public Agenda and The National Center for Public Policy and Higher Education, 2009), 3.

24. Peter Katopes, "The 'Business Model' Is the Wrong Model," Inside Higher Ed, posted February 16, 2009, http://insidehighered.com/views/2009/02/16/katopes.

25. Goldman Sachs Global Markets Institute, *Public Perceptions of University Endowments: Key Findings from a Survey among University Donors,* January 26, 2005, http://www2.goldmansachs.com/citizenship/global-initiatives/research-and-conferences/.

26. Rockefeller Philanthropy Advisors, http://rockpa.org/ideas_and_perspectives.

27. Responsible Endowments Coalition, http://www.endowmentethics.org/campaign.html.

28. Peter D. Hart Research Associates, Inc., for Association of American Colleges and Universities, *How Should Colleges Assess and Improve Student Learning? Employers' Views on the Accountability Challenge* (January 9, 2008), 6. http://www.aacu.org/LEAP/documents/2008_Business_Leader_Poll.pdf.

29. Board of Directors, Association of American Colleges and Universities, *Our Students' Best Work: A Framework of Accountability Worthy of Our Mission,* 2008, 1. http://www.aacu.org/publications/pdfs/StudentsBestreport.pdf.

30. The College Sustainability Report, http://www.greenreportcard.org.

31. Judy Touchton, *A Measure of Equity: Women's Progress in Higher Education* (Washington, DC: American Association of Colleges and Universities, 2008).

32. David Moltz, "Academic Accountability in Athletics," Inside Higher Ed, posted March 9, 2009, http://insidehighered.com.

33. *Accountability for Better Results: A National Imperative for Higher Education,* 21–22.

34. Bardo, 53.

35. Ibid., 7.

36. Voluntary Accountability System, http://www.collegeportraits.org.

37. Edelman, *Edelman Trust Barometer 2008,* http://www.edelman.com; World Economic Forum, "Trust in Governments, Corporations and Global Institutions Continues to Decline," press release, December 15, 2005, http://www2.weforum.org/site/homepublic.nsf.

38. *Squeeze Play 2009: The Public's View on College Costs Today,* 6.

39. David Glenn, "After the Crash, Scholars Say, Higher Education Must Refocus on Its Public Mission," *The Chronicle of Higher Education* 55, no. 32 (April): 10.

40. R. Edward Freeman and John McVea, "A Stakeholder Approach to Strategic Management," Working Paper No. 01–02 (Charlottesville: The Darden School of Business, University of Virginia, 2001), 3.

41. Global Reporting Initiative, http://www.globalreporting.org.

42. Peter T. Ewell, "Accountability and the Future of Self-Regulation," *Change* 26, no. 6 (1994): 25.

43. Ibid.

44. Vedder, 64.

45. David E. Leveille, *Accountability in Higher Education: A Public Agenda for Trust and Cultural Change* (Berkeley: University of California, 2006), 8.

46. National Association of State Universities and Land-Grant Colleges, *Returning to Our Roots: Executive Summaries of the Reports of the Kellogg Commission on the Future of State and Land Grant Universities,* (Washington, DC: NASULGC, 2001), 12. https://www.aplu.org.

47. Freeman and McVea, 11.

48. Daniel Yankelovich, "Unenlightened Self-Interest: The Wrong Response to Market Capitalism," *Leaders on Ethics,* ed. John C. Knapp (Westport, CT: Praeger Publishers, 2007), 17.

49. Leveille, 13.

CHAPTER 2

Universities and the Business Practice of Marketing

Curtis Carlson

For centuries, universities have held a lofty view of themselves. Cardinal John Henry Newman in his classic 19th-century book, *The Idea of a University,* said about a university, "It professes to teach whatever has to be taught in whatever department of human knowledge, and it embraces in its scope the loftiest subjects of human thought, and the richest fields of human inquiry. Nothing is too vast, nothing too subtle, nothing too distant, nothing too minute, nothing too discursive, nothing too exact, to engage its attention."[1]

Much later, in 1994, the late Ernest Boyer, noted educator, author, and former President of the Carnegie Foundation for the Advancement of Teaching, held up a lofty goal for higher education, again speaking specifically to the service mission and promise of colleges to address and improve "the human condition." Writing in the *Chronicle of Higher Education* about what he termed the "New American College," he said this college "would be committed to improving, in a very intentional way, the human condition. As new clusters of such colleges formed," he predicted, "a new model of excellence in higher education would emerge, one that would enrich the campus, renew communities, and give new dignity and status to the scholarship of service."[2]

Against this historical backdrop of the academy's self-image and Boyer's "New American College" vision for the future, it is jarring to associate colleges and universities with descriptors commonly attributed to the values, culture, practices, and terminology of business: profit-oriented, top-down management, sales force, and cut-throat competition. Now, for many within the ivory confines and sacred halls of academe, these ideas have been a hard pill to swallow. It is difficult for some administrators and faculty to admit that a university or college might be more effective in delivering on its mission if it adopts business practices, especially marketing, branding, institutional advertising and related practices—the primary business functions addressed in this chapter—when the implementation of such activities is driven by a strong campus CEO.

An anecdote may illustrate a common misperception among business people about the executive power of the president or chancellor. While walking across campus one afternoon with a member of an external advisory group (a vice president of marketing for a large Fortune 500 corporation) and a colleague from academic administration, the visiting executive commented about the difficulty we were encountering on getting the faculty to "buy in" to a particular marketing strategy we wanted to launch. "Why doesn't the president just tell the faculty that this is what you are going to do?" she queried. "You must understand," replied the administrator, "on a university campus, when the president asks for something, some faculty take that as their cue to do exactly the opposite!" While this may be an exaggeration, the story does illuminate in graphic terms the relative ineffectiveness, in comparison to corporate culture, of "top-down" authority when exercised by a university CEO in relation to faculty, especially tenured faculty.

Even though the campus culture resists a command structure, the president is not without power. James Fisher and James Koch write: "Power is a subject about which leaders—perhaps especially college presidents—are seldom candid . . . The secret seems to be to contrive a pose of refined disinterest and modesty behind which one wields all the power possible."[3] Stated a bit more gently by Ernest Boyer, a top campus executive "mainly has, or should have, the power of persuasion; appeals to a larger vision are limited only by the ingenuity of the leader."[4]

However, the debate as framed by this book set about the extent to which colleges and universities should be thought of as businesses has become a hollow debate on most campuses, especially those—like the university where I am currently employed, the University of Nebraska at Kearney, a moderately sized public campus in rural Nebraska—whose margin for strategic and operational error is thin. Business-driven competition is, in fact, a defining, and even all-consuming, characteristic of operational practice at most successful colleges and universities. It *is* the 800-pound gorilla in the room in councils of higher-education institutional management these days, along with the demand for top leaders who understand and embrace methods that have come out of the business world such as marketing and branding. The question has become "*how* to increase the effectiveness of your marketing spending," not necessarily *whether or not* to embrace marketing and other business practices.[5]

As early as 1986, noted marketing scholar and author George Keller made a proclamation that "Strategic marketing has experienced a volcanic eruption on campuses across the country."[6]

For purposes of this chapter, to avoid debates about differences in meaning among the communications, marketing, public relations, and other external relations disciplines as applied at most universities, "business practice" means all of these, plus the strategic planning and audience research that is, or should be, integral to all effective external relations activities.

COMPETITION DRIVES UNIVERSITY BUSINESS PRACTICES

While many powerful universities and colleges, large and small, that are well-established and well-endowed financially, would like to project and maintain an image of pure altruism as described by Cardinal Newman, and thus to be seen as above the fray, they are not exempt from the intense pressure of competition: competition for the best students, for the biggest amounts of federal research support and private endowment, the most citations and prominent placements of institutional and faculty "expert" stories in national media reports, and, perhaps most telling of all, the highest rankings in *U.S. News & World Report*'s annual beauty contest. Competition even among the permanently established and very secure Ivy League institutions—and Ivy League wannabes—though piously denied in some circles, is, in actuality, a prominent driver of business decisions, as it is at higher education institutions of all kinds, including at AASCU-affiliated universities like the University of Nebraska at Kearney (UNK), for example. The embrace of marketing practices in response to competitive forces has been a trend for many years at most institutions, but only more recently with less self-consciousness. While we "did it" 25 years ago, marketing was still a dirty word among many faculty and academic administrators.

Now, faculty and administrators whom I know and with whom I work on a daily basis not only embrace the terminology of marketing and marketing practices, they clamor unabashedly for *more* marketing, branding, advertising—you name it. Motivated by the threat and pain of increasing budget constraints amid uncertain economic times and teetering enrollments at many institutions, *anything* that will gain positive attention for the institution and drive more prospective students into our enrollment pipelines is welcome. A caveat: we're not yet to the point where *all* faculty members fully understand their own crucial role in this process. Some faculty would prefer to leave the process of marketing and student recruiting to the "experts," even though marketing cannot be effective without their support and participation.

John L. Pulley, in a 2003 cover story in the *Chronicle of Higher Education,* described reasons for the rush by colleges and universities to "stand out in a crowded market":

> Institutions have had to rethink their disdain for commercialism in a hurry. Colleges are competing among themselves and against non-educational institutions for state and federal appropriations, research money, and foundation grants and private gifts. Competition is heating up to land the smartest students, the best scholars, and the highest rankings in surveys of institutional quality. And for-profit educators, un-burdened by the high cost of conducting research, are gobbling up educational market share on the cheap. Suddenly, the name recognition enjoyed by a breakfast cereal with a well-known slogan ('Cuckoo for Cocoa Puffs') looks pretty good.[7]

While these pressures to keep one step ahead are parallel to the corporate world's drive to grow and be profitable, I would argue that higher education's track record in keeping the lid on excesses—such as we have too often seen in recent years in the world of big business and finance—is marginally more successful, as evidenced in part by the high levels of confidence demonstrated by the American public in the expertise of faculty and also by the continuing, and growing, demand for a college degree as the ticket to a successful life and career. Danger enters the picture for academe when its leaders allow pure, unexamined business practice—and the drive for increasing profitability for profitability's sake—to cloud or overtake the essentially altruistic mission of educating young people upon which colleges and universities were established. It is also this mission of human-oriented altruism that perhaps has helped to preserve higher education—along with institutions of religion—as among the most enduring type of institution in the world.[8]

MARKETING AND EXTERNAL RELATIONS MOVE TO CENTER STAGE

It is instructive to illustrate from my own experience how the influence of marketing, communications, and public relations disciplines has moved from the fringes of management where we are providing services, to center stage as a crucial management function. In 1985, at Berry College, I wrote my first "Public Relations Plan" as an academic administrator. In the introduction, reflecting the tone of the times, I was careful to downplay the role of public relations. "It is important to note," I wrote, "that it is primarily the function of this document to propose PUBLIC RELATIONS policy as it affects the institution, not INSTITUTIONAL policy. There is a great difference between establishing policy to improve the IMAGE of an institution and establishing OPERATIONAL policy. There is also a need to distinguish between public relations goals (To enhance the image of . . .) and institutional goals (To improve the performance of . . .)."[9]

Ten years later, at Emory University, I wrote a slightly more ambitious planning document entitled "Public Relations Themes/Goals." In it I stated, "PR Themes provides a framework for the development, over time, of a comprehensive work plan for public relations activities at Emory University."[10]

Flash forward another 10 years, still at Emory; I had developed a much better understanding of the strategic importance of the marketing and communications disciplines and more confidence to express that understanding to my colleagues. The first bullet point in a list of objectives for an Emory University "Public Affairs Plan" for school year 2004–2005 stated, "Develop and execute a university-wide, integrated marketing campaign to support the University's Strategic Planning Process and progress toward the goals expressed in the University Vision Statement."[11]

Finally, the latest plan that I recently authored at my present institution, UNK, shows how the marketing, public relations, and other external relations functions, labeled together as "University Relations," has emerged as a full partner in setting the future direction of the institution. In the Executive Summary of UNK's "Phase II Implementation Plan for University Relations," I stated that this plan "is one of eight major components of an action plan for the University of Nebraska at Kearney that was commissioned to be developed (by the Chancellor and the Cabinet) upon the completion in 2006 of the UNK Strategic Plan." The summary concluded that the "University Relations strategy will address the central challenges of UNK, as defined in . . . the University of Nebraska Strategic Framework."[12]

A NEW VOCABULARY TO ACCOMMODATE UNIVERSITY "CULTURE"

One of the more intriguing characteristics of higher education's history as a business enterprise is the extent to which the "academy" has evolved an entirely new vocabulary for business practices. "Fund-raising" became "development" and then "advancement." "Publicity" became "public relations" and then became any number of designations such as "public affairs," "university relations," "communications," and the like. A "news bureau director" became a "public information officer" and then a "media relations specialist." It is as if in the search for terminology that describes what we do, there is some advantage in being fuzzy, unlike business which has never abandoned such straightforward titles as "sales manager." Are there "sales managers" employed at colleges or universities? Yes. However, rather than use business language, they are designated "recruitment officers," or, better yet, "enrollment managers."

In spite of this camouflage terminology that is strange to the non-higher-education world, the underlying business practices that they represent have strongly gained a foothold within colleges and universities, and will grow in importance in the future. Universities will continue to learn from the business community, just as many of the more successful leaders in the business community have embraced cultural and operational practices more often associated with universities, such as the culture of decentralization in much decision-making and consensus-building among team members, leaders, and staff employees alike.

"ADVANCEMENT" EMBRACED AS A PREFERRED DESCRIPTOR

Now, I turn to an examination of the origin of one of the camouflage terms noted above, "advancement," that has gained a firm ascendency by its association with fund-raising, and by its incorporation into the very name of the largest and most important of the professional associations that serve the business development demands of higher education, the Council for Advancement and Support of Education (CASE).

Public Relations was the first "corporate" or "advancement" tool embraced by higher education institutions. My personal experience in higher education "advancement" traces to Southern Adventist University, while a student there in the 1960s. Then, there was no marketing department, no vice president for advancement, only a very enigmatic and effective director of public relations, the late William H. Taylor. Bill was oversize, silver-haired, and in possession of a booming, friendly voice and a strict work ethic. From my young perspective, he seemed to know personally, and be on good terms with, every editor and reporter in Chattanooga. He was the university's chief student recruiter and chief alumni cheerleader. He was also my professor, a mentor who first made me aware of PR in higher education as an attractive and exciting profession. His class in PR 101 is where I learned about the business practice tools of strategic planning and what was then labeled "audience or public relations research" but is now known generally as "marketing research." He clearly demonstrated to me the importance of well-designed research as a tool to help achieve the strategic objectives of student recruiting, fund-raising, and positive external relations among all university constituents—or "publics," as I was taught.

To trace the entry and full integration of business practice tools into the arena of higher education, it is instructive to follow the history of professional trade organizations specifically related to these functions. Public relations practice (of a type) in higher education dates back to the first alumni association, at Williams College in 1821. Some 90 years later, the first association of alumni professionals was formed. Twenty-three men, and they *were* all men, gathered at Ohio State University to form the Association of Alumni Secretaries, which later became the American Alumni Council (AAC). Their stated purpose: "The bottom line was getting the alumni to understand the goals of the university and promoting good will toward it."[13] The American Association of College News Bureaus, later named the American College Publicity Association and then the American College Public Relations Association (ACPRA), was founded in 1917. All of these early organizations represented fund-raising only as a fairly minor function of the job descriptions. "Marketing" was not in their vocabulary. It was much later, in 1949, when the first university staff fund-raisers joined ACPRA because they did not have an association home in the university setting. Through most of the first half of the 20th century, professional fund-raising was guided by outside consulting firms.[14]

Finally, with an increased recognition that the need existed for a coordinated PR, alumni, and fund-raising effort, in 1958, a historic gathering took place at the Greenbrier Hotel in White Sulphur Springs, West Virginia. It was underwritten by the Ford Foundation, and co-sponsored by the AAC and the ACPRA. The Greenbrier Report which came from that conference recommended that PR, fund-raising, and alumni relations be integrated equally under the umbrella of institutional advancement, with one high-level officer in charge, assumed to be knowledgeable and skilled in each of the practice areas now encompassed by "advancement."

Sixteen years later, in 1974, AAC and ACPRA merged to form CASE, still the major association incorporating all the advancement functions for higher education.[15] Interestingly, "marketing" as a critical operational component was not officially adopted into the CASE umbrella until 2003, when the name of the national CASE Commission on Communications was changed to "Communications and Marketing."[16]

While "integrated marketing" is a concept that is also being increasingly embraced within the university setting, direct marketing activity in support of student recruiting and admissions is more directly supported by the National Association for College Admission Counseling (NACAC), with its more than 10,000 members.[17]

DEVELOPMENT EMERGES AS THE "HARD" ADVANCEMENT DISCIPLINE

Perhaps it was inevitable that the critical need of institutions for money, lots of it, and the fund-raisers who had the skills and experience to find and bring it into the universities' coffers, would quickly influence the meaning of "advancement" and move fund-raising to center stage as the principle CASE agenda and fund-raisers to the VP positions within institutions. While the numbers of public relations and alumni relations officers relative to fund-raisers who are members of CASE has ebbed and flowed since the forming of the association, PR and alumni membership has ebbed in recent years. At the last CASE conference I attended (Denver, 2007), nearly two-thirds of the attendees comprised fund-raisers and disciplines directly associated with fund-raising, such as stewardship officers, event planners, and grant writers. Marketers and communicators—and conference content of interest to them—were in a distinct minority. The imbalance is a topic of concern, or worse, for many public relations and marketing professionals in higher education, who share, theoretically, the "advancement officer" label, leading inevitably to a rethinking of priorities and even organizational structure at many institutions.

> Despite its movement toward greater professional competence and standing, educational fund-raising remains an evolving field. . . . Tension and rivalry still exist among the various specialties of institutional advancement, and some campuses have moved away from the advancement model of organization recommended by the Greenbrier conference, separating administrative control of development from that of communications and marketing programs.[18]

Adding to the idea of fund-raising as the only "hard" advancement discipline, with the exception of marketing in support of student recruiting, goals for public relations, communications, marketing, and alumni relations functions are not as directly measurable as the often clearly-stated and publicized goals for fund-raisers. PR and related areas are seen as "soft" while fund-raising, or development, is seen as "hard." The term "advancement" has evolved to the point where it is now virtually synonymous with "development," meaning first and foremost, and for many, exclusively, fund-raising.

THE DECLINE OF "PUBLIC RELATIONS" IN HIGHER EDUCATION

While PR never actually threatened the dominance of the fund-raiser in higher education, as recently as 1998, fund-raiser and scholar Kathleen Kelly wrote a book proposing the idea that fund-raising should be an organizational subset of public relations, not the other way around as it is at many institutions.[19] Her conceptualization of public relations defines constituent relationships at a very high level, strategically formed in the top councils of the university, and guiding all other "relationship" functions, (i.e., media relations, community relations, financial and investor relations, internal relations, public affairs, marketing, marketing support, and consumer relations).[20] According to Kelly, in support of her idea about fund-raising's position in the hierarchy of management, the Public Relations Society of America's (PRSA) 1988 Body of Knowledge Task Force "clearly intended that fund-raising should be defined as a component of public relations."[21]

Kelly made her case quite clearly in her book, *Effective Fund-Raising Management*:

> Fund-raisers, by definition, concentrate on one stakeholder group: donors. When public relations and other functions such as alumni relations are subsumed under fund-raising, there is danger that relationship efforts will concentrate on the concerns and demands of only donors. Such situations describe *fund-raising encroachment*, when public relations is managed by a fund-raiser and is viewed as a support function for fund-raising objectives. Its practitioners are cast in technician roles and isolated from decision making. Strategic publics that can affect the organization's success and survival seldom are brought to the attention of the dominant coalition because public relations practitioners are denied access, and the manager who does have access—the fund-raiser—is trained and rewarded to concentrate on donor publics. The organization is then handicapped by *environmental blinders* that prevent it from 'seeing' problems and opportunities related to non-donor publics. Systems theory predicts that resulting imbalances produce crises and, eventually, dysfunction.[22]

In retrospect, her reasoning did not adequately account for the power relationships driven by the bottom line that would ultimately define how these groups work together, and in what organizational framework. While development officers have often risen to vice presidential levels, public relations and communications offices (on some campuses more than others) have come to be seen, in the words of Jane Taber of Golden

Gate University, as not much more than "publications vending machines. Campus clients place their coins into the PR machine, and their products emerge."[23] Others—*not* the PR and communications staff—set the strategy, define the audiences, set goals, and are held accountable for the results.

In spite of this reality and the organizational struggle to maintain balance among the advancement disciplines, CASE has taken steps in recent years to recognize and promote the communications (and marketing) functions as critical partners in the advancement mix. In 2004, the CASE Board adopted a set of "Principles of Practice for Communications and Marketing Professionals at Educational Institutions." It states:

> Educational institutions face an increasingly challenging environment in which to attract students, faculty, benefactors, alumni allegiance, government support, and public respect. As a result communications and marketing professionals perform increasingly strategic and complex roles as champions of the institution's mission, stewards of its reputation, monitors of its competitive environment, and liaisons to its many constituencies.

Operational Principles

Communications and marketing professionals are most successful at advancing their institutions when:

- Their efforts are carefully designed to support the institution's strategic plan, to manage its reputation, to monitor those issues most likely to affect its future.
- They are present in the inner management circle, where they provide strategic and crisis counsel to the institution's leadership, convey the viewpoints of the primary publics, and participate in the formulation of policies affecting those publics.
- They base their work on research that informs their understanding of the institution's primary publics and that measures progress toward established goals, expressed in terms of desired attitudes and behaviors among those publics.
- They undertake ongoing, targeted programs of communications and marketing, employing multiple channels appropriate to the audience and the message.
- They engage in two-way communication with primary publics and actively seek feedback to help the institution align its services with existing and emerging needs of its intended beneficiaries.

- They involve internal constituencies across the organization in delivering not only the messages but also the academic and service excellence on which the institution's reputation depends.
- They employ proven methods, as well as promising new approaches in the field, as part of a commitment to continuous improvement.[24]

OVEREMPHASIS ON DEVELOPMENT AND MARKETING PUTS INSTITUTIONAL REPUTATIONS AT RISK

Later in this chapter, I will argue for a full, balanced implementation of *all* the advancement disciplines. First, I will examine a debate about the critical role of public relations in higher education, as fully developed over the years by very able public relations practitioners, and as strongly linked to the enlightened utilization of public relations techniques and tactics espoused by the 25,000-member Public Relations Society of America (PRSA), the largest and most influential professional association of communications and public relations practitioners in the nation and world.

PRSA has recognized the value of segmentation of its own audiences, through the active division of its energies by geographic area, as well as—crucially—by subdisciplines. Starting with the prestigious "Counselor's Academy," the first of PRSA's "Sections," the organization's membership through the years has created numerous other focused sections such as the "Health Academy," the "International" section, "Employee Communication" section, and, most relevant to this discussion, "Counselors to Higher Education" (CHE). These groups begin their dialogue based upon PRSA's extensive Body of Knowledge about the practice of public relations, and then move on to apply this knowledge and best public relations practice in each section's specialized arena. CASE, on the other hand, starts with higher education as an organizing principle, reaching out to best practices within multiple disciplines. Each approach has its merits, and many practitioners have affiliated with both, or others, in meeting their professional development objectives.

In the meantime, speaking directly to a problem that public relations is perhaps best designed to address, are colleges and universities losing respect and support in this country? If the amount of public funding for higher education as measured by percentage of state budgets is a valid indicator, yes, support is declining. Critics dating back to then-Education Secretary William Bennett during the Reagan administration have "helped propel this rising tide of skepticism throughout the 1990s and into the new millennium," including a blistering attack on the value of a college degree in a PBS documentary entitled, "Declining by Degrees, Higher Education at Risk."[25]

According to Anthony C. Peyronel of Edinboro University of Pennsylvania, "Ask any campus public relations manager to name the biggest challenges facing American higher education today, and the response is likely to include something about increasing levels of public scrutiny."[26] He quotes C. S. Stepp, author of a recent article in the *American Journalism Review,* that examined media coverage of higher education, who described the situation this way: "In an age of accountability, as tuition surges and consumers squeal, colleges have begun sliding off the pedestals they once occupied as privileged, seldom challenged local shrines."[27]

According to a recent research report in the *Journal of Higher Education,* there is ample evidence of declining support, at least for public universities:

> Facing shrinking budgets, competing priorities, public resistance to increasing state levies, and prohibitions on deficit spending, state legislators more and more often find themselves in the unenviable position of debating the relative essentiality of state services, including postsecondary education. As a result, higher education, a discretionary budget item in most states, has often been moved to the end of the state funding queue, resulting in state governments allocating a smaller share of their spending towards higher education.[28]

Some within the academy attribute to market forces a decline from the glory years of higher education, whenever that was, to the defensive position in which many institutions find themselves today. One definition of market forces is "that a college education in fact contributes more to individual advancement than to the nation's social fabric."[29] Philip Altbach has described a "pact" that has broken down. "The unwritten pact between society and higher education that provided expanding resources in return for greater access for students as well as research and service to society has broken down, with significant implications for both higher education and society."[30]

Whatever the causes of higher education's alleged loss of public esteem, one thing seems clear: In an era of intense public and media pressures, colleges and universities can ill afford to ignore employment of enlightened, well-conceived public relations and communications strategies, distinct from (the also-necessary) marketing and fund-raising priorities.

THE RISE OF PROFESSIONAL DEVELOPMENT OPTIONS

An unintended consequence of CASE's evolution to an association with a majority of fund-raisers is, as noted earlier in this chapter, the reduction of its membership representing the other disciplines, and a corresponding decrease in professional development programming and services related to nonfund-raising tasks and strategies. In spite of gallant and even inspired efforts by CASE leadership to be more relevant to communicators (John Lippincott, CASE's current president, himself emerged from the communications disciplines and was a surprising choice to lead the fund-raising-dominated association), it has long been the view of this writer that CASE has developed, and still has, a serious image problem among nonfund-raisers in the academy. It will be a difficult cycle for CASE to break out of, though it is *still* hard to argue with the original premise upon which CASE was founded: "Advancement" means a balanced and integrated approach to building up our institutions. It just hasn't quite worked out that way.

What to do for the legions of PR/marketing/communications professionals disenchanted with CASE is a difficult challenge for the higher education professional development community. No other association has the staffing or resources to provide even the possibility of the range of services and programming in these areas as does CASE. Counselors to Higher Education (CHE), on the other hand, as a section of PRSA, is run by a volunteer Executive Committee, with one or two support staff at PRSA headquarters in New York. CHE runs an increasingly successful and highly focused "Spring Summit" every year, and provides a session and some networking opportunity at the International PRSA Conference each year. Besides that, the membership produces an occasional white paper, conducts several teleseminars each year, but not much more.

NAICU and AASCU each offer an annual meeting/seminar focused on communications and marketing topics. These meetings have emerged only in recent years, presumably, again, to help fill a need unmet by CASE. The AAU Public Affairs Network conducts one of the best annual meetings for university communicators, but membership and attendance is currently restricted to 62 elite public and private research universities. These institutions, deviating from the norm of the "advancement model" espoused by CASE, provide a working example of the enduring importance of public relations as a top management discipline. Most of these institutions operate with their chief communications officers as cabinet-level positions—vice presidents or vice chancellors of, usually, "public affairs." These positions, increasingly, also include marketing in the job description.

Several private groups, Keith Moore Associates for one, also offer excellent programming. In Keith Moore's case, he has developed a track record for an annual event that has come to be recognized as the best media relations conference available. CASE's annual conference for senior public relations and marketing practitioners is also noteworthy, as is its annual meeting for magazine editors. But these, too, are narrowly focused and don't even come close to covering the professional development needs of PR and marketing officers and staff professionals at the more than 3,500 universities nationwide.

Coming back to CHE/PRSA as an example, I was involved in the start-up of that organization, and was privileged to have a front-row seat to observe the dynamics of a start-up organization intended to fill a perceived void in service. Organizationally, and with limited resources, CHE is a part of PRSA—with the advantages and disadvantages that linking with a huge umbrella organization brings—and is challenged to grow much beyond its current membership, between 350 and 400. The logistics of managing a much larger group are simply beyond the ability of volunteers, however dedicated and idea-filled they may be.

THE ASCENDANCE OF "MARKETING": WHAT HAS BEEN GAINED AND LOST?

My first position as a chief public relations officer in higher education was at Berry College (Georgia) in 1985. "Marketing" was not in my job description, nor was it a concept that could be discussed easily with the faculty or academic leadership. Although the college was very successful recruiting students during the five years I served there, marketing for students was primarily the responsibility of a very successful director of admissions, George Gaddie. Although Gaddie outsourced design and production of much of Berry's marketing material and publications to a firm that specialized in these services, I quickly found ways to support the student recruiting effort through creation and placement of billboards and the development of a unique tool using personalized videos sent to every student who was accepted. During my tenure at Berry, more than 300 billboard placements were donated by a national outdoor advertising company (whose CEO happened to be a trustee). Also, several thousand individually edited videos were sent each year to accepted students, each with a 30-second, on-camera, personalized message by Gaddie attached to the beginning of the tape.

Even though the Berry College billboards were (almost entirely) donated, there was at first a firestorm of skepticism that we, *a college*, would stoop to such crass marketing tactics as billboards. After all, as the argument went, billboards are for advertising restaurants and cars, not pristine and prestigious institutions of higher education. Excellent and appropriate design, along with positive feedback from alumni and other constituents, soon prevailed, and billboards became the norm at Berry College during those years. Nevertheless, we never did publicly admit that we were "marketing" the college. Likewise, the use of personalized videos as a "marketing" tool became quite a sensation for a while, even attracting a feature news story on an Atlanta television station. Campus constituents for the most part described these activities not as "marketing," but rather as "good public relations."

Another experience at Illinois State University (ISU), where I worked as director of university relations from 1990 to 1994, convinced me that the world of higher education, at least *that* public university, was not yet fully subscribed to marketing as a legitimate function. As a part of a branding project (though we called it "institutional identity," and never "branding,"), it was my responsibility to sell a new slogan to the campus, "Gladly we learn and teach," adapted from the famous Chaucer line in *The Canterbury Tales*, "Gladly wolde he lerne, and gladly teche."[31] While conducting a meeting to explain the new strategy to a department chair, I was challenged with the comment that ISU's slogan ought instead to be, "Gladly we learn and *market!*" Clearly, this exercise in branding and messaging—two bedrock principles of marketing practice—was seen by this academic as frivolous at best, and extravagant and useless at worst.[32]

Later, while serving at Emory University as vice president for public affairs (1994 to 2001), we created the university's first office of university marketing. Marketing as a discipline had been employed there for many years in service to the university's large health care enterprise—a necessity for building patient numbers in a highly competitive urban healthcare landscape. Never before, officially, had marketing strategies been followed in order to "position" the institution for competitive purposes and to create consistent advertising messages on behalf of the university's strategic plan.

From my own experience, I have observed marketing as a full-fledged professional discipline move quickly over the past decade into the mainstream of most colleges and universities. In the gushing words of marketing guru Bob Topor in a 1997 issue of his electronic newsletter, *Marketing Higher Education*, "The time has arrived! You can't imagine how long I have waited for this: More schools, colleges and universities are finally organizing their staff and resources for higher education marketing. It has taken a long time."[33]

Presently, those of us with leadership responsibilities in these areas, it seems, are unable to embrace marketing quickly enough—only due to lack of sufficient resources—and enjoy all the benefits and advantages that a well-planned and executed marketing program can bring.

Clearly demonstrating the progress made in academe, for the first time in a 23-year career as a chief marketing and communications officer in a college or university setting, one of the central planks in my current job description is "marketing." As evidence of how marketing has come of age within the academy, University Relations with its strong marketing agenda at UNK is a cabinet-level partner with other major divisions of the university—business and finance, academics, campus life, and so on—in developing the university's Strategic Plan. We not only *may* participate, we *are expected* to participate in full recognition that the university will not reach its goals without a well-conceived, researched, and implemented marketing plan.

BRANDING: NOT JUST FOR CATTLE RANCHERS ANYMORE

The term "branding" is one of those marketing terms that, to say the least, has been embraced slowly by higher education, though it has been a staple of the corporate world for a very long time. But in recent years, universities have caught the branding bug, big time. At virtually every professional development conference on marketing and/or communication for colleges and universities that I've attended or known about in the past five years or so, no matter the organization providing the event, "branding" is a topic of at least one workshop, and sometimes several at the same conference. In fact, entire conferences devoted to branding are not uncommon. How is branding a university similar, or dissimilar, to branding a steer on a ranch? There are more similarities than one might imagine!

With regard to evolution of the terminology of branding, universities have remained true to form. In the earlier stages of academe's embrace of branding, the term in vogue was "institutional identity."[34] Correctly, universities had become concerned about how they were identified, including in my case leading an institutional identity program for Illinois State University. We recognized that using the same initials, "ISU," as at least three other major universities (Indiana State, Idaho State, Iowa State) was a problem. In addition to creating a set of distinctive graphics, we also issued guidelines for news releases and other marketing and advertising materials specifying the term "Illinois State" was to be used in place of "ISU." We did not use the term "branding" to describe the program, even though we created a new logo and a "wordmark" to be used as a mark of the institution.

Shortly after my arrival at Emory University in 1994, the marketing department of Emory University Health Care System (EUHCS), fondly pronounced "You . . . sh," realized the need for a new way of describing the large collection of clinics, hospitals, surgery centers, and other clinical services under the Emory health care umbrella. Though I was not responsible for the marketing department of the health care units, I took advantage of the momentum for a branding program in the health care units to build support for a university-wide branding effort. Again, even as late as 1996, we were more comfortable speaking of the need for a unified and coordinated "graphic identity system," and new campus and unit "identifiers," but not necessarily "branding," per se.

Thankfully, these name games no longer seem necessary. It is possible—even demanded—that we call branding and marketing by their names, with no hesitation. That is surely what we are doing at UNK, where we have recently developed and launched a new campus icon, as a part of a comprehensive marketing and branding strategy.

At its core, in my view, branding is simply—and profoundly—the process of creating a memorable visual look representative of the institution's values and culture. A well-planned and executed branding program will create associations between the institution, as represented by its graphics and slogans, the central essence of the place—its "promise," if you will. Like a brand seared on the hindquarters of a cow, the university's logo is a mark of ownership, identification, and, one might say, an instantly recognizable institutional "seal of approval."

Peeling back the layers, many other dynamics are also at play in a well-conceived branding program. First, *everything* is important in the presentation of an institution to its important audiences. A brand can represent high quality, distinctiveness, peculiarity, culture, value, among other characteristics. How can it be that so many great universities—among them some of the best known—can for so long carelessly ignore the manner in which they present themselves in their literature, signage, Web site, and collateral material?

A classic technique of a branding services salesperson is to collect, and lay out on a table or post on a wall, hundreds of printed pieces generated by the university and its many units and departments, sometimes no two pieces of which look anything like they came from the same institution. Dozens of wildly uncoordinated unit logos in this mishmash of visual images often add to the impression of disorganization and lack of cohesion.

Forward thinking college and university leaders really are beginning to understand the importance of good branding as a core component of marketing, and many are branding themselves very well, indeed. Numerous consultants and marketing firms now specialize in higher education branding, and job descriptions for professional marketing and communication staff are more likely than ever to include knowledge of branding strategies among the requirements of the job. A quick purview of university and college Web sites will show the progress made by academe—and, of course, the *lack* of progress by some.

A REALITY CHECK ON *U.S. NEWS* RANKINGS

Since the mid-1980s, colleges and universities have fretted over—and often celebrated—their rankings in *U.S. News & World Report*'s annual "Best Colleges" guide. Upon the rankings' release in the early fall each year, most institutions' public relations officers will pore over the rankings data, looking for and promoting those factors they see as advantageous to their reputation and positioning among peer and competitive institutions. If, as happens with some regularity, an institution moves down a notch or two in a particular year, the rankings are ignored. When the rankings, like the tides, move back up the next year, claims are made of institutional progress—"confirmed" by the positive ranking movement.

One would think that those universities that consistently show up in the top 20 in their categories, especially the crème de la crème list, Best National Universities, might be satisfied with their stratospheric positioning relative to the other 3,500 institutions in the nation. Having worked more than a decade for one of these universities, Emory University in Atlanta, I can confirm that the higher one's positioning on the list, the *more* worrisome is the competition. When the rank slides by a point or two—say, from 18th to 20th—this is usually a cause for complaints by students, and sometimes faculty, that "quality is slipping," or some such nonsense. While officially these universities are usually much too genteel for public bantering and teeth gnashing over such "unimportant" things as rankings, behind the scenes a great deal of attention is paid to strategies that, it is thought, may influence the rankings.

What, then, are colleges and universities to make of the rankings, not only the best known *U.S. News* rankings, but the growing number of other rankings of one sort or another? Much has been written about college rankings, frequently by college and university presidents who deride their importance and their methodology. Should rankings be regarded in the same category as, say, broadcast ratings in the media business? Or the Billboard charts in the music business? Or the Best Sellers lists in book publishing? Or, put another way, do students always receive the best education from those universities that are ranked high on the lists? And, if rankings measure popularity or prestige, are these good enough reasons to seek one's education at high-ranking schools? In short, how much stock should students and institutional leadership place in the U.S. News rankings?

To help answer some of these questions, Joe Brennan, a researcher and communications administrator at the State University of New York at Buffalo, led a team to examine five years of data from the popular magazine's survey reports, especially the reputation data that many schools attempt to influence with aggressive public relations campaigns. Surprisingly, Brennan found that "nearly half of the 248 schools had exactly the same [reputation] score in 2005 that they had in 2001." Another 46 schools experienced gains or losses by an insignificant 0.1 point, establishing in his study that "Clearly, peer assessment scores don't change much, if at all, over time."[35]

Perhaps his most significant finding, Brennan suggests that direct attempts by schools to significantly affect their position in the rankings are usually futile, even though "many schools surge bravely forward in their efforts to climb the rankings ladder, perhaps because they believe prospective students pay attention to the rankings." To this question, he cited an Art & Science Group survey that found that "just 20 percent could recall reading any articles or reports that ranked colleges. And only 8 percent said they used rankings information in the decision process."[36]

A Lipman Hearne study, also cited by Brennan, agreed, concluding that "college-bound students rated rankings guides among the least influential of information sources they consider, with 'direct sources'—campus visits and conversations with current students and faculty—at the top of their lists." Two-thirds of the students in the Lipman Hearne survey, in fact, said they ignored rankings altogether as an information source in choosing a college.[37]

WHAT MARKETING DOES NOT ACCOMPLISH

Though my ideas in this section may seem to contradict an earlier statement in this chapter to the effect that I would not draw distinctions among the various terms I've used to describe communications practices, the debate between advocates for the use of "marketing" and those who see "public relations" as the preeminent discipline deserves some comment.

The historical antecedent for this debate may be found in Kathleen Kelly's work, previously cited, that speaks of all these functions as falling under the "constituent relationship" function and properly named "public relations."[38]

The current debate was well represented by a panel of college and university public relations and marketing leaders at the 2008 Counselors to

Higher Education (CHE) Spring Summit meeting in Washington, DC Panelist Don Hale, vice president for public affairs at the University of Texas at Austin, articulated much of what he had previously written in a CHE monograph. First, he described the challenge of moving away from the "news bureau" model as a vestige of a narrow pursuit of "publicity," (i.e., "getting the word out is what they pay PR people to do"). These functions, he declared, have been outdated for two decades. Hale argued that our [PR] roots in this news bureau function hamper us to this day. If we are defined by this function, we are destined to fail.

"In the last few years," continued Hale, "we've been assaulted by the new higher education buzzword 'marketing,' and the highly acclaimed 'integrated marketing communications.' Here's another misnomer that is potentially lethal to public relations. . . . Isn't managing communications with all of an institution's key audiences something [that] public relations is supposed to do?" Warming to his topic, Hale explained what he sees as the core, and necessary, distinction between marketing and public relations:

> The sad truth is that these institutions who claim to be doing marketing are really just doing one aspect of it—product promotion. Their turn to marketing is an indictment of public relations. We have failed to meet our presidents' expectations. We haven't gotten the word out and we haven't delivered the press attention or public recognition that these presidents, our faculty and alumni know our institutions deserve.

The rise of marketing and the demise of public relations should be a wake-up call for each and every one of us. It's time to do some public relations for public relations. We must connect public relations to the business of our institutions. Let's demonstrate how we contribute to the success of admission, development, the research enterprise, and other sources of support for our colleges and universities.

- Close our news bureaus and abandon our in-house journalists' mentality.
- Capture the marketing function for public relations.
- Strengthen on-campus relationships, manage expectations, and build understanding of public relations.
- Improve our chief executives' understanding of and appreciation for public relations.

The success of our institutions is rooted in the relationships we build with our key publics. And those relationships are built on trust, on developing a mutually beneficial relationship based on an honest and open sharing of information. For the most part, these are not marketing relationships built on a transaction between buyer and seller. Just ask yourself, as an alumnus of your college or university, if you'd prefer to be part of a target market or a partner in a lifelong relationship with your institution. The answer is obvious.[39]

Contrary to Hale's strong defense of public relations, advocates for the "marketing-first" idea dismiss public relations as a "soft" discipline that is not as easily measured against the bottom line. Valuable, maybe, critics argue, but PR is seen clearly by marketing advocates as a support function for the *really* hard work of the institution, *marketing*.

ACHIEVING SYNTHESIS: BUSINESS PRACTICES WITHOUT COMPROMISING VALUES OR CULTURE

I have attempted to establish in this chapter that:

1. Business practices at American colleges and universities have become ever more refined and sophisticated in the face of increasing national and international competition between and among postsecondary educational institutions of all kinds, including public universities whose original tax-assisted missions were originally focused on serving the state in which they are located.

2. Business practices such as public relations and marketing have long been embraced by academe, though the vocabulary defining these functions has taken much longer to adopt.

3. Professional associations of communications and other advancement disciplines within higher education have struggled to stay abreast of trends driven by competitive forces, and have evolved—some say "splintered"—in the face of divergent philosophies of governing and prioritizing these disciplines.

4. Marketing and fund-raising have emerged as the dominant functions over public relations, but with serious concerns on the part of some professionals that the larger goals of the institution (serving the larger society, producing truly "educated" students) may easily be compromised in this process.

5. A subdiscipline of marketing, "branding," has gained acceptance and priority across academe, sometimes as a magic bullet cure-all, but more often as a welcome tool for defining and projecting the distinctive promise of institutions to its constituents.

6. Rankings such as those published by *U.S. News & World Report*, though seen by many as artificial and inaccurate measures of quality—and even dangerous by some— nevertheless are driving the almost universal quest among colleges and universities for prestige and perceived market position.

7. Marketing, if not defined and deployed in the fullest sense that goes way beyond publicity and promotion to true long-term relationship and reputation building, may push institutions toward decisions that, while driving the bottom line, may also drive them away from the long-held and cherished mission of higher education that would seek to change the world by positively affecting "the human condition."

Leaders of higher education will serve their institutions best by taking a broad, informed view of communications-related business practices. Terminology is certainly important. But truly great and effective advancement work has been done, and continues to be done, under any and all of the descriptors that are discussed here.

Every college and every university needs an experienced, savvy public relations practitioner, well-connected to the managing coalition, plying her craft according to time-tested best practices—developed first in the corporate world and migrated over time to academe.

Every college and every university needs an experienced and effective marketing specialist, one who understands the market forces that drive audience decisions, and has the creative talent to produce a compelling case for positive action on behalf of the institution.

And, certainly, every college and every university needs a professional who is well-trained and experienced in the art and science of raising private funds to supplement traditional income streams such as tuition and public funding.

These disciplines are all complementary and necessary, and must be exercised with every bit of sophistication and nuance in delivery that can be mustered, however they may be organized to work together within the organization. Professional associations, especially CASE with its focused resources, might "advance" higher education and the professions it represents with a reexamination of the term upon which it was founded, "advancement." Perhaps the coining of a new term is in order that harkens back to the original intended meaning of "advancement" as defined in the historic Greenbrier Report, which certainly carried a broader meaning than only "fund-raising."

Finally, as I've said time and again to my students and to staff colleagues, I can think of no more satisfying lifelong profession than the one I've had, and continue to have, of advocacy by whatever name for higher education, in the interest of students of whatever age, and, yes, in the interest of a better world.

NOTES

1. John Henry Newman, *The Idea of a University* (New Haven, CT: Yale University Press, 1996), 218. First published in 1899.
2. E. Boyer, "Point of View," *The Chronicle of Higher Education*, March 9, 1994, A48.
3. J. L Fisher and J. V. Koch, *Presidential Leadership: Making a Difference* (Phoenix, AZ: Oryx Press, 1996), 12.
4. E. L. Boyer, *College: The Undergraduate Experience in America* (New York: Harper & Row, 1987), 249.
5. R. A. Sevier, "Marketing: The Big Questions Answered. How to Increase the Effectiveness of Your Marketing Spending," *University Business,* May 2008, http://www.universitybusiness.com/viewarticle.aspx?articleid=1059.
6. G. Keller, notes from conference entitled, "Essentials of Strategic Planning and Marketing," CASE Conference, Baltimore, MD, October 15–16, 1986.
7. J. L. Pulley, "Burnishing Their Brands," *Chronicle of Higher Education,* October 24, 2003, A30.
8. C. Kerr, *Three Thousand Futures: The Next Twenty Years in Higher Education* (San Francisco: Carnegie Council on Policy Studies in Higher Education, 1980), 151.
9. C. K. Carlson, unpublished, "Public Relations Plan: Berry College," December 27, 1985.
10. C. K. Carlson, unpublished, "Public Relations Themes/Goals: Emory University," September 25, 1995.
11. C. K. Carlson, unpublished, "Emory University Public Affairs Plans for 2004–2005," September 1, 2004.
12. C. K. Carlson, unpublished, "University of Nebraska at Kearney Phase II Implementation Plan: University Relations," June 4, 2008.
13. K. S. Kelly, *Effective Fund-Raising Management* (Mahway, NJ: Lawrence Erlbaum Associates, 1998), 141.
14. Ibid., 143.
15. Ibid., 152.
16. C. K. Carlson, personal notes from membership on the CASE Commission for Communications and Marketing, 2004.
17. National Association for College Admission Counseling, http://www.nacacnet.org/.

18. M. J. Worth, *New Strategies for Educational Fundraising* (Westport, CT: Praeger Publishers, 2002), 31.

19. K. S. Kelly, *Effective Fund-Raising Management*, 382.

20. K. S. Kelly, "Fund Raising: Functional Element in Public Relations Education," *Journalism Educator* 47(2) (1992), 19–25.

21. Ibid.

22. K. S. Kelly, *Effective Fund-Raising Management*, 382.

23. J. Taber, notes from conference call of the Executive Committee of Counselors to Higher Education, 1999.

24. CASE, "Principles of Practice for Communications and Marketing Professionals at Educational Institutions," July 2004, http://www.case.org/Content/AboutCASE/Display.cfm?CONTAINERID=127&CONTENTITEMID=4384&CRUMB=3.

25. Public Broadcasting Service, "Declining by Degrees, Higher Education at Risk," 2005, http://www.decliningbydegrees.org.

26. A. C. Peyronel, "Public Relations, Ethics and Gaining a Seat at the Leadership Table," *PRSA Counselors to Higher Education 2005 Monograph Series* (New York: Public Relations Society of America, 2005), 3–4.

27. C. S. Stepp, "Higher Examination," *American Journalism Review* 25(1) (2003): 18–25.

28. J. J. Cheslock and M. Gianneschi, "Abstract: Replacing State Appropriations with Alternative Revenue Sources: The Case of Voluntary Support," *Journal of Higher Education* 79, no. 2 (2008): 208–29.

29. R. Zemsky, ed., "To Dance with Change," *Policy Perspectives,* 5(3), (1994): 1–4.

30. P. G. Altbach, *American Higher Education in the Twenty-first Century* (Baltimore, MD: Johns Hopkins University Press, 1999), 15.

31. Milner Library, Illinois State University, http://people.coe.ilstu.edu/malorber/seal.html.

32. C. K. Carlson, "The First Step of Marketing a College or University: Finding and Projecting Its True Identity" (paper presented at the 1992 Symposium for the Marketing of Higher Education, Chicago, Illinois, 1992), 5–13.

33. B. Topor, "Organizing an Institution of Higher Education for Effective Marketing: A New Paradigm," in *Marketing Higher Education,* (San Francisco: Topor Consulting Group International, 1997), 1–4.

34. C. K. Carlson, "The First Step of Marketing a College or University: Finding and Projecting Its True Identity," 5–13.

35. J. Brennan, "Be Careful What You Promise Regarding Your *U.S. News & World Report* Ranking." Counselors to Higher Education, 2008, http://www.prsa.org/networking/sections/che/documents/Brennan_monograph_rankings_2008.pdf, 3.

36. Ibid.
37. Ibid.
38. K. S. Kelly, "Fund Raising: Functional Element in Public Relations Education," *Journalism Educator* 47(2) (1992), 19–25.
39. D. Hale, "Public Relations in Higher Education, a Retrospective and Forecast," Counselors to Higher Education, February 2001, http://www.prsa.org/networking/sections/che/monographs1.html.

CHAPTER 3

Marketing the Academy: Benefits and Barriers

Larry D. Lauer

Marketing higher education has become a hot topic all over the world. The interest in it in institutions from the United States to Asia is intense, but there are also concerns about the possibility of commercialization. Competition for students, the increasing sophistication of consumers, the growing need to find new sources of revenue, and the increasing difficulty in gaining positive visibility all suggest that the academy must become more sophisticated in indentifying its audiences and telling its story.

No one argues that competition is not intense. However, some still have the "build it and they will come" attitude about colleges and universities. These people believe that quality speaks for itself, and that traditional admissions work is all that is needed. They usually are scholars with traditional academic training and have legitimate concerns about just giving the students what research tells us students and parents want. Their standard argument is that educators know better than high school students what college students will need to learn, and that making "we will meet your needs" promises to lure them in will diminish the academy.

Those who work in the admissions and communications fields on a daily basis, however, are unavoidably aware of how aggressive competition has become. Past enrollment indicators no longer help very much. They know that defining and developing basic institutional strengths, and identifying and understanding specific market segments, is the only way to keep an academic institution viable in this rapidly changing world. They have also come to see that meeting student and parent needs is only the first step in the life-changing educational process. Once they arrive on campus, it is up to the faculty to show students a whole new world.

This same type of marketing thinking applies to building a reputation and raising funds. The more precisely competitive advantage and strengths can be defined, the more effectively a reputation can be built. Likewise, the better donors' needs are understood, the more effective fund-raisers can be in knowing how to attract their financial support. This is what marketing offers higher education: understanding institutional strengths, as well as the perceived and real needs of constituents while systematically building a relationship between the two.

INTERNATIONAL TRENDS

There are a number of other factors that add even more intensity to the need to market institutions. The most basic is that government roles in higher education are changing. Most governments, in one way or another, are actually cutting back funding. The specifics change in different parts of the world. In some places, governments are setting national defense and social priorities believing that, between fees and private fund-raising, most universities are now able to do more to take care of themselves. Others are investing in science and technology, but not in overall academic support. Some are investing primarily to make their institutions more competitive and now need sophisticated marketing to make their efforts better known. The consequence is that when one institution initiates an aggressive marketing program, others follow, and when everyone is doing it, the marketplace becomes intensely competitive. In the case of the business of higher education, this more competitive market is also becoming more international.

Other international trends include the recognition of the power of the Internet to allow any business or educational institution to be competitive from any place on the globe. The world indeed has become smaller, and anyone from anywhere can participate in the global marketplace. I call my local bank, but talk to someone in India. I may sit in India and take a course offered in the United States. The consequence is a sense that the world is the market and each university can be a truly international institution.

For example, most agree that the world economy is moving east toward Asia. More and more universities, therefore, want to offer an "Asia savvy" education. They also find that, as they look for students who desire this kind of education, and look for donors, it is gradually becoming easier to find new ones outside their own country's boundaries. Partnerships with other institutions closer to Asia, new campuses in the Middle East and Asia, distance education, and study abroad—all of these developments arise out of the realization that an education today must be global, and so it has become imperative that the marketing of higher education become international as well.

Once an institution looks outside its borders for one new market opportunity, it also soon looks for others. Thus, institutions in countries such as the United Kingdom, India, China, and Australia are now looking for graduate and undergraduate students and money in the United States, pointing out that they offer increasing quality, growing prestige, and an "Asia savvy" international experience. Many of them can also offer entire degree programs in English.

MARKETING IS A WAY OF THINKING

Academics fear the commercialization of the academy, and they should, so it is important to understand that when adapting the subject matter of marketing to colleges and universities, it must become a way of thinking and cannot be allowed to become a way of commercializing. The way to think about it is that marketing is only a matter of being able to consider programs and services, price, program and service distribution, and communication strategies and tactics simultaneously. In the traditional academic institution, programs are developed first, and later in the process someone is called upon to communicate them.

The marketing oriented institution is more sophisticated. First, a study is done of the market trends, and then they are matched to institutional strengths. The institution only moves ahead when there is alignment. It will not move ahead when the needs suggest a program the institution is not equipped to offer or if the program does not match its strengths. The marketing oriented institution also considers price, but not so much because it needs the money. It does so because it connects with market realities and makes itself more competitive. Such an institution also sees distribution in terms of the total institutional experience, from housing to food service, to recreation, to bureaucratic processes, and to the service attitudes reflected in human discourse. Finally, it considers how the new world of communication integrates with these other factors. In integrated marketing, all this is done simultaneously.

WHY "INTEGRATED" MARKETING?

The marketing-oriented institution realizes quickly that striving to get everyone on the same page with respect to their understanding of strengths and competitive advantage is another necessary competitive goal. Of course, not everyone will ever be on board, but the reality is that, in the Internet world, word of mouth is the most powerful of the marketing tools and that getting as many students, staff, faculty, alumni, and friends as possible to tell the same story to everyone they know is essential to achieving ongoing success.

Integrated marketing really is a matter of orchestrating an entire institution. It mobilizes talented people no matter where they are found in the institution, gets most of them to tell the same story, and influences how they spend the resources in their program units and what new programs they develop. It therefore results in coordinating decentralized departments and schools and getting everyone tuned in to advancing total institutional goals as well as their own.

Academic marketing must be based on research. Research answers key questions: Have people in target market segments even heard of us? If so, what do they think about us? What do they know about us? The fact is that research usually reveals that even the closest stakeholders know very little about an organization, but in the final analysis it is most important that they have heard of the organization and have a high opinion of its quality and importance in the world. The marketing-oriented university therefore bases its program and communication targets on research, so that weaknesses are addressed and strengths are reinforced. Research informs the institution about student markets, current students, staff, faculty, alumni, community opinion leaders, and donors.

In order to utilize research effectively, key process tools must be infused into the management culture. For example, task forces are often used to bring key people in the institution together to define strengths and identify barriers and problems. Creative teams are used to bring planners, writers, designers, and others together to implement special marketing initiatives. Leadership is developed to "walk the talk" and champion the integrated process. All of this is focused on relationship building and is what makes the whole integrated process work. Remember, building relationships is the institution's most effective and enduring competitive advantage.

A new program initiative can achieve temporary competitive advantage, but competitors can and will match a new program. A relationship that makes students, parents, and donors feel that they are more comfortable dealing with this institution becomes the best competitive advantage of all. This integrated approach to marketing also translates strengths into what marketers call a "brand."

WHAT IS A BRAND AND WHY SHOULD INSTITUTIONS DEVELOP ONE?

An organization's name first has to be known in the places where it does business. It is virtually impossible in today's media world for academic institutions to be continually name recognized all over the world. Thus, picking target markets and the most effective media tools for use in them is a critical part of the professionalism of marketing. Most important of all is the knowledge of how to do this with a simple and direct message that communicates the institution's strengths and differentiates it from others.

In its most basic form, a brand is a feeling. It is a feeling that "I know what this institution stands for, I can rely on it to be consistent, and I can trust it to be honest." This feeling must be built systematically and maintained over time. It also requires that a few message themes be repeated over and over and that any contact with the institution reinforces the truth and consistency of what the institution promises. A brand, then, is really a promise made and a promise kept.

Developing a brand takes time and requires that a simple message be surrounded by a consistent and compelling design. An effective brand design will consist of shapes, textures, or colors that come to stand for the institution itself. They are selected by an artist because they artistically reinforce the substance and feeling of the brand message. This design can include a mark or symbol, referred to as a "logo," but a logo is not the brand. The brand is the sum total feeling the consumer has about the essence of the institution. Over time, however, and with consistent communication, the logo can come to stand for the brand and evoke the brand feeling in the consumer. This is why brands are so important, and especially so in a competitive situation where institutions need to stand out in a differentiated and compelling way. Both branding and marketing, then, are ways of thinking and ways to help make and keep an institution relevant in a rapidly changing world.

Integrated marketing also provides the process tools for getting the brand embedded into the internal culture of an institution. To accomplish this, small groups that represent all the constituents of the institution should be formed to brainstorm and prioritize strengths. A list is then reduced to the several most differentiating ones. Most academic institutions share similar characteristics, but their differentiation comes in how several key ones come together and are accompanied by unique design elements.

The groups that have helped clarify the brand can now be used to help merge it into the culture and conversation of the institution. This is an internal communication function, and it is an extremely important aspect of integrated marketing. Campus banners, messages in internal media, talking points for executive speeches, message boards, presentation at staff meetings, new employee orientations, and so on are all communication tools that are used. The longer professionals work in integrated marketing in academic institutions, the more they come to see the importance of defining the brand.

THE PLACE OF SUBBRANDS

Many academic institutions are composed of individual colleges, schools, and programs that have become "silos" promoting themselves without acknowledging their common institutional bond. Eventually this leads to a larger institution struggling to clarify and maintain its identity. It must be recognized that a school or college brand identity in the long term is limited by the reputation of the institution of which it is a part. Many deans and directors do not see it this way in the short term. After all, they have been hired in many ways as "mini-presidents" expected to find good students, raise money, and build their program's reputation.

Nevertheless, in the final analysis, the parent institution is a ceiling, and the only way for each individual program to continue to advance into the future is for the institution to advance as well.

Individual colleges, schools, and programs in integrated marketing are therefore treated as subbrands of the institutional brand. Bringing this about requires an integrated process. For example, a business school must look like a business school, but it also should reflect the look and identity of the parent institution as well. With creative writing and design, this can certainly be accomplished while maintaining individual school and college identity and distinctions.

INTEGRATED COMMUNICATION

At one time, marketers talked more about promotion and publicity than total communication. Integrated marketers today talk more about integrated communication. In other words, communication has become far more sophisticated. All of the tools in the communication tool box are used, and the challenge is to select the right ones for each market segment. Integrated communication, then, simply focuses the best combination of tools to converge on a specific market segment for maximum intensity and impact.

With the dramatic decline in newspaper readership and the rapid development of new media, the promotion element of marketing has gone through a dramatic change. Today, the more direct and interactive the media, the better it works, and so new media, such as email, pop-up ads, Web sites with Flash video, podcasts, RSS feeds, and so on are now combined with regular mailings, phone calls, personal calls, print advertising, special events, branded gifts, and the like to create a convergence of messages that is intended to cut through the clutter of an oversaturated media world. Some have actually declared mass media dead. This is not the case; rather, opinion leaders and stakeholders are targeted, and the aim is to ultimately generate word-of-mouth support. All of this changes the old news service or information office approach of sending out press releases into more of an internal marketing and communication agency working with all the media to develop total impact communication plans. This new digital media world is therefore opening up academic marketing to a whole new generation of creative professionals with a whole new set of communication tools.

THE BARRIERS TO MARKETING

There continue to be barriers to bringing this more sophisticated marketing approach to the academy. What are they, and how should they be addressed?

At the end of a summer institute on academic marketing, students were asked what they thought they would face when taking some of the ideas and strategies they learned back to their institutions. Their answers invariably included the comment: "If only I did not have to deal with the politics, I could be more effective." And the response given back was: "Not only will you not be able to avoid the politics, if you are going to be successful in this work, you had better learn to love the politics!" Here are some typical barriers that require some political savvy to address:

1. *Academic attitude that marketing is commercial and not appropriate in the academy.* Approaching this problem requires empathy. Professional marketers need to express understanding first and assure scholars and career teachers that, especially for academic institutions, marketing is a way of thinking and the last thing it should do is commercialize. Marketing research defines trends and identifies ways to make contact with consumers. The process that follows builds relationships with them and then turns them over to professors to take them in to a whole new world of possibilities. If anything, good marketing makes the academic mission better understood and appreciated. Most academics will come to understand and support sophisticated marketing and communication when they are first approached with a sincere understanding of their concerns.

2. *Unit heads that feel threatened by opening their units to participatory processes.* Some admission deans, for example, respond to creative teams and outside participation with the attitude that they have

been hired to do the job and they want to do it their way. After all, they are experienced professionals and they do not want their work guided by a committee. They will live or die by their decisions. Many of these people can be won over, however, when they experience how effective well-facilitated teams can be. They see that, while credit for successes must be shared, failure must be shared too. By thinking and acting outside the box, they are bringing more minds to problem solving, and their work actually becomes more satisfying.

3. *Lack of support at the top.* Sometimes it is the president and/or provost who lack appreciation for marketing, even though someone just below them sees how essential it will be to the future of the institution. Without support from the top, marketing has little hope of long-term success, especially integrated marketing where process participation is essential. It is when the president appoints a campus-wide marketing task force and asks people to participate that they will take it seriously, and when ideas and recommendations come back to the president, they have a much better chance of being implemented. So, if the president needs to be persuaded to try marketing, find the people who most influence him or her, and then work on influencing them. Persistence combined with diplomacy and savvy can win the day.

4. *Lack of money.* The fear that there will be no new money to spend on marketing keeps many institutions from taking the first step. The fact is that the integrated planning process will usually get better results merely by spending differently what currently is being spent. The best approach is often to begin with what money is there and make expenditures more effective through creative team interaction, a more precise brand identity, better market targeting, and integrated convergence communication. Once better results are produced, more resources are likely to follow. This works best, however, when the president has been a part of the whole integrated process.

5. *The person championing marketing is seen with suspicion.* Academics often have a difficult time listening to a professional marketer who has little or no experience as an academic. Outside agency people, consultants, or former corporate executives often come on too strong, use too much commercial language too soon, and lack the patience to show the empathy necessary to communicate with lifelong academics. Once the faculty has been exposed to someone like this, it takes a while to turn the situation around.

The answer is to have someone with academic experience and who also understands marketing take the lead inside. If outside people or firms are used, they will need to be willing to learn about the academic world, respect those in it and their attitudes, and be willing to demonstrate the patience necessary to build understanding and trust.

6. *The dean who has been hired as a little president.* Many deans are hired with the understanding that they are to ramp up the visibility and reputation of the program, find the best students, and raise money. When someone from central administration shows up wanting to integrate the marketing and branding with the institution, such deans are likely to respond negatively. It is very difficult for them to see the longer-term benefit to them of lifting the institution's visibility and reputation, so the strategy for them, too, must begin with empathy and understanding for their situation and then proceed by convincing them that the goal of integrated marketing is to help them develop a total marketing plan for their school and to bring them additional resources in the form of talent and staff time. Breaking down silos has become the strong objective of many larger college and university presidents in these more competitive times.

CONCLUSION

Marketing academic institutions has become one of higher education's hot topics because of recent intensification in the competition for students, money, reputation, and visibility. The topic has generated international interest and practice as a consequence of changing government roles, the competitive possibilities of the Internet world, and the movement of the economy toward Asia. Integrated marketing is the process of getting everyone in an institution onto the same page and using creative teams and integrated convergence communication to enhance marketing effectiveness. The barriers include academic fears of commercialization, lack of understanding in the administrative leadership, distrust of the person championing the idea, department heads who dislike out-of-the-box group processes, and deans and department heads who want to focus on their own silos. In the final analysis, however, marketing well done and carefully adapted to the academy will strengthen the academic integrity of academic institutions and broaden everyone's understanding and appreciation of the greater good contributions of the academic world.

FURTHER READING

Adler, Roy D., and Thomas J. Hayes. *University Marketing Mistakes: 50 Pitfalls to Avoid.* Washington, DC: CASE Books, 2008.

Friedman, Thomas. *The World Is Flat: A Brief History of the 21st Century.* New York: Farrar, Straus, Giroux Publishers, 2005.

Kim, W. Chan, and Renee Mauborgne. *Blue Ocean Strategy: How to Create Uncontested Market Space and Make the Competition Irrelevant.* Boston: Harvard Business School Press, 2005.

Lauer, Larry D. *Competing for Students, Money and Reputation: Marketing the Academy in the 21st Century.* Washington, DC: CASE Books, 2002.

Lauer, Larry D. *Advancing Higher Education in Uncertain Times.* Washington, DC: CASE Books, 2006.

Senge, Peter M. *The Fifth Discipline: The Art and Practice of the Learning Organization.* New York: Doubleday, 1990.

Sevier, Robert A. *Integrated Marketing for Colleges and Universities: A Step-by-Step Planning Guide.* Washington, DC: CASE Books, 1998.

Sevier, Robert A. *Building a Brand That Matters: Helping Colleges and Universities Capitalize on the Four Essential Elements of a Block-Buster Brand.* Hiawatha, IA: Strategy Publishing, 2002.

Trout, Jack, with Steve Rivkin. *Differentiate or Die: Survival in Our Era of Killer Competition.* New York: John Wiley and Sons, 2000.

CHAPTER 4

Seeing Is Believing

Malcolm Grear

Design is a form of art. If it is approached as an art, a certain dignity can be sustained to help ward off the venalities of the marketplace.

There is no substitute for seeing the big picture, the entire system.

When we meet someone for the first time, we get a sense of that person from several sources—voice, demeanor, handshake, gestures, even smell—but usually the dominant signals are visual. This *first impression* is quickly formed. With time and frequent contact under varied circumstances, this impression is modified, made subtle and complex through interactions that deliver more signals, more information. Still, the original impression lingers in memory, shaping our view of that person henceforth. The same is true with organizations.

Whether a corporation or university, an organization likewise reveals to us its character and purpose in diverse ways—the behavior of its personnel, the quality of its products, performance, or services—but, as with a person, its visual presentation remains a strongly influential force.

Visual presentation—and, more broadly, visual communication—is the scope of graphic design. The dictionary definition of graphic, "giving a clear and effective picture," reveals a key function of graphic design: to convert information. As with music, design must set a mood, generate tension, surprise, or calm; it can startle or seduce. But all of these emotional states, and many others, are for the designer a kind of information.

Music in a movie tells you what to think or feel about what's going on. In a sense, design does the same thing—it tells you how to respond to the rest of the message embodied in the graphics—and again, like music, or like smell, the visual signals shoot straight to the emotions. That is the power of graphics.

Graphic design is not an independent, private art, such as painting, sculpture, or music, although it draws upon these disciplines. It is a public enterprise, devising ways to communicate information through form, color, texture, and the other visual signals.

"Professional" design can be said to have started in earnest in the United States in the 1930s—although designing is an activity as ancient as the human species—and it came more clearly into focus in the 1950s, locating itself between the fine arts and advertising art. The first generation of graphic designers wanted to separate themselves from advertising, which some saw, rather preciously, as the sleazy side of graphic communication, since they considered it tainted by commercial intentions.

This disdain for and suspicion of commerce was in part a response to the perceived need for more objective, more ethically responsible graphic communication.

These pioneers of graphic design wished to see themselves as more socially responsible than their cohorts in the world of commercial advertising art. They wanted to use images and type, color and form, and other design elements to convey information vividly but honestly instead of dressing up hard-sell copy to seduce buyers. Despite these efforts at separation, the distinction between graphic design and commercial art is often blurred, since both serve the needs of business.

Graphic design at its best, however, attempts to deliver direct visual communication, while most commercial art is meant to entice, but enticement is a form of communication, too, and often a worthy one. Further, it should not be said that all advertising is without integrity or that those inventing it have no concern for truth and aesthetics. It is simply that those involved in advertising as a profession need not focus on such matters. Their purpose, quite sensibly, is to sell, whereas those involved in graphic design have a different purpose: to communicate information graphically, which includes values as well as facts.

Because its purpose is to communicate, graphic design remains neutral with respect to the industry it serves, so whether applied to a corporation or a university, graphic design functions to communicate something about the organization, typically its identity, character, and purpose. This is the true whether what is being designed is a visual identity, publication or other print matter, signage or wayfinding, or any number of other applications of design.

When done well, graphic design helps to identify an organization and thus improve its performances *externally* within its market—and here I mean market in the broad sense, where universities as well as corporations have a market. Design also helps improve performance *internally* within the organization itself. There is nothing exotic about this phenomenon. Workers at all levels within an organization can get an emotional boost from the power that their organization's visual identity, including environmental graphics, generates. Where does pride come from? We shall leave that answer to the psychologists or maybe the genetics and evolutionary biologists. There is no question, however, that pride is a motivating stimulus—sometimes a politically destructive one (think of Nazi pride)—and there is no question that being proud of one's organization can prompt a person to work hard to fulfill its mission. Put simply, no matter what type of organization a body is, good design is good for the organization, inside and out.

The most effective graphic design, or visual communication, then, captures and conveys an organization's personality, including its mission, vision, values, and goals. It does this through the use of images and symbols that assert the organization's meaning and significance.

IDENTIFYING THE PERSONALITY OF AN ORGANIZATION

Each of us has what psychologists call a *personality,* and we all know intuitively what is meant by that term. It means the muddled assortment of dynamic actions that, taken together, are seen to be the person himself or herself. We are consistent creatures. We have a way about us. Each of us has an array of attributes, attitudes, mannerisms, and quirks—a uniquely complicated pattern of moods and behaviors—that, taken together, become, to ourselves and others, the *way* we are, indeed, who we are. I'm calling that composite thing our personality, our spirit, and I am saying that organizations of various sorts can have one, too.

A designer needs to discover—and, sometimes, help to create—an organization's spirit, and then devise a symbol that conveys it. Helping an organization create its spirit or personality is a substantial part of the designer's job. Unlike an individual, whose personality is, for the most part, set and inescapable, even if difficult to define, an organization might have failed to achieve a state of maturation that allows it to see itself, and to be seen by others, as having any distinct identity at all. When this is so, when the organization's identity, for whatever reason, remains amorphous, a strong symbol, properly presented, can give it a distinct, easily recognized, and favorable personality.

Consider how design helped Apple. In this era of casual attire, the "clothes" an organization wears, its visual devices (logo, signage, package, letterhead, and so on) have great meaning as an expression of, among other things, its personality. Apple has generated an upbeat mood in the marketplace for computers not just because the hardware works well; the look counts, too. Product design and promotion design in all its ramifications have pulled that company out of the "valley of the shadow" and back onto the playing fields of business. If an organization lacks a distinct and positive personality, the designer can provide one—and I mean an authentic one, not just a superficial dressing up that fails to stand the test of time.

To get at the organization's authentic personality, a designer must catch the essence of the enterprise, understand its nature, history, purpose, intentions, virtues, and dilemmas. Without this profound understanding of the organization, a designer has no way to invent—or reinvent—a strong visual identity that gains and holds the attention of those who matter in the organization's sphere of action. No composer can write effective music for a movie without first reading the screenplay. Most such music is written after a draft of the film is already in the can. The same goes for the designer. You need at the outset to see the operation in action, to get to know the enterprise inside and out.

Whether new business or old, we at Malcolm Grear Designers begin with interviews, talk to the head of the organization and to its directors, management, staff, and members of the target audience: customers, clients, and so on. We pose questions about the business plan and the competition, examine the product or service, and use them if possible. We look closely, too, at what competitors are offering; we consider and compare. Through this research, we become members of our client's effort, take it to heart, and make it our own. Only then can we begin to design.

When we have completed research and analysis, gained the requisite understanding of our client and audience, tested the products and services, taken for ourselves the client's goals, and made them our own, we begin the thrilling part; we begin to design.

Sometimes our client asks whether we will be showing them a set of proposed designs from which they may choose a favorite. "NO!" is the answer. It cannot be done. Design is a creative act, in our case a collaborative endeavor among members of our studio and, during the research stage, among ourselves and members of the client's staff. During this process, we will surely develop a number of possible solutions; but we keep these to ourselves until we settle upon the one that works best, which then becomes our point of focus.

Consider this parable:

A fishmonger commissions an artist to draw a fish for a sign to attract customers. A long time passes. The fishmonger can wait no longer. He goes to the artist's studio to demand his sign. He says, "I need that image of a fish."

The artist promptly draws a uniquely beautiful fish, the perfect sign.

The fishmonger says, "That took you just a few minutes! Why didn't you get back to me ages ago?"

The artist opens a closet door; hundreds of sketches of fish fall to the floor.

SYMBOLIZING AN ORGANIZATION'S PERSONALITY: THE LOGOTYPE

The world is increasingly cluttered with signals clamoring for attention. Designers need to take this circumstance as a sign of cultural and economic vitality and a challenge to our ingenuity, even though much of the resulting visual and auditory tumult can be exasperating. How, in the thick of this clutter, do we create for our client a visual identity that reaches the audience and earns its attention and allegiance? How do we help the client distinguish itself among competing symbols in a crowded marketplace?

There is no easy answer. But there *is* an answer. One can devise a symbolic form—a logotype—that stands for the enterprise, making it salient amid the noise of daily commerce, and that symbolic form must last; it must work over the long haul, entering the minds of its audience, gaining respect, even affection, as it gains familiarity. Certainly, the character of the enterprise itself, the quality and integrity of its products or services, will be crucial. These attributes will determine public response, and this is as it should be. What the logotype must do is *symbolize* these attributes, assert their importance, and serve as an insistent and welcome reminder that the enterprise is alive, strong, enduring, and reliable. You can count on it!

Creating an engaging and meaningful logotype is the first step in constructing a whole identity scheme, the interrelated visual mechanisms that embody the personality of the entity being symbolized.

A logotype is a simple tool, like a hammer; it has a straightforward function. Anything that gets in the way of that function weakens the effectiveness of the tool. Keep it simple. You do not need an elaborate hammer, one with adornments. The same is true for symbols. Simplicity, clarity, and elegance are key; by elegance, I mean the sort of form that a wide diversity of viewers will find visually active and easily remembered. Being memorable matters a lot. If the form is ornate, it cannot stick in memory.

Such simplicity is hard to achieve if what you are after is attractive, memorable simplicity that carries your message without ambiguity. Simple and ugly is easy; simple and boring is easy; simple and vague is also easy. How, then, does a designer go about achieving this simple result, a hammer that hammers, a symbol that symbolizes? The answer itself is simple; it is the process that is hard. Study the client, study the audience. This is all about communication. The client sends, the audience receives. The symbol is the signal, so the designer must understand what the client needs to communicate to its audience and must also understand how the audience can best receive that communication.

At best, a symbol that becomes part of the organization's signature is an important part of its visual identification. It serves as common linkage for publications, advertisements, and building signage. The wide exposure of a symbol ensures its position as one of the single most important aspects of visual identity.

To design a symbol, one worth having, is one of the most challenging jobs a serious designer can undertake. This is especially true if he believes that the symbol must be unique, memorable and as timeless as possible, not moving in and out of vogue, and if he foresees its being used large and small, in two dimensions as well as three, and will not accept any image that exhausts its meaning at first glance. The symbol should convey an idea rather than a literal picture. It can certainly be pictorial, although it may have a short life span—as a single picture soon becomes obsolete—and it will have little flexibility. An idea, well conveyed, does not exhaust its meaning quickly; its message of identity or functions seems inevitable and timeless.

An example that some may think goes against my philosophy on pictorial images is the symbol that Malcolm Grear Designers created for the Presbyterian Church USA. During the process, we designed some really nice pictorial images but ruled them out, feeling that they would have a short life because they were too pictorial. Our final design, which was hugely accepted, was what I call a transformative image (see Figure 4.1). This symbol had an entire book written about it, with a chapter dedicated to each of its seven components: the cross, the pulpit, the dove, the cup, the fish, the fire, and the book.

Developing a strong visual identity is a major concern for most aspiring organizations. Before distinctive imagery can be designed, the organization must establish clear, specific, and unique goals, as was the case with the Presbyterian Church USA. Sign and symbol must sing a message.

The majority of the visual identity programs that Malcolm Grear Designers creates include a symbol incorporated with the name of the organization. This becomes the logotype. If the name of the organization

Figure 4.1

is short, strong, and direct, then the name, all by itself, may be used as the logotype. The word becomes the symbol, making the symbol's meaning clear and direct. This was the case when we were hired to design the logotype for Emory University and Bates College (see Figure 4.2). Both organizations have short names, easily remembered. We use this strategy often in our work on visual identity, mainly to make explicit what the symbol means.

Abstractions can be attractive, but our central task is to send a message. We *mean* Bates College; we *mean* Emory University; these are the messages that matter, that establish and sustain the identity.

Visual identities for colleges and universities are a unique design challenge, as often there are numerous subentities (i.e., schools, colleges, departments, and programs) that want their own identities to stand out.

They may think they are so strong, well organized, and independent that there is no need to appear as if they are part of the whole picture, under the institution's umbrella. They may even already have an existing

Figure 4.2

EMORY
UNIVERSITY

visual identity without considering any juxtaposing relationship to the university's visual identity.

If we are successful in our task, this closed viewpoint will change during the research process, when the individual units begin to understand the importance and benefits of companionship with the parent.

In the case of Emory University, we designed a shield system that could be used in conjunction with our new Emory wordmark. We redesigned Emory's historic shield and developed a system where the individual schools could adopt this official shield or use the shield framework to contain their own visual identity. These identities needed to follow specific guidelines. The system allowed for individuality within the university, but also created a cohesive structure that reinforced the strength of Emory as a whole (see Figures 4.3 and 4.4).

In our quest for an effective visual identity, we generate hundreds of possible versions. Almost all of these will be off the mark; a few will show promise. It is only through this kind of visual exploration that an effective symbolic form begins to emerge. This procedure is common in nature and in human endeavors alike.

Think of nature's ways: millions of seeds are released, a single plant takes root; there are millions of sperm, but just one uniting with the ovum to form a single offspring. Think of the artist's ways. A few years before he died, Harry Callahan, a great photographer, turned over to the Center

Figure 4.3

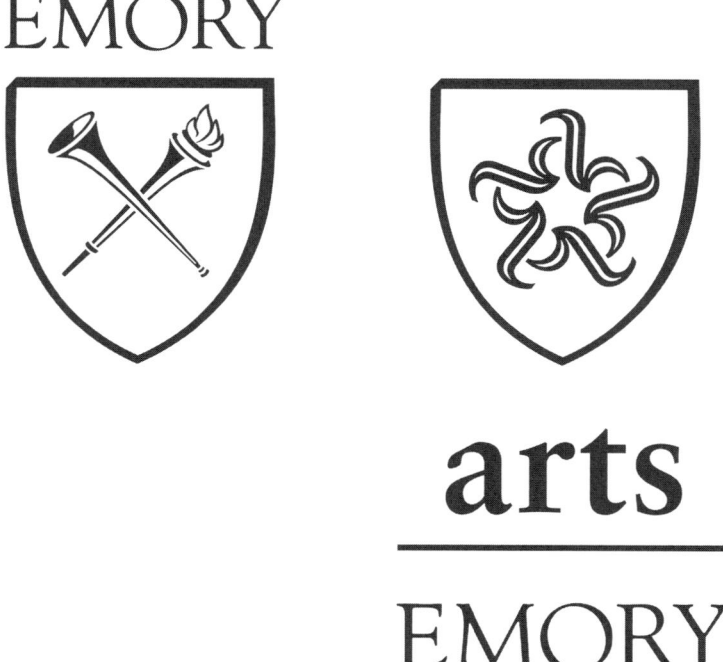

for Creative Photography at the University of Arizona more than 100,000 negatives that, by agreement, would never be printed. I asked Harry about this profligate abundance. He said, "I shoot a lot of film before I get a picture that I like."

Often, a few of the numerous variations we produce during the beginning phase of identity development are delightful to look at; it is not the absence of visual appeal that disqualifies these candidates. Indeed, it is often disheartening to see them set aside. Function alone determines the outcome. We are looking for an image that captures and conveys the essence of the client's enterprise. Beauty is never enough. From those few forms that survive the cut, we close in on the strongest, and this becomes the center of our focus. Now we enter the realm of nuance, the designer's state of grace. Subtleties abound: form and counterform, light wells, and a host of other elements that greatly influence the final outcome but will escape notice of all but the sharpest eye.

How does Bach get from the "Goldberg Variations" its universe of emotional power? Ask Glen Gould. The rest of us remain enthralled by

Figure 4.4

Source: Courtesy Jon Rou, Emory University Photo Dept.

that power and mostly ignorant of its technical origins. The angels are in the details.

Once we have invented a logotype, we spell out for the client the many ways in which it can be used in particular contexts. These instructions and suggestions—a set of guidelines with examples of various applications—are both liberating and constraining. We want the client to make optimum use of the symbol; we very much want it not to be misused. There is always ample room to adjust relevant design elements to suit particular applications (e.g., stationery, packaging, advertising, three-dimensional displays). Colors may vary within prescribed limits; placement may sometimes be adjusted to suit particular purposes and media, as long as these adjustments fit one or another of the grid formats that we provide in our guidelines.

A major goal for any visual identity is to build familiarity within the target audience, to prompt the viewer to "identify" the symbol with its source, the entity being symbolized. Consistency, that much-maligned hobgoblin, plays, in this case, a constructive, even essential, role in the optimum use of the symbol.

In addition to guidelines on paper, we give our client a DVD that shows the ways in which the logotype can be employed across a wide range of applications. When appropriate, we create a Web site (accessible to the client only) that provides essentially exhaustive guidance. Not all applications can be anticipated—institutions and corporate entities evolve—but basic principles of use can be clear enough to allow the invention of new variations as needs arise, while still sustaining the consistency so crucial to successful application of a visual identity.

TO REDESIGN OR NOT TO REDESIGN

It also seems worth mentioning that, in some cases, where we have been asked to design a new logotype for an organization that already has one in existence, we will recommend they keep it.

In these cases, our initial research has led us to conclude that the organization has a huge investment, through exposure, in the one that exists. Such was the case with Wolf Trap Foundation for the Performing Arts and John Hancock Companies. In both cases, we recommended simply cleaning up the one they had and making changes that were related to improving reproduction.

Something that happens too often in the not-for-profit sector is what I call change for change's sake. This can occur, among other reasons, when the leadership of an organization mistakes the personality of its leadership for the organization's identity or personality. Visual identities or images are created for an organization, which, presumably, will outlast its leadership at any point in the organization's existence. When a visual identity, starting with a logotype, has been embraced locally, regionally, nationally, and even internationally, over a considerable number of years, its exposure represents a substantial and effective investment. It becomes irresponsible to abandon the equity that has been built up as a result of this recognition. If an organization's visual identity were changed each time it had a change of leadership, it would cost the organization dearly in terms of public recognition as well as actual dollars to change everything that uses that visual identity to communicate who it is, such as signs, stationery, Web site, and so on.

Having said this, let me add that while it is inadvisable to change a visual identity for the sake of new leadership alone, it is possible—even advisable—to create a new look (i.e., branding strategy) for an aspect of the organization or a time-limited event, such as a fund-raising campaign, a theater season, or the like. A visual identity (symbols, logotypes, colors, typography—a kit of parts) should have enough flexibility to visually work in any situation. Whether an organization is structured as a for-profit or a not-for-profit, it must realize that it has a market that is built upon year after year, exposure after exposure, and that its logotype, as the core of its visual identity, is an important legacy.

ATTAINING VISUAL HARMONY, VISUAL GRACE

We hear these days that "image is everything." This is not so, of course. Reality prevails. The quality of production or service remains critical to success in the marketplace, but it *is* a marketplace; competitors clamor for attention, and it is dangerously easy to get lost in the crowd. Any serious organization must seek to distinguish itself from competitors and, with pride, claim the attention of its customers and clientele. We are visual creatures in a Darwinian world. An organization's visual identity is like a nation's flag, an ancient device that stands for the institution and asserts its meaning and significance.

Most of us are strongly affected by the signals that reach our brain through our eyes. We seem able to tolerate an astonishing diversity of visual noise generated by urban crowding and decay, but we are soothed by the look of trees and fields, the ocean, open sky, art and architecture, and other signs of visual grace—any object, place, or creature that we find attractive.

At the risk of sounding grandiose, I will mention what I regard as a beneficial side effect of good design. Ugliness can be emotionally costly; it can be stressful in the same the way that harsh noise is stressful. Visual dissonance, like a wrong note in music, can set the mind on edge. Some of us have a high tolerance for disorder and feel no unease in an ugly place, we do not even see it as ugly, but most of us find such environments dismaying, even depressing. I have no data from research to support this contention: that our public health, in general, would be much improved if we were to both design with greater care our public spaces, our cities, towns, suburbs, and all the manufactured components of our physical world. We seek solace in natural settings, and we are increasingly aware that those wild places must be protected from damage of human exploitation. We are failing, though, to defend ourselves against the damage that urban and suburban ugliness can cause to human health. Some will say that beauty and ugliness are subjective concepts, that what you find attractive, I might well find repulsive. How, then, are we to determine an optimum visual experience for the human population as a whole? I think this argument, which sounds reasonable, is probably wrong. It seems to me that there is a human nature that we have in common across cultures, a sense of visual harmony that brings us ease and a sense of visual dissonance that brings us discomfort.

Showing visual elements at random and in cacophonous discourse makes them compete, fragmenting instead of reinforcing the organization's image. I feel it is important to establish a unified system starting with a symbol and/or logotype and an identifying color palette that provides a clear, forceful, and unmistakably individual statement. The image must be flexible and versatile and evoke humanistic qualities.

During our intense interview and research process for Vanderbilt University, we learned that the campus was an active arboretum and discovered two symbols long associated with the university: the oak leaf (strength and steadfastness) and the acorn (seed of knowledge). When we presented our design concept incorporating these elements into our symbol, the university and its many individual units enthusiastically embraced this unifying visual identity. (See Figures 4.5 through 4.8.) Malcolm Grear Designers was credited with having an enormous impact on Vanderbilt rethinking its own culture, helping the university to formulate a better strategic plan, and resulting in a more focused and more interesting place of learning.

Figure 4.5

Figure 4.6

CREATING SIGNAGE

It seems clear to me that a university concerned with high level education is obliged to present itself with visual harmony, encompassing everything from a strong, well-thought-out and designed logotype and all promotional materials to a clear, well-designed sign system that includes identification, wayfinding, and, of course, donor recognition. As it is with a book or Web site, we feel better when we know exactly where we are at any given time.

One of the major forms of communication for a university is the sign (signage). The real problem is information, not signage. Information and signage require a communications expert, someone who is involved with communications on many levels—intellectual, ethical, social, and economic—responding to people's needs. The message must be right. It is unlikely that the best designer for a university's signage is an in-house person, whether from an architectural firm or college staff. A graphic designer should be a member of the design team in the earliest stages of planning a new building, not brought in after the fact. He can contribute greatly

Figure 4.7

Figure 4.8

in planning spaces. Too often architectural firms will design signs that fit only their building, with little or no regard for the school's identity. In other words, a good system can respond to both the architecture and the university's image.

The function of messages in the campus facilities may be relatively simple, but signs must have distinctive visual identity, organized visually in an aesthetic, efficient, and economical way. A unified, consistent communications program, from stationery to environmental graphics, will help identify the university facilities.

A total graphic communication system can be both lively and vital to the day-to-day and, at times, minute-to-minute functions of the university facility. Purely pragmatic concerns, such as directions, are not the only part of the messages. Human and highly emotional issues must be met. Each level of information and each application of an image must respond to the environment and the need. As people and faces may change daily, as spaces must serve multiple functions, the graphic elements should provide a visually cohesive system, but also allow flexible application.

Even though the idea of electronic signs, such as holography, seems exciting, I am of the opinion that, at this time, such information systems are impractical and somewhat inhuman, although this may not be the case if it is a school of technology. For example, most reception areas are, in general terms, well enough designed, furnished, and maintained. Sometimes, there is, however, a feeling of desolation and impersonal monumentality that makes these areas look more like uninhabited showrooms than the warm reception areas they should be. This does not mean that I advise a formal redesign. I simply recommend that making these areas more inviting is a goal, and electronic signage will not help. Although, it makes good sense to have LCD screens located in such areas as student and faculty communal spaces, lounges, and cafeterias so that current events and news can be immediately announced, helping the faculty and students to become aware and involved.

The most downright problematic public spaces are usually the connecting circuits. To improve the social quality of these untidy but vital arteries, a merely functional signage system will not suffice. However, an informative, well-designed, dignified sign system—one that will not move in and out of vogue—can distract attention from vastness, guiding the visitor through the labyrinth.

Messages and graphic elements should be simple and direct. The clarity of the message is primary; the supporting material should be kept neutral. There is also a need for a positive approach in the messages the signs deliver. The stern, reprimanding tone on instructions and regulations could, in many cases, be presented in a more sensitive manner.

I feel that it is wrong, in most cases, to have a symbol and/or signage that visually tries to imitate the environment in which it is placed—unless, for example, the purpose is to identify a particular thing, such as a tree. Signage should be juxtaposed in a natural way to its habitat. Signs should not try to blend—that defeats the purpose; they should be simple, well-designed messages.

WAYFINDING FOR GOOD DESIGN

As with clinicians, designers are in the problem-solving business and must see problems in context. A designer needs to take account of the nature and needs of the people who are to use the design. The users are not just those who hire the designer; users also include the consumers of the design. If this entire set of circumstances, the state of the total system, remains unexamined, the designer is in danger of plugging in preconceived solutions without taking full account of the problem at hand. The designer who solves a problem within its context will not have to worry about doing something original. The outcome will be new because the problem was solved in accord with its context. Each context is unique; a successful solution will likewise be unique.

I like the adage that for every problem there is a solution that is simple, obvious, and wrong. A problem worthy of the name is seldom accessible to sudden and simple solution. It may appear that way at times, but usually this is because the solver, even unconsciously, has been steeped in the problem and its various ramifications and thus is able to experience revelation or sudden insight, as though it sprang full-blown from a brilliant mind. It is best to take it that problem solving is hard work, and from the designer's perspective, he or she might as well enjoy it.

Constraint, of course, is the name of the game. Problems confronted by professional designers are defined by the purpose a design must serve and the constraints imposed by unavoidable circumstances. Such constraints can involve time, money, materials, dimensions, audience, media, and a host of other factors.

There are no easy solutions, and no quick ones. Remember the value of the *prepared mind*. Sudden inspirations, eureka moments, spring mostly from such minds. Linus Pauling "thought up" the alpha helix (a basic molecular component of protein structure) while in bed with a cold. He had been seeking the answer for years. James D. Watson, fiddling with cardboard cutouts one Saturday morning, February 28, 1953, hit upon the base-pairing combination that forms the *double helix,* the structure of DNA, the veritable "secret of life." He and Francis Crick had been consumed by this mystery for more than 30 months. Note that each of these achievements—both leading to Nobel Prizes—was a visual breakthrough, each solution was a form in three dimensions. For me and my colleagues, these two bits of intellectual history—nature's molecular designs at the root of life itself—are a lesson on the nature of insight and inspiration. We expect no glory or grand prizes, but, through experience, we have come to know what we must get to know if we are to arrive at successful design.

At Malcolm Grear Designers, the work on a new job begins when we receive an invitation to submit a proposal. The invitation usually gives a reasonably full account of the design problem that we must address.

We begin proposals with a description of the project as we see it, and we follow with a list of phases that we think will lead to a satisfying conclusion.

I am making this process seem bloodless, a perfunctory routine that leads to quick agreement with the client. Reality, of course, is sharply different. We live in a competitive world. Other designers or architects may be contending for the same job, so as you read the steps we take, please imagine a studio galvanized to win the day. There is tension, spirit, and determination in these efforts to close the deal—an essential and demanding part of the business.

Phase 1: Information Gathering

Our first phase is research and analysis. We need to discover what the design must accomplish. The depth of the research is determined by the complexity of the project.

The designer meets with designated representatives from the university facilities in order to be briefed on the organization's objectives, to arrange a schedule of personnel interviews and a facilities tour, and to collect available information relating to:

1. Primary goals and objectives
2. Facilities and basic functions
3. Facilities policies, codes, and regulations
4. Public relations and community role
5. Personnel organization and responsibilities
6. Physical layout and equipment

Phase 2: Concept Development and Presentation

The second phase involves the preparation and presentation of design ideas in considerable detail. Clear communications between client and designer at this point can save hours of ill-conceived effort. If we have misunderstood the client's circumstances and purpose, discussions during the presentation can put us back on track.

It is best to work directly with the individual or individuals empowered by the organization to make final decisions.

During the course of this phase, the designer reviews these materials, collects additional information as necessary, conducts interviews, tours and documents facilities as needed in order to identify crucial issues, determine constraints, and defines the options for the development of a graphic system.

Phase 3: Final Concept Development and Presentation

In phase three, we present a final concept, which includes all aspects of the project. The previous phase and this one are normally the most time consuming; they are also the most energized, creative, and exciting. Preparing presentations may require hundreds of sketches. It is great fun, sometimes.

Phase 4: Graphic Identifiers and Graphic Standards

Upon approval of the previous phases, the designer prepares art and copy for Graphic Standards to include:

1. Graphic Identifier/s and guidelines for their use and application
2. Stationery System guidelines for typography, color, paper, typing, formats, and application of Graphic Identifier/s
3. Signage guidelines, including size, color, format, grid structures, typography, shape, material, location, and methods of fixing, positioning, illumination, and construction.

Phase 5: Production Preparation

In phase five, we complete finished art for printing or, if the project is architectural, we generate drawings to guide fabrication.

Phase 6: Production Supervision

Phase six, the supervision of production, is our chance to make sure we get the product that we want. Then we send a bill, the final phase of any project. The time and fee schedule, which may cover weeks or years, is, of course, an important element in the initial proposal.

For new clients, a proposal allows them to evaluate the designer's ideas and skills. For the designer, preparing and presenting the proposal can help shake out chaff, reducing the project essentials.

This whole process of devising, presenting, discussing, and revising a proposal is a necessary mechanism for communication between a client and designer who do not know each other. Once a working relationship is established between client and designer, it is unlikely that the client will need ornate proposals on future projects. A brief account of design ideas will probably suffice.

THE INCREASINGLY SIGNIFICANT ROLE OF GRAPHIC DESIGN

Our world is overstocked with images—mostly clutter—from computer monitors, movie and television screens, product packaging, billboards, magazines, and other print media. We are bombarded by a numbing array of visual information. There is little chance of slowing down this high-speed, high-tech culture. We have to adapt. One adaptation that will reduce confusion and offer solace is improved graphic design.

It is for this reason that graphic design has an increasingly significant role to play. Along with architecture, resource management, and environmental planning, it helps to shape much of our world and will shape more of it in times to come, so it matters that designers of visual communication do their work with a sense of responsibility.

Designers serve a human need for clear, engaging forms of visual communication. This need is more profound and pervasive than we might think. It is not for nothing that we—and all cultures—spend so much time and substance arranging our environments to satisfy this need. It is not for nothing, too, that we pay so steep a price in stress-related ailments when we neglect the need for visual harmony.

If you track a design from beginning to end, it is not so different from work in other professions, say that of a writer, doctor, or lawyer. Designers stay with the project until they get it right and include whomever and whatever may be needed to accomplish the goal.

The designer may serve as choreographer, but most jobs depend on many dancers to bring an idea to fruition. A designer may forget that his work involves many people, including the client. Those involved may be writers, photographers, illustrators, editors, architects, engineers, computer specialists, publishers, typesetters, and printers—a host of people who hold the job together and make it work. If communication among collaborators breaks down, if vanity intrudes, the project suffers. In this quickly changing world, it is now more important than ever that graphic designers solve problems in an open, collaborative, responsive, and flexible manner. A designer must welcome others into the effort; it is a social transaction.

CHAPTER 5

Coping with Crises: Special Challenges for Universities

Andrew Westmoreland

There was no reason in particular that May 9, 2008, should have been an unusual day at Samford University in Birmingham, Alabama. It was the last day of classes for the spring term, the semester was winding down, and students and faculty were preparing for final exams. Circumstances changed, however, at 4:15 A.M., when a campus safety officer reported encountering a man with a gun in one of the university's parking decks. Thirteen months following the mass killings at Virginia Tech, heightened sensitivity to a report of "a man with a gun" demanded that I, as Samford's president, immediately activate a complex crisis emergency process.[1] Were we prepared for the task?

The Virginia Tech massacre was the worst incident of mass murder on a university campus since August 1, 1966, the day the nation listened in disbelief for 96 minutes as Charles Whitman killed 16 and wounded 30 from a sniper's perch atop a tower at the University of Texas. The incident ended when Whitman was killed by police officers. Before his rampage, Whitman left a note indicating he had consulted the university health clinic about his painful headaches, his psychiatric condition, and his fears that he felt overwhelmed with violent impulses. Whitman also requested an autopsy be performed on his body, which later revealed he was suffering from a brain tumor.[2]

School shootings, though rare, are sadly regular enough to cause preparation for prevention and response. Such plans are largely the result of the 1999 shooting spree at Colorado's Columbine High School, during which two seniors, using automatic weapons, murdered 12 students and one teacher. An additional 24 victims were injured in the 45-minute attack.

According to the U.S. Department of Education, an annual average of 31 homicides occurred in the nation's schools in the seven years prior to the Columbine tragedy. In response to the mass murder, schools increased security and preparedness by installing security cameras, requiring identification badges, banning backpacks, conducting random searches for contraband, and implementing zero tolerance policies and regular lock-down drills. For the seven years following the events at Columbine, the average of school homicides was cut in half. The evidence appeared to support the idea that efforts to keep students safe were being rewarded. Then came Virginia Tech.

Perpetrated by a mentally disturbed student, Seung-Hui Cho, the series of events that took place at Virginia Tech on April 16, 2007, revealed flaws in many university safety systems. When the bodies of two students were discovered in a residence hall around 7:30 A.M., police first thought this to be an isolated incident of domestic violence. Two hours after the bodies were discovered, Cho, carrying two weapons and 400 rounds of ammunition, had barricaded himself in an academic building to continue the slaughter of 30 additional victims before committing suicide.

The Virginia Tech massacre raised myriad questions. Cho had a long record of criminally frightening and bizarre behavior that raised warning signs. Given a student with known mental illness, how should universities balance the privacy rights of students with the need to assure safety? Faculty and staff are reluctant to intervene for fear of breaking privacy laws and the resulting threat of lawsuits. With his public record of mental illness and unstable behavior, how was Cho legally able to purchase the weapons? The most pointed questions were reserved for the Virginia Tech administration. In the cloud of uncertain facts following the first shootings, why was no immediate attempt made to warn the campus of the potential of a threat?[3]

LEARNING FROM THE VIRGINIA TECH TRAGEDY

In the aftermath of the Virginia Tech tragedy, confronting the potential for such threats moved to the top of the agenda on most college campuses, including Samford. Enhanced security and immediate emergency notification systems and procedures were suddenly a necessity.[4] Administrators focused on improving communications with local law enforcement and evaluating timely response to a crisis. One lesson from Virginia Tech was the faulty reliance on e-mail as the only means of emergency notification. Virginia Tech sent out e-mail messages during the attacks, but an insufficient number of people saw them. Many students, for instance, do not read university e-mail messages on a regular basis. The consensus opinion throughout higher education was that future crisis communication with students and employees must be immediate.[5] Universities evaluated public-address systems, alarms, emergency telephones, and the use of personal messaging to cell phones.[6]

Within a few months after the Virginia Tech attacks, Samford University had new plans for coping with campus crises. The university reviewed and updated its emergency response program, planned a joint "active shooter" training exercise with local law enforcement, installed additional video monitoring cameras at strategic locations on campus, devised a system to sound warning alert bells from the university carillon, and implemented an emergency university-communications system provided by Rave Wireless, Inc.[7]

When voluntary registration for the Rave system began at Samford in February 2008, administrators were concerned about the relatively low response. Privacy laws prohibit the university from unilaterally registering students and employees or even requiring such registration. Despite repeated university-wide announcements, and the well-known lessons of the events at Virginia Tech, only a few hundred of Samford's 5,500 students and employees had signed up before the successful first test of the system on April 14, 2008.

EMERGENCY ACTIVATES NEW SYSTEM

Days later, on the evening of May 8, as violent thunderstorms with possible tornados descended upon the Birmingham area, the chief of campus safety made the decision to activate the Rave system to alert the campus of the threatening weather conditions. Violent crime is just one threat to which universities must respond, and other institutions had successfully used the Rave system to warn of dangerous weather. We found the system to be effective, as students prepared for the gathering storm. Finally, the weather cleared and the campus settled in for a restful night.

With the passing rainstorm, one of our patrol officers reported for his assignment on the night shift, reporting to Shift Supervisor Chris Feigl. According to police records, early Friday morning the junior officer—unarmed—was on routine patrol of the lower level of a vacant parking deck on the northeast corner of the campus when he reported seeing a man, dressed in black, on the west end stairwell. The officer called in to dispatch to report a suspicious person. He reported that when he confronted the subject, the man pointed a gun at him. The officer took cover and radioed dispatch to advise that the suspect was armed. He said the man leaped over a low wall and headed north, away from campus. Supervisor Feigl arrived on the scene and, following a search of the area, notified Deputy Chief Steve Inman and then enlisted the local police department for assistance.

Upon his arrival on campus at about 5:00 A.M., Deputy Chief Inman called Campus Safety Chief Bobby Breed to inform him of the details of the intervening minutes. Breed instructed Inman to notify residence life and facilities services to begin the process of locking down the campus. Samford's gated 180-acre campus has only two vehicle entrances. Both gates were locked, identification was checked for anyone arriving or leaving campus, and all arriving traffic was directed to a parking lot on the opposite side of campus from the alleged incident. At 5:30 A.M., Breed activated the Rave system to alert the campus to the potential danger. I was notified of the situation and immediately began the 20-minute drive from my home to the campus, calling key administrators and the chair of our Board of Trustees, en route. During this time, Samford safety officers and members of the local police force initiated a search of two residence halls near the site where the gunman was alleged to have been seen. In addition, members of our staff contacted administrators at the local high school, located near the Samford campus, to warn them of the potential threat.

As soon as I arrived on the campus, I asked Chief Breed to take me to the site where the gunman was seen. Step by step, he explained the details of our officer's account of the incident. I asked several questions, then I turned to Chief Breed and said, "Bobby, do you believe that this event actually occurred." He replied, "I will admit that there are parts of the story that don't add up." I agreed, but then I added, "Regardless of our suspicions, we need to treat this situation as a genuine emergency. As calm returns, let's see if we can get a complete story."

Meanwhile, members of our staff were calling and texting each other, alerting them to changing circumstances. Philip Poole, executive director for university communication, was reading the message from the Rave system when Sarah Latham, assistant to the president, called to provide additional information. As he made his way to the campus, Poole called the vice president for university relations, Randy Pittman, one of Samford's media relations officers, and the university Web administrator to let them know that they were needed on campus. The Web administrator was already headed to the office, and they talked briefly about how to get updates on the university's Web site for parents, employees, and others who would be seeking information.

MEDIA AND PUBLIC COMMUNICATIONS

Local media, having heard police monitors, already were headed to campus and calling the university's media spokespersons. Arriving on campus about 6 A.M., Poole began to respond to media inquiries. The Web administrator and Poole quickly posted a notice on the university's home page, passing along all available information.

Officers staffing the campus entrances were instructed to route media to the same parking lot as employees and commuters. The first media representatives arrived on campus at about 6:20 A.M., and Poole and I began doing live interviews shortly afterward. At the same time, both CNN and Fox News had posted news alerts on their Web sites, creating national concern about the situation. We made the decision to have someone available for every interview request and to give up-to-date information as quickly as possible.

While employees gathered and the media frenzy expanded in the parking lot near the front gate, the search of the residence halls turned up nothing. An exploration of the area surrounding the parking deck and nearby woods yielded no suspect. No footprints of an intruder were found on the ground where he was alleged to have jumped over a low wall, although the soil was soft and moist following the heavy rains from the previous evening.

About 7:45 A.M., we removed the campus from lock-down status. An update was posted on the university's Web site. By about 8:30 A.M., we had completed the first round of media interviews and the television trucks began to leave the campus. Meanwhile, members of the local police department continued the investigation by beginning a lengthy interview with the officer who had witnessed the gunman.

As the campus began to return to normal, I asked several staff members to meet in my office, where we reviewed information and determined the next steps. We drafted a university-wide e-mail message, which I sent at 9:05 A.M., including comprehensive information about the situation. Among other things, the message stated: "At this time, as part of the ongoing investigation, the officer who made the initial report is being interviewed by the Homewood police department. Campus safety has extra personnel on duty and they are continuing with their due diligence. At this point, our safety officers are looking for evidence for why the person may have been on campus. The Homewood authorities will continue to monitor the neighborhood surrounding the campus." The full text of the message was posted to our Web site.

Throughout the morning, the university's media staff responded to calls and requests for interviews during noonday newscasts. They also kept information updated on the university's Web site.

QUELLING RUMORS, ANSWERING QUESTIONS

The university grapevine, always active, was alive with conversation and gossip. To respond to rumors and questions and to continue to provide a flow of information, just after noon I sent a second e-mail message to students and employees. I stated that there was no indication of attempts at forced entry for any vehicles or buildings, that the local police department remained at work in looking for clues on campus and in the surrounding neighborhood, and that there had been no additional reports of sightings of anyone matching the description of the person.

I also responded directly to questions that were circling the campus: Why did we declare an "all clear" notice before the person was apprehended?

"The rationale for allowing regular activities to resume was, first, that the person was observed fleeing from campus, rather than toward campus. The room-by-room searches and other activities were undertaken as precautionary measures. After campus safety and Homewood police officers were convinced that there was no threat, I approved the decision to resume normal operations. If we had waited until the person was apprehended to open the campus to regular traffic, we might never have opened the campus," I said.

Why are we allowing the normal flow of traffic through the gates?

"The person who was seen on campus this morning may be within a few blocks, or he may be 200 miles away. Regardless, we have no reason at this point to disrupt the normal routine."

I added that there was no reason to believe that the person was accompanied by someone else, but as an added precaution we would be expanding the safety presence on campus for the remainder of the spring term.

Throughout the day, as we worked on campus to manage the delivery of information, the local police continued to interview the safety officer who claimed to have seen the gunman. Finally, we received the news that many of us felt was inevitable: Our employee confessed that he had fabricated the entire story. He said that he wanted to create a crisis so that he could help his colleagues to receive additional funding for the campus safety program.

I quickly gathered the members of our crisis management team in my office to brainstorm our communications plan. As it turned out, we did not have much time; the local police department released the information to the media within minutes of receiving the confession from the safety officer. Anticipating his confession, I had already begun work on yet another e-mail message to the campus. Working as a committee-of-the-whole, our crisis team helped me to revise the message and I hit the "send" button at 3:27 P.M. Among other things, I wrote, "After an intense investigation, we have learned that there was no mystery gunman on campus this morning. The safety officer who filed the initial report has admitted that the event did not happen. Appropriate disciplinary measures are being taken." While I contacted trustees and fielded additional telephone calls, our media relations officers coordinated interviews for Sarah Latham, assistant to the president, and Randy Pittman, vice president for university relations, with the television and newspaper outlets. Very quickly, key decisions were made on campus about responding to the situation. The media coverage on the evening news was highly sympathetic to the university, and friends of Samford were able to breathe a sigh of relief.

LESSONS FROM SAMFORD'S EXPERIENCE

What did we learn?

First, although the report from the safety officer was a hoax, we were slow in responding. Too much time expired between the alleged sighting of the gunman and the series of notifications of key staff members, including the president. For almost one hour, the episode lacked coordination. Similar situations in the future will call for immediate implementation of the crisis response plan.

Even though the public safety office was open throughout the crisis, it would have been helpful to establish an emergency operations center near the site of the investigation. By doing so, public safety officers could have effectively communicated with the president's office, local police, and media relations. The lack of such a center created many issues related to communication and—in some cases—probably delayed the making of decisions.

Our campus communications office responded quickly, but these staff members should have been provided with additional notification as the crisis emerged. Media outlets monitor police radios. In order for the university's media response to be proactive rather than reactive, our staff members in that area must be in the first line of notification.

Although accessibility was not an issue in this case, we now have back-up plans for Web access and a media center when the campus is in lock down or key facilities are not available.

Our mystery gunman hoax provided us with an opportunity to prove that the university's Rave alert system does work. We continue to perform periodic tests of the system to ensure that it remains functional. Many of the parents of our students have asked why Samford does not require everyone to sign up for text alerts or automatically register them in the system. Federal privacy laws prohibit that level of enforcement, but the number of registrants skyrocketed in the aftermath of the hoax. We have now implemented a process of announcing the Rave system during freshman orientation and encouraging students and their parents to sign up. Participation is high.

An alert system for the contract housekeeping, food service, and landscaping personnel who work on campus has been devised. Most are not allowed by their various employers to have cell phones on their person while working. Many of these employees already were on duty when the alert was issued but did not know about the situation until after the campus reopened.

Two months after the events described in this case study, Samford hosted an active-shooter, SWAT situation training for campus safety and several local law enforcement agencies. Ironically, the training had been in the planning stages before the May 9th hoax. We received favorable media response due to continued interest in the gunman story, and we were able to demonstrate that the university is prepared, as best as possible, for other crisis situations.[8]

A HIGHER STANDARD

In the matter of crisis management, universities are often held to a higher standard than the business community.[9] Federal law requires the publication of on-campus crime statistics. New legislation mandates that universities promptly inform students and employees of immediate danger. Students expect, and parents demand, that the university is prepared to provide an effective and immediate response to any crisis.[10] While thousands of acts of adolescent foolishness occur unnoticed and unreported each year, if the adolescent is a star athlete at a major university, the incident will become a significant news story. When members of the Duke University lacrosse team were accused of sexual assault, for instance, the story was followed with great interest. The charges proved to be false and the district attorney in the case was forced to resign and ultimately disbarred for unethical conduct.[11] One wonders if the case would have been so vigorously prosecuted if this had been an anonymous group, unrelated to a university.

When Hurricane Ivan threatened the Alabama gulf coast in 2004, Samford was swamped with phone calls from anxious parents demanding a quick decision as to the university's plans to close in advance of the storm. Any university emergency communication must consider the relationship with parents. In the Rave communication system, students may register multiple phone numbers. We encourage the listing of at least one parent.

In his 1991 book, *The Crisis Years,* Michael Beschloss writes of the efforts of the Kennedy administration to ensure secrecy and time for reflection during the six days of the Cuban Missile Crisis: "Kennedy's six days of quiet deliberation were a gift that no American President in a similar quandary will probably ever enjoy again. Were the Missile Crisis to occur in the political and journalistic culture of three decades later, an American television network with access to a private satellite might well have discovered the missiles and announced them to the world only hours after the President had learned about them."[12]

Indeed, we inhabit the earth in an era when moments of secret reflection are rare. In times of campus crisis, when police vehicles and media trucks are streaming past our manicured lawns, reflection is measured in seconds, not in days. Wisdom and intuition serve as guides, but they are no substitute for planning.

Our episode of May 9, 2008, involved many aspects of Samford's plan: the emergency alert system, media relations, campus lock-down protocols, and the establishment of an emergency operations center. University leaders must be ready to respond in any emergency from weather disasters to acts of domestic violence, to public health emergencies or massive acts of terrorism or violence. The events of May 2008 were not catastrophic; instead, they were a learning experience to improve Samford's emergency management efforts.

NOTES

1. Harvard Business School, "Contingency Planning," *Crisis Management* (Boston: Harvard Business School Publishing Corporation, 2006), 35–50.

2. Paul Brown, "U.T. Tower Shooting: 40 Years Later," News 8 Austin, http://www.news8austin.com/content/news_8_explores/ut_tower_shooting/.

3. Lauren Stiller Rikleen, "Virginia Tech: the Challenge of Assuring Safety," *The Chronicle Review,* May 11, 2007, http://chronicle.com/weekly/v53/i36/36b01402.htm.

4. David Nagel, "Oklahoma Task Force Calls for Increased Campus Security Spending," *Campus Technology,* http://campustechnology.com/Articles/2008/01/Oklahoma-Task-Force.

5. Doug Lenderman, "What Changed and Didn't, after Virginia Tech," *Inside Higher Ed,* http://www.insidehighered.com/layout/set/print/news/2008/05/28/vatech.

6. Eric Ferreri, "Duke Installs Campus Emergency Siren System," *The News and Observer,* June 2, 2008, http://www.newsobserver.com/news/v-print/story/1092931.html.

7. Josh Rischman and Andrea L. Foster, "Dark Day in Blacksburg," *The Chronicle of Higher Education*, April 27, 2007, http://chronicle.com/weeklyv53/i34/34a01601.htm.

8. Sean Flynt, "Samford Hosts 'Active Shooter' Training," Samford University News Releases, http://www.samford.edu/News/72308_1.html.

9. Jeffrey Selingo, "College Leaders Wrestle with How to Prepare for Unknown Threats," *The Chronicle of Higher Education,* February 22, 2008, http://chronicle.com/weekly/v54/i24/24a01702.htm.

10. Lynette S. Merriman, "Managing Parent Involvement during Crisis," *New Directions for Student Services* 122 (2008): 57–66.

11. CNN.com, "Duke Lacrosse Prosecutor Disbarred," http://www.cnn.com/2007/LAW/06/16/duke.lacrosse/index.html.

12. Michael R. Beschloss, *The Crisis Years* (New York: HarperCollins Publishers, 1991).

REFERENCES

Beschloss, Michael R. *The Crisis Years.* New York: HarperCollins Publishers, 1991.

Brown, Paul. "U.T. Tower Shooting: 40 Years Later." News 8 Austin, http://www.news8austin.com/content/news_8_explores/ut_tower_shooting.

CNN.com. "Duke Lacrosse Prosecutor Disbarred," http://www.cnn.com/2007/LAW/06/16/duke.lacrosse/index.html.

Ferreri, Eric. "Duke Installs Campus Emergency Siren System." *The News and Observer,* June 2, 2008, http://www.newsobserver.com/news/v-print/story/1092931.html.

Flynt, Sean. "Samford Hosts 'Active Shooter' Training." Samford University News Releases, http://www.samford.edu/News/72308_1.html.

Harvard Business School. "Contingency Planning: Preparing Today for Tomorrow's Problems." *Crisis Management: Master the Skills to Prevent Disasters* (Boston: Harvard Business School Publishing Corporation, 2006), 35–50.

Lenderman, Doug. "What Changed and Didn't, after Virginia Tech." *Inside Higher Ed,* http://www.insidehighered.com/layout/set/print/news/2008/05/28/vatech.

Merriman, Lynette S. "Managing Parent Involvement during Crisis." *New Directions for Student Services* 122 (2008): 57–66.

Nagel, David. "Oklahoma Task Force Calls for Increased Campus Security Spending." *Campus Technology,* http://campustechnology.com/Articles/2008/01/Oklahoma-Task-Force.

Rikleen, Lauren Stiller. "Virginia Tech: the Challenge of Assuring Safety." *The Chronicle Review,* May 11, 2007, http://chronicle.com/weekly/v53/i36/36b01402.htm.

Rischman, Josh, and Andrea L. Foster. "Dark Day in Blacksburg." *The Chronicle of Higher Education,* April 27, 2007, http://chronicle.com/weeklyv53/i34/34a01601.htm.

Selingo, Jeffrey. "College Leaders Wrestle with How to Prepare for Unknown Threats." *The Chronicle of Higher Education,* February 22, 2008, http://chronicle.com/weekly/v54/i24/24a01702.htm.

CHAPTER 6

The Escalation of Consumerism in Higher Education

Michael S. Harris

Higher education faces pressures from a variety of internal and external sources to respond efficiently while also attempting to maintain its historical role and mission in American society.[1] The current sociopolitical environment challenges the traditional processes within colleges and universities in fundamental ways. Long-established notions of what is taught, researched, and promoted are confronted within this context. Additionally, who participates in decision-making and the academy more broadly are brought into scrutiny. The move toward a market model of higher education, particularly over the last 30 years, encourages institutional leaders to engage in a sophisticated competition for the best students and faculty. Moreover, the pursuit of revenue and prestige drives much of the current decision-making process, particularly given the value attributed to various rankings systems.[2] The creation and expansion of the market for students influences the product of higher-education institutions. The rise of this revenue-generating market, coupled with an escalation of student consumerism, leads to changes in how higher education operates.[3]

The goal of this chapter is to explore the rise and implications of student consumerism. I begin with a discussion of the larger marketplace as a means to contextualize the influence of consumerism within the academy. The emphasis on prestige within higher education, in combination with a general lack of information, challenges students to make decisions regarding colleges and universities. Although the rhetoric in higher education often touts the importance of service and a well-rounded education, students largely consider their own self-interest when weighing postsecondary options available to them. Student consumers hold a strong position within the marketplace, as campus leaders desire the flexibility gained from tuition revenue. An escalating arms race to attract students through a variety of amenities and convenient academic programs dominates the higher education marketplace. I argue that the rising influence of consumerism has led to a decline in the power of faculty with a corresponding ascendency of administration on campus. The result is an increased professionalization in administrative ranks that improves institutional management, but also potentially threatens the historical mission of higher education.

CONSUMERISM DEFINED

Higher education supporters hotly debate the notion of student consumerism, and many traditionalists are particularly uncomfortable with the concept. Geiger uses an instructive comparison between customer and client to demonstrate the difference.[4] Commonly evident in a retail setting, a customer desires a particular good or service to set parameters or taste. When ordering a filet mignon from a steakhouse, there is an expectation that it will be cooked to specification, and the customer decides if it is cooked enough or overdone. The well-worn mantra of "the customer is always right" typifies this relationship. Contrast this idea with a client relationship with a lawyer. A client expects that an attorney is an expert in the law, hired specifically for this expertise and representation. The seminal difference between these two ideas is who makes the decision. A customer determines the course of action, while a client typically defers to the "expert." For the purposes of this chapter, I use the term student consumerism to describe the actions, behaviors, and beliefs of students and institutions to position students as customers of higher education.

PRESTIGE AND LIMITED INFORMATION COMPLICATE THE STUDENT MARKET

The pervasive role of prestige and limited consumer information form two of the central influences on the operation of the student market in higher education. The limited number of options available for colleges and universities to successfully compete and gain additional financial resources only amplifies the significance of prestige and the lack of information. Increasingly, the prestige and revenue potential of the student market takes prominence in internal decision-making at many institutions.[5] Recessions in the 1980s and 1990s compelled higher education to rely increasingly on the tuition revenues available in the marketplace.[6] Tuition represents one of the few truly significant sources of income that the institution can control. The result is that campus leaders feel compelled to engage in a high-stakes competition for students to supplement declines in other sources of revenue—particularly state appropriations.

The value placed on rankings, most notably those issued by *U.S. News & World Report,* within the student market is an attempt to determine the quality and prestige of an institution. Various indices such as SAT scores, graduation rates, and the number of student fellowship winners that comprise the rankings are considered in decision-making on campus. The prestige generation tied to rankings fuels the desire to recruit progressively more qualified student populations. The competition over this relatively small number of students forces administrators to implement programs they otherwise may be disinclined to support because of cost or mission.

The American system of academic prestige likewise limits the ability to evaluate or coordinate the activities within colleges and universities. Administrators and faculty desire increased prestige, not simply to enjoy the benefits, but also to prevent losing position relative to peer institutions. The result exacerbates the market's inability to promote quality or price control within higher education. This leaves institutions with the freedom "to define quality largely in terms of what they already deliver."[7] Within this environment, the business community, state governments, and the general public question the lack of accountability of colleges and universities. Annual increases in tuition and at least the perception of inefficiency amplify demands for greater responsiveness. The argument of these external constituencies calls on higher education to become more accountable to the customers and governments that support its continued operation. With roots in K-12 school reform, this movement seeks to measure outcomes of student learning and faculty productivity.[8] Measurement and assessment become self-sustaining and self-perpetuating methods of accountability with little regard for the utility for improving higher education's significant activities. Moreover, simply defining the product of higher education presents a great challenge, particularly in an industry where the product is also the consumer.[9]

With these intrinsic challenges, very little concrete or easily obtainable information exists for students to make informed decisions within the student market. The philosophy behind a market-based system relies on informed consumers to serve an integral role in guaranteeing the self-regulation of markets. The ability to judge quality and price not only rewards those providing high quality, cost sensitive goods, but also eliminates those who are not performing well.[10] An example of the dangers of the lack of information is the scare in 2007 regarding Chinese-made children's toys containing lead paint.[11] With the increased globalization of our economy, consumers are unable to easily gauge where a toy is made or the production process at work. This limits the ability of the market to either drive out poor performers or to encourage improvements in product and process. Globalization blurs boundaries and complicates the information available to consumers.[12] Furthermore, traditional sources of consumer information often prove inadequate or unavailable given the complexities associated with globalization. As a result, companies operate more freely with limited influence from markets or consumers in this environment. Similar trends occur within the higher education marketplace due to the lack of information for consumers. For example, online diploma mills thrive in an environment where determining product differentiation is complicated and technology aids the ability to avoid government regulation.[13] The growth of both nonprofit and for-profit higher education institutions, along with a dizzying array of academic programs, confronts consumers seeking to make well-informed decisions regarding college. All of these various components only serve to convolute the decision-making process for students seeking the best fit for their academic and professional aspirations.

The widespread availability of options presents a challenge to students in choosing a postsecondary option best suited to their needs. Institutions present their academic programs and other services to meet the demand for education, training, and credentials. Students wade through the plethora of choices to narrow to a list of potential options, particularly those considering selective institutions.[14] Given the limited information on higher education and the difficulty in predicting individual student choice, colleges and universities seek to control their image and brand in hope of managing or influencing student decisions.[15] At a basic level, the purpose of a brand is to create differentiation in the marketplace for consumers.[16] The university brand becomes a valuable organization asset to develop and nurture as a result.[17] Institutions spend thousands on marketing consultants who predictably argue for complex, expensive, and comprehensive marketing plans.[18] Despite the incredible sums spent on branding and marketing, higher education fails to clearly delineate the differences that exist between institutions. Every school offers opportunities for exciting careers, boasts successful alumni, and sports a nationally ranked academic (or athletic) program.[19] As a result, marketing only perpetuates the information challenge for student consumers.

When making value-laden decisions, as in the case of higher education, consumers respond differently to marketing as a result of the inherent beliefs and assumptions of each individual.[20] The hope of university branding is to mediate the relationship between the institution and consumer by clearly projecting an institutional identity reflective of the institution's culture.[21] To this end, a brand can serve as a point of interaction between the university's activities and the expectation of consumers.[22]

CONSUMERS BEHAVE IN THEIR OWN SELF-INTEREST

The market offers a tremendous number of different options for students without the ability to easily receive sufficient data to make comparisons. Despite these inherent problems with the student marketplace, students and parents exhibit a remarkable economic rationality and price sensitivity relative to academic ability. When loans are a major component of a student's financial aid package, this behavior manifests itself to an even greater degree.[23] Family income and support factor into the college choice decision by providing or limiting opportunities on a financial rather than academic basis. The challenge for institutions lies in dealing with students and, increasingly, parents who are particularly savvy in navigating the financial aid and admissions processes.[24] An increased sophistication and the raw market power of students places tremendous pressure on institutions to adapt quickly or become relegated to a reactive position. In a proactive attempt to attract top students, colleges and universities compete with meticulously planned and researched financial aid packages, often with substantial amounts of merit scholarships. The role and influence of parents in the college choice and financial aid system favors high ability–high income students to the likely detriment of first-generation and low-income students.[25] This competition, fueled by student consumers, leads to lower net tuition revenue, which impacts institutional operating budgets, need-based aid packages, and academic programs.[26]

Once a student narrows down the potential number of institutions under consideration, other aspects enter the decision-making process. At this point, nonacademic features typically influence student consumers.[27] Institutions seek to attract students using amenities ranging from extravagant recreation facilities to wide-ranging student services. Adult and part-time students seek convenient, 24-hour access along with innovative program completion opportunities.[28] These types of services, both the luxurious and the convenient, become a component in students' comparisons of institutions. As a result, institutions include these offerings as part of their expanded efforts to recruit and attract students. Satisfying escalating student demands for services and facilities becomes as central to institutional efforts to recruiting and retaining students as traditional enrollment strategies.

A dramatic consequence of this emphasis on satisfying the desires of student consumers is the changes that have occurred in the area of student services and the co-curriculum more broadly. These moves are made with little regard for the potential influence on co-curricular engagement or student learning. We know little about how the changes made to satisfy student consumers influence their success, retention, or chances of graduating. High Point University in North Carolina provides an ice cream truck that travels campus dispensing free ice cream. The University of Montana-Missoula, along with many institutions around the country, offers a sizable, luxurious, campus recreation facility with an indoor rock climbing wall. Indeed, rock climbing walls seem as prevalent on campuses today as quadrangles, bell towers, and neo-Georgian architecture. Residence halls built today focus on student demands for living arrangements including access to high-speed Wi-Fi, laundry facilities, and private bathrooms. Apartment and suite-style living with kitchens and single occupancy bedrooms receive emphasis in planning discussions. Examples of elaborate student amenities offered by higher education institutions could easily fill this chapter, if not the entire volume. Despite the tremendous amount of resources and effort expended, however, higher education practitioners and researchers lack the data necessary at either the institutional or national level to understand the influence these amenities have on our students and institutions. Colleges and universities, regardless of size and quality, progressively continue to add services students seek. The desires of student consumers, largely based on individual needs and preferences, and the response of institutions to meet these requests, challenge many of the historical processes and aims of higher education.

ARMS RACE TO SATISFY CONSUMERS

The consumerism paradigm and its increased significance within higher education causes wide ranging impacts beyond the differentiation created among students. A worrisome and more pronounced separation between institutions also occurs, as "the rich get richer." Not only do affluent and superior academically performing students benefit as detailed earlier, wealthy and research universities also profit. In order to compete within the marketplace, institutions spend exuberant sums on merit based financial aid, new student amenities, and new academic initiatives. As a result, only those institutions that are able to absorb the costs of this escalating competition are able to succeed in recruiting the most highly valued students and meeting their desires in an institution.

The nexus between consumer desires and institutional responses with amenities lies in the college choice decision. As student "wants" enter the student decision-making process, the heightened competitive environment leads institutions to believe they must respond to satisfy the desires of students and parents. The fear of losing students to a competitor drives campus responses to the demands of the student marketplace. This arms race leads to ever-growing expenditures in areas outside of the traditional purposes of higher education.[29] The pressure to transfer resources away from core academic functions to areas perceived to influence student choice grows tremendously. In the current scenario, there is no mutually assured destruction to limit institutional actors. To the contrary, each institution moves to gain a competitive advantage with the full knowledge that only short-term gains will be realized as competitors quickly move to offer similar services for fear of losing students. The continuously cyclical nature of the phenomenon results in colleges and universities becoming more reliant upon student tuition to satisfy consumer demands. Institutions believe they must meet student desires in order to recruit students to pay tuition to create tuition revenue which is used to respond to consumers. These decisions cause inefficiencies within the market that inhibit their proper functioning as a mechanism to balance the demand of students and the supply of higher education across the states as well as nationally.

INFLUENCE OF CONSUMERISM ON THE ACADEMIC ENTERPRISE

Although the influence on co-curricular goals and outcomes is somewhat murky, consumerism's influence on the academic side of higher education is more pronounced. Many warn of the dangers of consumerism to traditional aims of higher education, including liberal education and public service. Beginning with the rise of the research university and continuing through the first half of the 20th century, faculty hegemony went largely unchallenged.[30] Regardless of institutional type, few inside or outside of academe questioned the role of faculty to determine and evaluate academic content.

Faculty dominance grew out of the specialization of higher education necessitated and reinforced by the expansion of research and graduate education. Armies of well-trained and well-credentialed faculty fanned out to institutions across the country arguing in favor of their expertise in disciplinary knowledge and the essential nature of the protections of academic freedom and tenure. The role of faculty and higher education during the two world wars and in helping create the military-industrial complex reinforced this notion in the public consciousness. Professors received a degree of reverence as the creators and inventors of the postwar period. Advancements in the sciences and technology grew at astounding rates with large, complex research universities replacing the Benjamin Franklins and Thomas Edisons.

The ascendency of the faculty saw its first sustained critique and attack from the counterculture movement of the 1960s and early 1970s along with governmental efforts to regulate institutions in ways favorable to students. David Riesman attributes the eventual decline of faculty hegemony largely to the rise of consumerism among students and government.[31] Although these groups held influence even during the expansion of faculty power, the consumerism paradigm eroded the support and deference enjoyed by faculty. Returning to the example of the customer and client, students and government are unable to assert control over the process and outcomes of higher education without attempting to diminish the extensive authority of the faculty. The need for additional revenue to both expand and compensate for a decline in appropriations during economic downturns dramatically escalated the market power wielded by students.

The expansion of student consumerism influenced the teaching and learning function of higher education from inside the institution.[32] This leads to the inclusion of student satisfaction as a key goal of colleges and universities. Many extol the significance of student satisfaction in ensuring the retention and graduation of students.[33] Administrators seized on the concept of satisfaction and elevated its significance within the academy. For example, class evaluations transitioned from a source of feedback to improve instruction to central elements in assessing faculty teaching performance.

Moves to add curricular innovation and exciting academic programs manifest differently within this context as well. These efforts are considered optional for students who seek them out or desire to engage with faculty outside of the traditional paradigm. Moreover, recruiters use these special programs to attract the most desirable students according to the institution's enrollment strategy. Honors programs and living-learning communities are among the initiatives used to attract students. As Bridget Terry Long details, the creation of honors programs in response to trends related to consumerism has grown significantly within the last 10 to 15 years.[34] Although the success of honors and living-learning communities in improving retention, student engagement, and academic achievement are well documented in the literature, there is great concern regarding the increased differentiation this creates internally within a student body.[35] In an effort to recruit the best students with these successful and popular programs, the preference given to the best and most engaged students raises questions regarding the quality of instruction and experience for the rest of the student population that is not given the opportunity or chooses not to participate. This becomes particularly troublesome given the long-standing concerns regarding access to higher education. The movement toward giving preference to these types of programs and students further raises the bar on populations with historically lower attainment rates, such as low-income or first-generation students. All of these trends taken together show how consumerism and the importance placed on satisfying student demands profoundly influence the academic endeavors of colleges and universities.

RISE OF THE ADMINISTRATIVE LATTICE

So far, I have detailed the rise of consumerism within higher education and the resulting decline of faculty hegemony, but I have not addressed the implications of this for higher education institutions today more broadly. Two key interrelated trends are central to understanding the influence of consumerism going forward. The rise of student consumers has given way to an administrative ascendency that potentially threatens the positive gains of both the faculty and student counterculture movements of the 1960s and early 1970s. Additionally, the tendency for institutions to support a conservative push for deregulation has encouraged the development of a professional bureaucracy on campus.

Although each movement was plagued by negative consequences associated with overreaching, the rise of faculty and students positively influenced American higher education in particular areas. The research success of faculty led to the prominent role of universities in fulfilling and advancing the scientific, medical, and technological needs of society. The student counterculture movement broadened the definition of who should study and what should be studied in higher education in a way few groups would have been able to transform. Increases in female and minority enrollment demanded appropriate attention within the curriculum, resulting in the rise of women's studies and African American studies programs nationwide. To reiterate, neither movement is faultless for the excesses each promulgated; yet, the lasting positive influence should be appreciated for advancing the cause and purpose of higher education.

Today, higher education is on the verge of a potential transformation with the growing supremacy of professional administration. One of the least understood and most profound changes since the Civil War, the growth of the professionalized bureaucracy became necessary to satisfy the expanding and increasingly complex organizational needs of the university. The creation of the administrative lattice, as Robert Zemsky describes the expansion, entails additional staff not only to operate the institution, but also to satisfy the demands of external constituencies for accountability.[36] Increased micromanagement by state governments and boards of trustees has resulted in "more paper, more procedures, [and] more staff."[37] Furthermore, at many institutions, the competition between academic and administrative units leads to unproductive struggles for additional resources. Faculty see themselves as the central business of the university, while professional staff proudly boast of their own ability to perform tasks with managerial efficiency typically found in businesses. Administrators have increasingly viewed themselves through a lens of professionalization similar to the ownership faculty feel about their disciplines. Professional staff, as a result of their administrative acumen, have acquired "the capacity to put into place their visions of how a well-run institution should look."[38] National associations and annual conferences exploded for administrators during the 1960s and 1970s, and a system of free agency developed with administrators moving between institutions to expand their responsibilities, prestige, and salaries. Ironically, the expansion of associations for staff occurred at the same time as a dramatic decline in the membership and influence of the American Association of University Professors.[39] State agency mandates and regulations, along with administrators' expansion of their own areas of responsibility, led to the creation and escalation of the administrative lattice.

Although state governments and increased complexity were initial causes of the ascendency of administrative units, student consumerism in the 1990s and 2000s caused a dramatic escalation. The pursuit of student consumers became and remains a significant administrative focus for institutions. This competition reigns supreme as colleges and universities desire the revenue and prestige associated with the best, brightest, and wealthiest students. Any edge to be gained is sought in this endeavor. Over the past two decades, college presidents shrewdly leveraged the desire of many in the state capital to limit higher education spending and a natural disposition to support deregulation on the part of conservative legislators. The presidents successfully argued that they could compete for students in the marketplace if only they did not have the burden of state regulations.[40] As a result, institutional leaders rely almost exclusively on responding to consumers in order to improve market position and long-term financial viability. Questions of mission, access, and knowledge production are secondary to attracting, satisfying, and retaining students.

The case of enrollment management is illustrative in demonstrating the expansion of administrative operations in response to student consumers. The traditional scope of admissions in the first half of the 20th century focused on processing the increasing volume of applications to higher-education institutions. Although a degree of this effort focused on constructing the most desirable class,[41] admissions offices largely managed paperwork. Today, admissions offices have grown into enrollment management, which seeks to direct student activity strategically and includes pre-admission stages, registration, and retention efforts. Sophisticated modeling is utilized to predict student behavior and where to recruit new students. Registrars and retention initiatives are also utilized in an attempt to manage and support students in their college experience through graduation.

To be sure, the expansion and professionalization of enrollment managers has improved the operations of institutions by bringing greater predictability to recruitment efforts, ensuring an incoming class of sufficient quality and quantity to satisfy administrative priorities. The enrollment process has also cemented the marginalization of faculty from the admissions decision. While faculty have removed themselves in a large measure to focus on other pursuits, particularly research, the complexity of new enrollment operations has necessitated the use of trained professionals to implement them.

Furthermore, enrollment units understand and to a large degree successfully reach and respond to potential student consumers and their parents. These successes have victimized the institution, as the revenue generated only encourages administrative leaders to transform their campuses to improve their ability to compete for students. The result is a series of decisions that administrators believe will improve the institution's marketability to student consumers, with often little concern for potential impacts for higher education broadly. Administrative attempts to appease student consumers more so than the consumeristic desires themselves become the driver of decision-making at the peril of the entire enterprise.

The move by institutions to expand beyond their traditional missions typifies the influence of administrators seeking to pursue student markets. New possibilities for prestige and revenue generation drive decision-making on many campuses. Academic drift or mission creep[42] is the development of initiatives and activities by colleges and universities characteristic of those institutions in the segment above them. This often occurs as a result of unchecked market forces leading to the creation of substandard doctoral and graduate programs, the proliferation of majors, and entrepreneurial endeavors. The justification of these moves often rests in the belief that a market exists for the program with little regard for potential impact on the existing and traditional aims of the institution. Administrators and faculty who are frequently complicit see the move as advantageous in terms of revenue and prestige generation. Faculty bear responsibility in failing to remain effectively involved in institutional operations, yet the speed and pace of administrative work negates any real ability to participate actively in meaningful ways in decision-making. Indeed, many view academic senates, a major vehicle for faculty involvement on 90 percent of campuses, as ineffectual, if not downright dysfunctional.[43] The result is a limited role of faculty in determining short-term courses for action, as in the case of academic drift.

The concern of many in higher education that I share is the sense that senior administrators view mission creep as personally advantageous and a proverbial notch on the belt. Beyond the concerns raised about the implications of prestige-seeking initiatives, administrative decisions too often appear to be based solely on the relative success in attracting institutional prestige. Indeed, much of the contemporary critique on the damaging influence of consumerism can be attributed to administrative responses to consumer behavior. Often couched in terms of improved efficiency, administrative decision-making too frequently favors expedience and increasing status in the marketplace.

THE FUTURE OF CONSUMERISM IN HIGHER EDUCATION

For nearly 20 years, the climate within higher education largely relied on the principle of a free market for recruiting students. With the cyclical rise and fall of state appropriations and other sources of funding, institutions turned to the flexibility of tuition revenue to better control their futures. The prevalent ideology of market deregulation and an aversion to tax increases in conservative statehouses across the country facilitated the growth of competition between colleges and universities. With the preoccupation of campus leaders on tuition, student consumers gained a powerful position within the market. Institutional responses to recruit, retain, and satisfy students influenced the activities and decision-making processes. Faculty dominance waned as professional administrative ranks swelled to meet growing student demands. The impact of this new administrative ascendency changed the internal dynamics of shared governance and resource allocation strategies.

Perhaps the greatest potential change in the future of student consumerism specifically, and higher education more broadly, rests in the premise of an ideological shift of the country as a result of the 2008 economic recession and as illustrated by the election of Barack Obama as president. The extent to which the excesses of financial institutions and real estate investors change public sentiment on government regulation presents the possibility for dramatic change in the higher education marketplace. Increased regulation by governmental agencies could result in "the values of the polity play[ing] a large role in affecting approved and disapproved activities."[44] As described earlier in the chapter, the market proved unable to self-regulate institutions as a result of the role of prestige, the lack of information for consumers, and the difficulty in defining the product of higher education.

The question before higher education fundamentally is one of balance. The concerns of administrators for securing resources, the role of faculty in making academic decisions, and the desires of student consumers form the basic components of the future of postsecondary education. Understanding how to weigh each of these elements becomes the challenge in moving beyond the illogical decision-making typified by the arms race to simply satisfy consumers. In the absence of governmental intervention through a limited system of regulation, it is difficult to foresee any substantial movement within the student marketplace to curb efforts to meet consumer demands in spite of the potential damage to the historical purposes of higher education.

To conclude my discussion of the challenges of consumerism, I present three recommendations for campus leaders to address in an effort to preserve the long-standing benefits of higher education: a renewed focus on shared governance; leveraging the nexus between consumer and institutional objectives; and a stronger emphasis on the mission of the college or university. Given the existing environmental context and pressures facing colleges and universities, the goal of these suggestions is to provide areas where institutional leaders can better achieve balance in decision-making. The first recommendation encourages internal stakeholders to respect the goals and intent of shared governance within higher education. Participating faculty should move with deliberate haste, recognizing the tremendous pressures faced by administrators. As an example, the traditional shutdown of faculty governance structures during the summer hinders involvement in decisions that require rapid resolution. External influences push for rapid change that often requires action that may not wait until faculty return to campus in August. Faculty committees exist to influence and contribute to institutional decision-making despite occasional uses to delay and derail administrative initiatives. Likewise, campus administrators ought to appreciate the goals and responsibility placed on faculty. Priorities such as protecting academic integrity and knowledge generation processes represent core areas that faculty rightfully safeguard. Administrators demonstrate a support for shared governance by presenting information regularly and asking for input before an issue escalates into a time-sensitive crisis. Forthrightly addressing pressures from student consumers in a spirit of appreciation for the unique responsibilities and mutual objectives of each group establishes a foundation for institutional success.

In addition to renewed support of shared governance, campus leaders can look for a nexus between institutional goals and those of consumers. Finding areas where consumer demands improve the teaching, research, and service functions presents an opportunity to advance larger priorities. Attracting consumers through improved teaching, state-of-the-art facilities, and small class sizes concurrently supports the academic mission. As discussed throughout this chapter, the escalation of consumerism challenges how higher education operates and warrants close scrutiny to protect core values. Establishing boundaries, which will vary between institutions, enables administrators and faculty to work on leveraging potential benefits from consumerism.

The key to thriving in this environment rests in the ability to understand the institution's mission and fundamental values. Agreement on mission provides the trust for various stakeholders to work together to advance the institution. In this context, a decision to start a new program or create a new student service exists within a larger, established social contract among faculty, administrators, and students. The revenues generated from meeting consumer desires represent an opportunity to advance core institutional activities and objectives. In the long run, success will largely result from our ability to self-regulate and continue to advance the traditional purposes of higher education.

NOTES

1. Derek Bok, *Universities in the Marketplace: The Commercialization of Higher Education* (Princeton, NJ: Princeton University Press, 2004).

2. Dominic J. Brewer, Susan M. Gates, and Charles A. Goldman, *In Pursuit of Prestige: Strategy and Competition in US Higher Education* (New Brunswick, NJ: Transaction Publishers, 2002).

3. Ibid.

4. Roger L. Geiger, *Knowledge & Money: Research Universities and the Paradox of the Marketplace* (Palo Alto, CA: Stanford University Press, 2004).

5. Brewer, Gates, and Goldman, *In Pursuit of Prestige*.

6. Arthur Hauptman, "Reforming Ways in Which States Finance Higher Education," in *The States and Public Higher Education Policy: Affordability, Access, and Accountability,* ed. Donald Heller (Baltimore, MD: Johns Hopkins University Press, 2001), 64–80.

7. Robert Zemsky, Gregory R. Wegner, and William F. Massy, *Remaking the American University: Market-smart and Mission-centered* (New Brunswick, NJ: Rutgers University Press, 2005), 140.

8. Rachelle Brooks, "Measuring University Quality," *The Review of Higher Education* 29, no. 1 (2005), 1–21.

9. Richard M. Canterbury, "Higher Education Marketing: A Challenge," *Journal of Marketing for Higher Education* 9, no. 2 (1999), 15–24.

10. Gabrielle Baldwin and Richard James, "The Market in Australian Higher Education and the Concept of Student as Informed Consumer,"

Journal of Higher Education Policy and Management 22, no. 2 (2000), 139–48.

11. Eric S. Lipton and David Barboza, "As More Toys Are Recalled, the Trail Ends in China," *New York Times,* June 19, 2007: A1.

12. Walter Truett Anderson, Jim Dator, and Majid Tehranian, eds., *Learning to Seek: Globalization, Governance, and the Futures of Higher Education* (New Brunswick, NJ: Transaction Publishers, 2006).

13. Dan Carnevale, "Federal and State Officials Discuss Cracking Down on Online Diploma Mills," *Chronicle of Higher Education,* February 13, 2004: A32.

14. For additional information on this process, Don Hossler, Jack Schmit, and Nick Vesper describe in detail the process of college choice in their book, *Going to College: How Social, Economic and Educational Factors Influence the Decisions Students Make* (Baltimore, MD: Johns Hopkins University Press, 1999).

15. J. Douglas Toma, Greg Dubrow, and Matthew Hartley, *The Uses of Institutional Culture: Strengthening Identification and Building Brand Equity in Higher Education* (San Francisco: Jossey-Bass, 2005).

16. David A. Aaker, *Managing Brand Equity: Capitalizing on the Value of a Brand Name* (New York: The Free Press, 1991).

17. Debra Grace and Aron O'Cass, "Service Branding: Consumer Verdicts on Service Brands," *Journal of Retailing and Consumer Services* 12, no. 1 (2005), 28–52; Kevin L. Keller, "Brand Synthesis: The Multidimensionality of Brand Knowledge," *Journal of Consumer Research* 29 (2003), 595–600.

18. Matthew Hartley and Christopher C. Morphew, "What's Being Sold and to What End? A Content Analysis of College Viewbooks," *Journal of Higher Education* 79, no. 6 (2008), 671–91.

19. Michael S. Harris, "Message in a Bottle: University Advertising during Bowl Games," *Innovative Higher Education* 33, no. 5 (2009), 285–96.

20. Donald E. Vinson, Jerome E. Scott, and Lawrence M. Lamont, "The Role of Personal Values in Marketing and Consumer Behavior," *Journal of Marketing* 41, no. 2 (1977), 44–50.

21. Toma, Dubrow, and Hartley, *The Uses of Institutional Culture.*

22. Leslie de Chernatony and Francesca Dall'Olmo Riley, "Modelling the Components of the Brand," *European Journal of Marketing* 32, nos. 11/12, (1998), 1077–90.

23. Michael B. Paulsen and Edward P. St. John, "The Financial Nexus Between College Choice and Persistence," *New Directions for Institutional Research* 95 (1997), 189–236.

24. Michael S. McPherson and Morton O. Schapiro, *The Student Aid Game: Meeting Need and Rewarding Talent in American Higher Education* (Princeton, NJ: Princeton University Press, 1998).

25. Alberto F. Cabrera and Steven M. La Nasa, "Understand the College-Choice Process," *New Directions for Institutional Research,* no. 107 (2000), 5–22; Edward P. St. John and Jay Noell, "The Effects of Student Financial Aid on Access to Higher Education: An Analysis of Progress with Special Consideration of Minority Enrollment," *Research in Higher Education* 30, no. 6 (1989), 563–81.

26. Edward P. St. John, "Assessing Tuition and Student Aid Strategies: Using Price-Response Measures to Simulate Pricing Alternatives," *Research in Higher Education* 35, no. 3 (1994), 301–34.

27. Geiger, *Knowledge & Money.*

28. Joann A. Brown, "Marketing and Retention Strategies for Adult Degree Programs," *New Directions for Adult and Continuing Education,* no. 103 (2004, Fall), 51–60.

29. Sheila Slaughter and Gray Rhoades, *Academic Capitalism and the New Economy: Markets, State, and Higher Education* (Baltimore, MD: Johns Hopkins University Press, 2004).

30. John R. Thelin, *A History of American Higher Education* (Baltimore, MD: Johns Hopkins University Press, 2004).

31. David Riesman, *On Higher Education: The Academic Enterprise in an Era of Rising Student Consumerism* (New Brunswick, NJ: Transaction Publishers, 1998).

32. Geiger, *Knowledge & Money.*

33. George D. Kuh, Jillian Kinzie, John H. Schuh, Elizabeth J. Whitt, et al., *Student Success in College: Creating Conditions That Matter* (San Francisco: Jossey-Bass, 2005).

34. Bridget Terry Long, "Attracting the Best: The Use of Honors Programs to Compete for Students," 2002, http://gseacademic.harvard.edu/~longbr/HonorsColleges.pdf.

35. Murray Sperber, "End the Mediocrity of Our Public Universities," *Chronicle of Higher Education,* October 20, 2000: B24.

36. Robert Zemsky, "The Lattice and the Ratchet," *Policy Perspectives* 2, no. 4 (1990).

37. Zemsky, Wegner, and Massy, *Remaking the American University*, 21.

38. Ibid., 22.

39. Scott Jaschik, "Change Ahead for AAUP," *Inside Higher Education,* January 23, 2007, http://www.insidehighered.com/news/archive/(year)/2007/(month)/1.

40. Frank Newman, Lara Couturier, and Jamie Scurry, *The Future of Higher Education: Rhetoric, Reality, and the Risks of the Market* (San Francisco: Jossey-Bass, 2004).

41. See David O. Levine's *The American College and the Culture of Aspiration, 1915–1940* (Ithaca, NY: Cornell University Press, 1986) for an

illuminating account of how Ivy League institutions addressed the "Jewish problem" in college admissions decisions.

42. Christopher C. Morphew, "A Rose by any Other Name: Which Colleges Became Universities," *The Review of Higher Education* 25, no. 2 (2002), 207–23.

43. James T. Minor, "Understanding Faculty Senates: Moving from Mystery to Models," *The Review of Higher Education* 27, no. 3 (2004), 243–63; Robert Birnbaum, "The Latent Organizational Functions of the Academic Senate: Why Senates Do Not Work but Will Not Go Away," *Journal of Higher Education* 60, no. 4 (1989), 423–43; Mary Burgan, "Academic Citizenship: A Fading Vision," *Liberal Education* 84, no. 4 (1998), 16–21; Martin Trow, "The Academic Senate as a School for University Leadership," *Liberal Education* 76, no. 1 (1990), 23–27.

44. Geiger, *Knowledge & Money,* 233.

CHAPTER 7

Academic Customer Service

Neal A. Raisman

"Customer service is an aberrant bastard wrought of the detestable marriage of commercialism and those who would corporatize the academy by pandering to students."

Or so stated an anonymous professor in a blog comment on customer service in higher education. His or her comment is one that is starting to become an academic relic as more and more people in higher education recognize that, though retail customer service may not be appropriate, academic customer service may well be.

This shift in thinking about what is important and primary at colleges and universities may not necessarily derive from any strategic restructuring of the academic hierarchy that traditionally places the needs and desires of faculty above that of students.[1] Students, after all, do not issue votes of no confidence. In fact, the growing focus on customer service in higher education, especially as a part of enrollment management, is seen largely as a means to feed the appetite of faculty and others on a campus. Customer service done well and correctly leads to increased retention, and increased retention leads directly to increased revenue. Additional money in the annual budget allows colleges and universities to fund what is considered important including salaries, increased benefits, release time, travel, research, hiring, equipment, supplies, capital maintenance, and other revenue priorities and needs. These aspects of the business of higher education are driving the interest in academic customer service.

In the past, higher education has been fully focused on customer acquisition, on enrolling new students. There has been little effort to retain customers, never mind up-selling them. In fact, turnover has been seen as a positive factor in the branding of the institution. The positioning of many schools was summed up in an old anecdote. "Look to your left" the president or dean would intone to the freshman class. "Now look to your right. By the end of the semester, at least one of you will be gone." When costs, salaries and benefits were low, competition for students limited, and market share assured, the poor business strategy of losing a third of the customer population was not merely a statement of academic integrity, but was fiscally viable. What a school lost in one year could be planned for and made up the next.

The loss of at least a third of the freshman class during tight budget years and against increasingly expensive times can no longer be tolerated. Retention must become a major fiscal strategy if schools are to succeed fiscally. Customer Service Factor 1[2]:

The formula [(population × attrition = students lost) × tuition] calculates the cost of attrition and illuminates the problem for colleges. A school with tuition of $10,000, a population of 5,000 students, and a 33 percent annualized attrition rate loses $16.5 million in potential tuition revenue.

Seventy-two percent of all attrition can be attributed to customer service issues,[3] as shown in Figure 7.1.

Three primary issues are the major factor for students/customers to leave a school, transfer to another, or drop out of higher education completely. First, they feel the school is indifferent to their needs and expectations (30%). Second, they encounter problems with staff or feel they receive

Figure 7.1 Why Students Leave

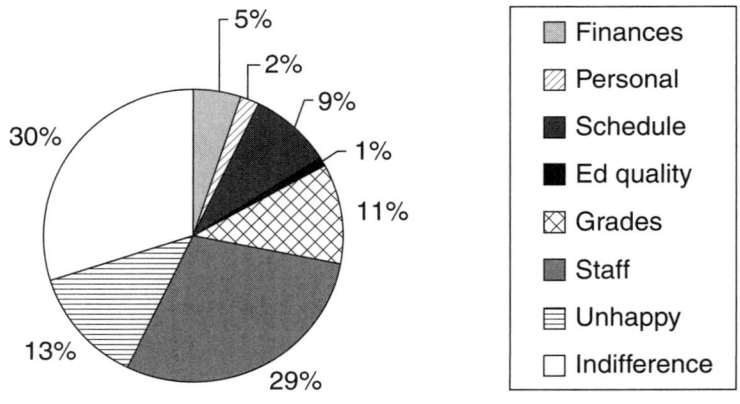

weak or poor treatment from them (29%), with staff defined as including faculty and administrators as well as clerical levels. Third, students were just plain unhappy at the school (13%). All of these are attributable to customer service or the lack of it. Weak or poor customer service leading to attrition directly accounts for the major portion of lost tuition revenue, which could be preserved if the students are retained. As a result, business and budgetary concerns are fueling the push for greater customer service awareness and practice in higher education. In turn, the business of education is strengthening the focus on student success and retention. Good academic customer service yields only positives for students, institutions, society, culture, and the economy.

ACADEMIC CUSTOMER SERVICE

The history of academic customer service as both an institutional concern and an academic research topic is but seven years old, starting with the book *Embrace the Oxymoron: Customer Service in Higher Education*.[4] In the book, customer service is initially defined as "simply fulfilling the real expectations of students—*expectations,* Not wants. Not desires but *expectations.*"[5] The expectations were enumerated as:

1. A positive reception and ongoing indications of appreciation
2. Response and action
3. Me-centered service
4. Educational value and quality
5. Educational return on investment.[6]

These five expectations still form a core part of what became a functional academic customer service definition. Research since the 2002 publication has broadened, refined, and refocused the definition.

Additional competition in the marketplace, as well as a tightening in the economy that started in 2000 and continues to the present day, has forced a primary shift from the 2002 considerations of academic customer service. There are simply more colleges, driving increased competition for new students (Figure 7.2). Each new college means additional seats to fill in the academic sector.

Most of the growth has been in the career college (for-profit), four-year sector that markets very aggressively to prospective students. This is an important point because the aggressive marketing by career colleges has increased the overall competition for students significantly. In one study of 300 four-year career college students,[7] just 14 knew the school they were attending was proprietary/for-profit. All 14 also indicated that

Figure 7.2 Number of Universities and Colleges, 2000–2006

	1999	2006
Public 4-year institutions	615	640
Public 2-year institutions	1,092	1,053
Private 4-year institutions, non-profit	1,536	1,534
Private 4-year institutions, for-profit	169	408
Private 2-year institutions, non-profit	184	113
Private 2-year institutions, for-profit	500	528
Total	4,096	4,276

Source: Chronicle of Higher Education Almanacs 2000, 2008.

they did not care or make any value distinction between for- and not-for-profit colleges. Meanwhile, 221 thought of their chosen school as a private college and that perception conferred some associative value on it. None of the 300 thought they would receive less than a very good to excellent education at the college. Through their responses, the students appear to indicate that not only have career colleges grown in number but also in stature, thereby allowing them to compete for students on an equal footing. As a result, the market for new students has tightened for all colleges alongside the growth in the number of career colleges which has only expanded the number of additional seats and choices for students.

Making entry quotas has become increasingly more difficult and more expensive for colleges outside of the top tiers. Even major name-brand colleges are finding it more problematic to complete their freshman quotas.[8] This shift has forced colleges, or at least began to nudge them, to realize that they cannot simply plan on revenue from increasing initial enrollment and fees.

The result of additional successful competition has been that colleges have been forced to focus not only on admissions but increasingly on retention. Colleges have to consider moving away from traditional front loading of sales and replacing students who leave with newly acquired students. Moreover, in an attempt to acquire a greater or targeted market share of new students, schools must subsidize tuition more and more, thereby decreasing actual incoming revenue. Tuition discounting at the levels indicated point out that the need to compete for new students is costing the colleges more than they can afford if they stay with a fully front-loaded admissions approach to producing more revenue.

> The most recent data . . . reveal that the (unweighted) average discount rate is 12.5 percent for public two-year colleges and 14.7

percent for public four-year institutions. In other words, these colleges and universities are spending a significant portion of their revenues creating different net prices for different students.

Over the decade beginning in 1994–95, the discount rate increased by about 6 percentage points in two-year public institutions,[5] 3 percentage points in four-year public colleges and universities, and 10 percentage points in private four-year institutions. Whereas the private four-year average discount rate has increased at a fairly steady rate of about 1 percentage point per year over the entire decade, the discount rate in the public sector peaked in 2002–03. The growth in the public two-year sector discount rate occurred between 1994–95 and 2000–01. The discount rate in public four-year institutions did grow over that period, but it leapt up in 2001–02 and has remained at that higher level since.[9]

Moreover, it has been calculated that every student a college attracts costs the institution an average of $5,460.[10] Institutions are also encountering average, annualized attrition rates of 32.6 percent.[11] That means to get one FGE (full-time graduate equivalent),[12] a four-year college must enroll six students, not just one. It also means the college will pay at least $27,300 more than if it simply retained that first student all the way through to graduation. It is worth noting that, according to IPEDS data, the baccalaureate college and university six-year graduation rate nationally is 56.4 percent, yielding an attrition rate of 43.6 percent. Colleges are losing almost as many students as they enroll over a period of six years.

All of this translates into millions of lost tuition and fee revenue dollars. In turn, academic budgets are falling short and have little chance to recoup lost dollars via new students. Moreover, there are moves underway in some states[13] to require public and state colleges and universities to increase their graduation rates. The result is that more and more colleges are realizing that retention is an increasingly important factor.

To increase retention and thereby improve revenue streams, colleges need to increase the services they provide their clients, their students. This has become a primary underlying reason why academic customer service has gained increased attention over the past four years in particular. AcademicMAPS, an academic customer service consultant group, reports that inquiries and demands for its services have grown by a factor of five since 2005.

RETURN ON INVESTMENT AND STUDENT EXPECTATIONS

Claes Fornell, director of the American Customer Satisfaction Index, writes "regardless of product, there are three general factors that determine how well a company's offerings correspond to the idiosyncrasy of consumer demand: expectations, quality and price."[14] Though higher education is a rather different business than most of the companies he works with, Fornell's overview fits much of academic customer service as well, as expressed in three return-on-investment (ROI) expectations brought to college by students and families. In fact, one might posit that good academic customer service has at its foundation providing the client/student with the means, ability, and services to be able to achieve three major ROI considerations (financial, emotional, and affective), which are key to student and family expectations of the school, while attending and graduating college in a way that makes the client feel valued and appreciated.

Academic customer service accomplishes the above by employing a student-centric approach—processes and protocols focusing on teaching, training, and learning in an encouraging environment that acknowledges a student's worth and existence to assure personal growth and success now and in the future. It does not assume coddling students or favoring them with unearned or higher grades. Academic customer service also does not include faux business concepts such as "the client is always right" (they take tests and quizzes after all).

ROI is normatively a financial formula (i.e., a positive or negative percentage indicating what financial return may or may not ensue from an investment), but the ROI concept in academic customer service is calculated not on a financial plus or minus percentage basis, but as a personal psychological formulation comprising a student's perceptions and judgments that his or her investment is worthwhile. If it is seen as such, the student is comfortable, even happy, and stays. If the student does not feel there is at least a financial, emotional, and associative equity between what his investment and what the school provides, a negative ROI will be perceived and the student will likely leave. If the student should stay, he will slog through, bad-mouthing the school whenever the chance arises. If the student graduates, he will not contribute as an alumnus.

The three major returns on investment that students receive and retain throughout college and into their careers are, in order of importance:

1. Financial ROI
2. Emotional ROI
3. Affective ROI.

Financial ROI has two formulations. The first, *Financial ROI 1,* is focused on present-day money invested and what is provided in return. This focuses on the perception of whether or not "I am getting my money's worth. Do I feel that the tuition and fees are well spent and spent on me?

Is the college using the money to give me what I am here for?" The second, *Financial ROI 2,* evaluates whether or not the student believes that staying at the school will finally lead to the job and career that he came to the school to acquire.

In determining *Financial ROI 1,* the student and her supporters judge the value of a number of seemingly disparate issues: perceived value of classroom instruction; faculty concern about students' understanding and learning; faculty availability for office hours and help; administrators' responses to problems; or treatment by staff. Even what might seem to some to be ancillary issues fall under the category of objective correlatives,[15] such as facilities, parking, lighting, and so on. These figure in strongly in formulating a financial ROI and have some importance in the calculation of an affective ROI, as has been discovered in retention audits of colleges conducted by the author.

Financial ROI 2 is a prediction of future career returns on the investment. The core of the calculation is the belief that one's investment in the school will or will not lead to and help one obtain a good job. Students must believe that the college will not only assist in preparing and certifying them to go out and apply for jobs, but that the school's reputation will make obtaining that job possible. If a college has good, available, and publicized career services that help them prepare and apply for jobs or, even better, if there is an active outreach to students on careers and assistance in locating possible jobs, the *Financial ROI 2* will remain positive. If the college can also point to a history of success stories for its graduates, this too strengthens *Financial ROI 2.*

Emotional ROI refers to the personal, nonfinancial investment that a student and family make in a school. When a student decides to attend a college, that person is making a commitment that is somewhat akin to a marital engagement. The decision to attend a college is like saying a student and the college will not date others. Trust, attachment, and commitment between the student and college arise in the student's mind and feelings, leading to a pledge that she expects to be reciprocated. That pledge is, "I will trust you to do right by me. I will put my education and thus my future in your hands. I will trust you to treat me fairly and provide me an honest opportunity to learn and get that job I want."

If this vow is not reciprocated by an institution's actions, the student does not perceive the emotional investment being returned and falls out of love with the college. Students cite two major reasons for ending an engagement with a school. First, they come to believe that "The school only cares about me for the money they get," thus seeing the school as placing money above the student in importance (too many adjunct faculty, not enough sections of courses, poor scheduling, canceling classes at the last minute, not enough staff, aggressive bursar and collections letters, etc.). Or second, the student feels the school does not reach out and show it cares about her as an individual with personal needs (cannot find faculty during office hours, cannot get extra help when needed, faculty do not seem to realize students have lives too, administrators do not care or solve problems, staff are cold or rude, no one smiles, students get the runaround also known as "the shuffle," issues go unresolved or with just a decision that is unexplained, etc.). Any of these can and will lead to a perceived weak *Emotional ROI*.

The last is *Associative/Affective ROI*, calculated on the sensation that attending this college says something about a student, his values and character. Valuations such as "attending this college is an investment in my reputation, self-value and social position, as its name defines me through association." The student is also calculating whether being part of this school will "make me feel good, improve my value and recognition?"

Associative ROI can be strong if the student feels that the school is well known and respected in the community. If this is not the case, the school may create strong associative value by providing excellent service to the student, who will then take pride in attending, thus also reinforcing the *Emotional ROI*. A college can overcome lack of current recognition (in, for example, the *U.S. News & World Report* rankings) if its services are strong enough. Excellent service and personal attention can build a student's desire to be associated with the college. Conversely, the student's belief in the school may be lost by ignoring concerns or by negative reports in the news. When this happens, the *Associative ROI* can be negatively impacted so that the student does not want to be associated with the school.

One way a school can judge if its associative value is up or down is by counting the amount of logo- or name-laden clothing that is sold in the bookstore. When students wear college branded clothes, it is done to make a statement to the world about the wearer. Wearing a brand-name college such as Harvard, **the** University of Michigan, or another high-recognition school is a statement meant to associate the wearer with the strength and value of the name.

STUDENTS AS CLIENTS

Students and colleges are not really in a customer-business relationship as one would consider in retail, for example. A retail customer relationship is based on time- and incident-bounded events. A specific need is identified and met. For instance, when a customer goes to a store to find an MP3 player, a salesperson welcomes her, perhaps smiles, locates the MP3 players, and answers questions. The customer makes a buying decision, the salesperson completes processing the purchase, and the event ends. A service person fixes an identified problem, in this case by supplying a desired product. The salesperson or service professional need not be concerned with establishing a meaningful relationship to complete the sale or service.

A student is making a decision to enter into a long-term relationship with a college based not on a purchase of a particular item, but on the acquisition of knowledge, skills, training, and assistance that will prepare him or her for a job, career, or the next educational step. The relationship between student and school is more analogous to a client–consultant one. The client (student) must believe that the consultant has the excellent skills, ability, experience, and successful track record required to help him make competent decisions or to provide the correct assistance for growth and change to move toward his goals of graduation and a job. The student must place faith in the integrity and services of the college and must feel that the provider of the services has his best interests as a central priority in everything that happens at the institution.

The relationship might be compared to that of a medical professional and patient. A patient comes to a doctor to live a healthy and long physical life, just as a student attends a college to have a meaningful and successful career and life. The patient chooses a doctor because of reputation, proximity, whether or not she is accepting new patients, and ability to pay the doctor's fees. The decision to stay with that professional depends on a number of factors. First is whether or not the patient believes the doctor is actually good at what she does and that health will result from following her advice and knowledge. The patient does not have to take the doctor's advice or follow her orders. If the doctor assigns the patient to lose weight and exercise, it is the patient's decision whether or not to do this. If he does, he may get healthier and move further to his goal of a long and good life. If he chooses not to be compliant, he will fail his next exam. In the same way, if an assignment from a class is not done, the student must accept the potential failing of the next exam.

Second, whether or not the patient listens to the doctor, or the student to the teacher, depends fully on trust of the provider and a belief that there will be a commensurate return on investment. A patient will be more compliant with a doctor's directions if he trusts her knowledge, ability and, even more, has faith in her. Commensurate with and the building block of faith is whether or not the doctor shows she cares about the patient. The last aspect is actually the most important: faith that the doctor really cares about him as an individual and has made an effort to show it. This can be seen in the work of malpractice litigator and researcher Alice Braunstein (formerly Burkin). In advising medical doctors on how to avoid lawsuits, she makes the case for faith and concern from the service provider as core issues.

> The most important factor [to avoid being sued] in many cases, besides the injury itself, is the quality of the patient's relationship with the doctor . . . [It is important to] establish good relationships with your patients, and to treat them with respect. That requires taking time to talk with them, and more important, to listen.[16]

Braunstein also discussed a patient who wanted to sue a doctor because

> she never took the time to talk to her and never asked about her other symptoms . . . the doctor has to take the time to explain what happened and to answer the patient's questions. To treat him like a human being.[17]

The trust and faith factors are also very strong in academic customer service. Students are investing a great deal of money and time, not just in their education, but also in their future. The student wants to believe he is a valuable part of the institution, as if his being there matters to people. He does not want to ever feel "like a number" or that the school "just cares about my tuition payments." Both of these statements are too commonly heard during customer service audits that AcademicMAPS performs for client colleges experiencing attrition above 30 percent. Comments from students are clear indicators that some are among those who will leave because they believe the institution is indifferent to them as individuals. They feel they have been treated as patients in a busy clinic where the doctor hangs in the door, jots down a prescription without listening well enough, and runs to the next patient. Often this characterizes the situation of a college with a large cadre of adjunct faculty who must run to their next paying academic gig. It also encapsulates most research universities wherein too many faculty teach because they have to, but see classes and students as getting in the way of "their important work as a researcher."

Trust is also formed by experiencing the work and truthfulness of the doctor. A patient most often comes to a doctor when he does not feel well or has some problem that needs remedying. If the doctor does not want to be forceful about a patient's unhealthy lifestyle, eating habits, or lack of proper exercise for fear of alienating him when hard truth or bad news is needed, she is failing the patient. Not being honest and complete with a patient can be a certain way to lose that individual's trust and faith. In turn, the doctor loses a patient to another doctor or can gain a malpractice lawsuit as a result.

In a similar manner, students come to college because they perceive weaknesses that will keep them from being able to perform well enough to obtain the job and then keep the job they want. They seek out the PhD doctors to make them strong enough for success. They place particular faith in their professors. They are ready to take harsh medicine if it will help them.

A third factor in the client relationship is the fulfilling of assigned trust by doing what is truly best for the student. A common example of professors failing to fulfill the trust placed in their professionalism and leadership is a failure to maintain the classroom decorum that they and most students know should be preserved. Faculty are becoming more and more bothered by what they see as inappropriate rudeness and improper classroom behavior, such as answering cell phones, searching the Web during lectures or discussions, and even sleeping, yet they do not insist on a proper academic learning environment. They allow nondecorous behavior to upset them and others in the class and say they do not wish to get into arguments with students or risk poor evaluations, or they claim they are just going along with "the administration's customer service push." This is not customer service. Failing to maintain the requisite decorum in a classroom is, at best, pandering to students and, at worst, cheating them of both service and a full return on their investments.

Academic customer service is in no way equal to pandering. Though many academics, mainly faculty, say that they believe customer service just means letting students do what they want or giving them easy grades, this is very far from what real service entails. In fact, giving easy grades is a disservice to students, to the school, and to the integrity of everyone involved.

Students come to college to be prepared for the future. This requires the institution to give them the best and most honest service possible, just as a medical doctor should be complete and fully upfront with a patient in terms of both diagnosis and treatment. To do less is to misrepresent learning, which must involve acculturation to the customs and demands of the world after college (an aspect of *Financial ROI 2*).

While it is true that students go to school to "become something" and get a job, a college also should prepare them to keep a job. This is an important service to academic customers,[18] teaching them to be responsible employees so they can succeed in the jobs they get. One important aspect of on-the-job success is using correct business decorum—showing up on time, not taking phone calls during business meetings or discussions, using language appropriate to the workplace, completing assignments on time and as requested, not walking out of meetings early, and following the codes, folkways, and mores of the workplace.

Therefore, it is an appropriate customer service to maintain classroom decorum that is appropriate to the learning environment, which is the students' workplace for the time of the class. Good service inculcates students with an understanding of behaviors that the workplace demands. Bad customer service allows students to engage in harmful behaviors when the professor does not wish to take a chance of upsetting them. A doctor who knows a patient is engaged in an unhealthy behavior has an obligation to provide the best medical service and inform the patient of the dangers of the behavior as well as what is healthy behavior. In the same way, a professor has a service obligation to inform students of inappropriate and unhealthy learning and future job behaviors as well as what is appropriate behavior. A doctor or professor who does not inform a client of dangerous behavior is rendering substandard service and shirking a duty.

A fourth factor in successful customer service is taking action to complete the service. If a doctor has blood drawn to determine if an illness exists, she must communicate and explain the results. If there is no review of the blood tests, even if they are all indicative of a healthy patient, she risks breaking faith. The patient has invested in the tests and the value of the doctor. To help fulfill this service obligation, many doctors have begun using computer programs that print the patient's test results alongside normal standards with explanations of any abnormal indications at the bottom or on an attached sheet. A cover letter offers additional explanation, a potential follow-up appointment and, at times, a personal note jotted by or for the doctor. Thus, the doctor proves she values the patient as an individual by fulfilling the client service proffered. This sort of response also strengthens bonds between the doctor and patient, in turn helping retain the patient in the practice, bolstering trust in the doctor, and making the client more compliant and accepting of both diagnosis and treatment. According to Braunstein, it may also reduce or eliminate the possibility of being sued.[19]

A college must do the same. Expectations created must be fulfilled by action. If a college says it will provide tutoring services, it must do so. If it sells itself on providing small classes, it must do so. If a faculty member gives an exam, it must be returned in a reasonable time period, marked and graded, and students must be able to get the correct answers to their wrong answers, or have their grades explained on essays or short-answer tests. A math teacher may go over each problem and how it should have been solved to get to the correct answers in front of the entire class. Multiple-choice tests may be reviewed with a discussion of answers as well. For essay or short-answer exams, it is helpful to provide a discussion with examples from good answers written by students in the class. All of these approaches also employ good teaching and learning devices. Going over an exam reinforces learning through repetition.

A professor may even use a method similar to that of the service-oriented doctor who provides detailed information of a blood test. This may take the form of an exam report sheet that takes each question and provides a correct or sample response against which a student may measure his or her own work.

BUYING DECISIONS AND ACADEMIC CUSTOMER SERVICE

Finally, academic customer service is quite different finally than that of retail operations. A college-buying decision is not a finite one that ends with enrollment. It is an everyday determination. Students do not come to college to make a singular purchase of goods or even a service, as when they go to the doctor, dentist, or dry cleaner. In these transactions, a problem is resolved and the customer need not return until another issue or need arises. A student makes a buying decision each and every day, each and every class, and each and every assignment, all based on an evaluation of whether the ROI will lead to his success in the future. If a class does not seem to be worth a student's time and expense, it will not be "bought." The student will not pay attention in class if attendance is required, or may skip it and its assignments, or even drop it altogether. If she feels the school does not care, or is indifferent to her and her needs, she will end the buying relationship. If she does not feel she is getting a full ROI from classes or from employees who may not treat her with the attention, respect, honesty, or the assistance she feels she is due, she may seek another college or university.

Students are investing in a long-term series of purchases over a long period of time. They make buying decisions every day, every class, and these are influenced by every encounter with employees of the institution. Certainly every scheduled class in a day leads to a decision. As the time for the start of each class arrives, a student must decide whether or not she will go to the class and thereby *purchase it*. Granted, the student does not actually pay daily for attendance, as was done in the days of the medieval guild college, but just as the medieval student determined how much to pay based on the value of the information received, today's student invests the prepaid time and effort to attend a class based on whether or not she perceives it is worth it. The important concern here is that if a student decides that a class is not worth the outlay, she essentially withdraws a part of her investment in the institution. If that level of withdrawal increases to a tipping point, she may leave since she does not perceive an acceptable

ROI. The concern will be balanced against the future ROI benefits that the name on the diploma can provide.

It is important to realize that, in the eyes of the college's customers, everyone in the institution, from the president on down, is there to serve them, their needs, and their goals. Today's students are not all that intimidated by concepts of top and bottom tiers in the academic hierarchy. Thus, they have little or no trepidation at starting with the president to raise an issue or service problem. Moreover, they judge everyone's interaction as more or less equally important in serving them when they need assistance.

By contrast, students also have greater expectations of having their issues serviced the higher up the academic ladder they go. They are aware of the various levels and titles and expect a quicker and more positive resolution of their issues at each higher level in the hierarchy. They do not subscribe to the normative academic protocols that ask them to follow a pattern of action that begins at the lowest possible level of resolution. For instance, a classroom issue may start with the faculty member and progress to the discipline coordinator, the department chair, the dean, the vicepresident, and then the president—moving up the ladder only as each lower level has been approached. Academic mores apply pressure at each level to protect the colleague(s) below. The discipline leader does not want to expose a faculty colleague. The department chair does not want to publicly disagree with the discipline leader or be seen as not supporting faculty. This pattern continues through the next layers of administrative structure. The taxonomical problem-solving approach almost always adds to the student's frustration, particularly as the code of unity does not resolve the issue but just passes the student on to ever-increasing levels of aggravation.

In most colleges this moving of a student from one office to another and another is referred to as *the shuffle*. It is also a common *dis*service creating a large number of angry customers on campus. The shuffle, also known as *turfing* (i.e., removing a problem from one's own area of responsibility or turf), is a major causal factor for increasing student discontent, which becomes especially acute when, at one point in the shuffle, the student is sent back to an earlier point as if landing on a chute space in the game Chutes and Ladders. It is then that a student often decides to drop the issue and start shopping for another school.

Turfing also increases the likelihood of a rebuff at the end of the shuffle. The student may, for example, start the process because of a simple disagreement with a member of the college community that may just need clarification. If the student endures the shuffle long enough and exhausts lower level employees and/or offices, turfing starts the student moving further up the academic hierarchy. This leads most often to a final negative response from a vice president or even the president who will certainly not want to overrule all the colleagues in the process that led to his or her door. As the shuffle draws to a close, a tipping point may be reached in the student's decision to stay or leave. When she no longer buys into the value of the college, the decision is made.

It is unfortunately paradoxical that, though the issue-resolution protocol places such primary importance at starting at the lowest rung, the decision-making ability stays at the higher levels, compounding the problems for students attempting to gain service. Ironically, the lower one's level of authority to resolve issues, the more pressure one feels to do so, with some exceptions for teaching faculty. There is some variance for faculty being able to resolve issues in their own classrooms, recognizing the classroom professor is both the highest and lowest authority in a classroom—highest if she can resolve it, lowest if the issue goes beyond her because she does not resolve the issue in a way the student does not accept.

Administrative and clerical staff members are also in a paradoxical customer service situation. They are lower on the hierarchy, yet primary in contacts with students. They are the first line in the customer service chain as providers and recipients of student services. The first person a student normally makes contact with at a college is the one who answers the telephone calls or greets potential students when they arrive on campus. The person a student most often turns to learn where to go with a problem is an administrative or clerical staff member, even though they have little or no empowerment to solve problems at the lowest level where the protocol actually says issues should be resolved. Moreover, since the administrative/clerical level encounters most complaints, this group can be a very important resource for identifying customer service issues and sources, yet because of their low stature they are much too often prevented from resolving or bringing forward issues.

Colleges that have empowered all levels of employees to attempt resolution of student service issues have been rewarded with higher student and employee morale.[20] The program to empower all employees requires that employees must be able to answer three questions when determining a service solution for a student:

1. Does the possible solution meet the laws, rules, and regulations within which the college works? This requires that every employee be trained in the laws, rules, and regulations that are in force.
2. Is the action ethical and one that I should be taking? For example, faculty and academics must resolve grading issues.
3. Is the solution in the best interests of the student? It may be that a solution could make the student happy but finally will not

help provide the fullest benefit for him, such as letting a student drop a required course he is not doing well in rather than obtain tutoring. It is important that everyone involved realizes that academic customer service is not equal to making people happy each and every time.

If an employee is certain she can answer all the questions positively, then it is appropriate to proceed. If the employee is unsure of the solution, then the student should be directed to someone who can make the appropriate decision right then and there. The employee should do this after ascertaining the correct person to resolve the issue, repeating the issue to the contacted administrator for the students, and arranging a time when the student and the next person can and will meet for discussion. Next, the employee should provide the student with the name, directions to the next person, and the appointment date and time to be sure there is not a break in communication and show of personal concern.

In the program developed to accomplish fuller empowerment, employees who solve problems must also communicate their actions to the administrators who may be affected in any way. This communication is not for approval but to inform, as the action may affect other students and employees. What is one student's problem will often be found to be that of a larger cluster or even most of the student body.

CHEERS UNIVERSITY

The personal nature of academic customer service and the fulfillment of the *Emotional ROI* can be understood in Principle 1 of the Principles of Good Academic Customer Service: All Students Want to Attend Cheers University: Where Everyone Knows Your Name and Everyone Is Glad You Came.[21]

The television show *Cheers* was set in a bar that was home to a cast that can best be described as losers. Each member of the cast was flawed and did not seem to fit in socially anywhere outside of the bar. Some, like Cliff, even stretched the patience of some of the other cast members, and Carla was anything but the epitome of appropriate customer service to most patrons. Outside of Cheers, each was inadequate, unappreciated, and without a sense of full value, but once within the confines of the bar, each became a member of a community that gave them meaning and worth.

Norm was a slovenly, obese, socially awkward failed accountant, painter, home decorator, business owner, even a failed beer taster who seldom even had money to pay for the beer he drank. Yet, he is a primary example of how Cheers and Cheers University work. When he came down the stairs and into Cheers, he went from a failure to a very important member of the community, so much so that he was greeted at the start of most every episode with a large communal "NORM!" as he walked in. He in turn said, "Hello, everybody," and someone would ask him how he was, or some such inquiry. This led to the punch line, but more importantly it displayed how a community provides a very important service to its members. It accepts, recognizes, and welcomes its members with warmth and pleasure.

The members of the community returned to Cheers every day, making it their home. Even though they did realize at some level the bar and they were not really fully adequate, they never thought of abandoning Cheers for its rival, Gary's Olde Time Tavern. Gary's would win every competition and even humiliate them publicly, but they would never think of transferring from Cheers. The reason was that each and every Cheers community member was recognized and embraced by the other members of the community. No one was too flawed or unimportant for a greeting, a discussion, criticism at times, and support at others. Community members took the time to get to know one another, even if they did not socialize with one another. They gave each other recognition and value.

Students want to receive the same treatment from the college they attend. They wish to be accepted not just into the college but into its community. They want to feel as if the community recognizes their existence and values their coming there. They want to feel as if they belong, even if they may be out of place elsewhere or even in some locations on campus. They may not be accepted at a sorority or fraternity, but they want to feel as if they are full members of the college community. This is the key to providing an *Emotional ROI* that will sustain students as continuing customers of the college.

The college can take some simple steps to start making the campus into Cheers. Call on every member of the community to say hello to students as they pass them. The simple act of recognizing another's existence with a hello is at the core of making another feel acknowledged and part of the community. Try to get everyone to take the time to ask students how they are and then listen to the answer. Have employees ask students if everything is going all right, and then try to resolve anything that may not be going as they might wish.

Most important to making a college into Cheers University is to realize that it is the patrons of the school, the students, who count the most. People need to understand that the college would not exist if it were not for the student body. All members of the college community need to understand that every student who leaves the college is both rejecting it and them, as well as reducing the amount of revenue to accomplish the mission. Customer service is fulfilling expectations and the three ROIs. Finally, much of academic customer service can be summed up in the following 15 principles.[22]

1. Every student wants to attend Cheers University and every employee wants to work there! "Where everybody knows your name and they're always glad you came."
2. All members of the community must be given courteous, concerned, and prompt attention to their needs and value.
3. Students come before personal or college-focused goals. Students really are more important than you are or I am.
4. Processes, rules, and products should assure that students and learning are at the center of the institution. If not, rethink them.
5. Be honest in all communications. Do not patronize.
6. Students can never be an inconvenience.
7. The goal is not to recruit the very best students, but to make the students you recruit their very best.
8. Just because someone else did a disservice or harm does not relieve you of correcting the injury.
9. Students and employees all deserve an environment that is neat, bright, welcoming, and safe.
10. Students are not really customers. They are professional clients.
11. The customer is not always right. That is why students come to college and they prove it on tests.
12. Satisfaction is not enough and never the goal.
13. Do not cheapen the product and call it customer service. No cheap grades. No pandering.
14. To every problem there is more than one solution, and it may be external rather than within academia.
15. Not everyone is capable of providing good customer service. That does not mean they do not have value somewhere.

NOTES

1. To simplify language, the word "college" will be used to represent not just colleges but all two- and four-year public, private, and career colleges and universities.

2. Neal Raisman, *Customer Service Factors and the Cost of Attrition* (Columbus, OH: The Administrators Bookshelf, 2008), 19–25.

3. Neal Raisman, *The Power of Retention: More Customer Service in Higher Education* (Columbus, OH: The Administrators Bookshelf, 2008), 119–23.

4. Neal Raisman, *Embrace the Oxymoron: Customer Service in Higher Education* (Horsham, PA: LRP Publications, 2002).

5. Ibid., 17.

6. Ibid., 23.

7. The study was conducted by the author at four different four-year, for-profit schools in 2005. One hundred and fifty students at each school were surveyed, 75 freshman and 75 sophomores at each.

8. Elyse Ashburn, "After the Deluge, the Drought? How Admissions Offices Are Preparing for a Shrinking Pool of Traditional Applicants," *Chronicle of Higher Education,* May 2, 2008, http://chronicle.com/weekly/v54/i34/34b00501.htm; Eric Hoover, "For Admission Deans Waiting List Roulette Gets Trickier," *Chronicle of Higher Education,* May 30, 2008, http://chronicle.com/weekly/v54/i38/38a00102.htm; David Prizinsky, "State's for-Profit Schools Experience Rise in Enrollment; Some Say Programs Help Fill Need for Trained Employees," *Crain's Cleveland Business,* April 7, 2008, http://goliath.ecnext.com/coms2/summary_0199-8002513_ITM.

9. Sandy Baum and Lucie Lapovsky, *Tuition Discounting: Not Just a Private College Practice* (Washington, DC: The College Board, 2006) 6.

10. Neal Raisman, *The Power of Retention: More Customer Service for Higher Education,* p. 129–33; *Customer Service Factor and the Cost of Attrition,* 25.

11. Calculated from college-provided rates in *US News & World Report, 2009 Edition.* The rates provided are often even better than what are really experienced by the school as found in working directly with some colleges that have reported one rate to *US News & World Report* but experienced a higher one.

12. Neal Raisman, *The Power of Retention,* 126.

13. For an example, see Eric C. Fingerhut, *Strategic Plan for Higher Education, 2007–2017* (Columbus, OH: Ohio Board of Regents, 2008).

14. Claes Fornell, *The Satisfied Customer: Winners and Losers in the Battle for Buyer Preference* (New York: Palgrave Macmillan, 2007), 92.

15. Neal Raisman, *The Power of Retention,* 204–6.

16. Berkeley Rice, "10 Ways to Guarantee a Lawsuit," *Medical Economics,* July 8, 2005, http://www.modernmedicine.com/modernmedicine/article/articleDetail.jsp?ts=1222211385943&id=168737.

17. Malcolm Gladwell, *Blink: The Power of Thinking without Thinking* (New York: Little Brown & Co., 2005), 42.

18. Neal Raisman, *The Power of Retention*, 171.
19. Berkeley Rice, "10 Ways."
20. In a forthcoming study by Neal Raisman on client colleges that have implemented training to empower all employees to be service-solution providers.
21. Neal Raisman, *The Power of Retention*, 259–60.
22. Ibid, 257–60.

CHAPTER 8

The Pre-College Quagmire

Rachel Toor

As with many of the random, out-of-the-blue phone calls I get, this one was from someone who wanted me to do something. The guy explained, in rather too much detail, that he and a partner were in the process of creating a service to help students fill out their college applications using artificial intelligence. This sounded, on its face, like a truly idiotic idea—something rendered possible by technology and made appealing because of the prospect of, well, filthy lucre. The guy explained that they had started with a program for business school applicants. It asked a series of questions using fuzzy logic and then made suggestions from an expert database on how to improve the answers. Finally, it gave the odds of being admitted. The program was available in a beta-version on their Web site. I should try it, he said.

But he also said that the MBA applicant pool was too small for this to be a profitable venture, so naturally they looked to dip some toes into the ocean of undergraduate admissions. They wanted a partner with expertise, someone who could help them come up with questions that would be useful in sussing out an applicant's strengths and weaknesses, someone with a name that would lend some credibility to the enterprise. To say that I was skeptical would be giving me more credit for tact than I actually displayed. I was irritated and annoyed.

After we talked for longer than I would have liked, I told the guy that I wasn't the girl for him. The notion—that a computer program could tell a student what to stress on the application—was antithetical to everything

I believed and knew about the college admissions process. Having worked in undergraduate admissions at Duke, and now, as an independent college counselor, what I know is that filling out the application is one of the least important parts of the process. Good grades, a rigorous high school curriculum, excellent board scores, and teacher recommendations that go beyond the typical and obvious, are the necessary but not sufficient conditions to gain a spot at one of the nation's prestigious colleges or universities. Beyond that, there's a scary, rarely discussed degree of subjectivity that goes into the weeding out and selection of applicants. Things like the individual preferences of the admissions officers (one of my colleagues at Duke loved Eagle Scouts who played lacrosse; I was partial to green-haired runners who wrote poetry and hated high school) or what time of the night (or early morning) they get around to reading the application during the mad rush between January and March. It can matter at what point in the marathon-length committee meeting the applicant's school falls and what the collective blood sugar level of the people making the decisions is. These are things applicants, supplicants, can't do anything about. The things they can control—which activities they list and in which order, what they choose to write their personal statement about—are relatively trivial.

"Yeah, but," said the persistent guy with the fuzzy logic, "some activities are going to look better than others." This is true. But applying rules to these conditions makes even less sense. At some high schools, National Honor Society is a joke; at others, it is in fact an honor. Some students do community service because it is required; for others, these activities can represent an expression of commitment and passion. It's not so much what you do, but how you describe it that counts. Filling out the application is the easy part. The place where the human component comes in is in the essay. "We're not going to touch that," the guy said, other than to give some pointers on which topics to use, how to write it, and maybe helping to come up with an outline. *Oy,* I said to myself, and pointed out to him that it's plain ridiculous to give generic advice like this. I've read many great essays on topics students are commonly told to avoid, such as sex, drugs, politics, or religion. I lied and said that I had a meeting to get to.

"Just do one thing for me," the guy said. "Try out the MBA version on our Web site. Just look at it and tell me what you think."

I tried it. I answered as honestly as I was able, given my limited choices. Many of the questions were not relevant to my experience: 12 years in scholarly publishing; three in a college admissions office; another eight doing admissions counseling. Oh, plus a graduate degree in creative writing and a current job as a college professor. I was told that I had a 100 percent chance of being admitted to the top 40 business schools.

I kept lowering the GMAT score I reported, but it did nothing to hurt my odds. I suspect an undergraduate degree from Yale, and a self-reported assessment that I would have stellar recommendations, are what made the program think I was a strong applicant. I'd had no real fiscal responsibility in any of my jobs, and had, at most, managed one assistant. But, hey, I thought, maybe I should apply to a B-school. There's something warm and fuzzy about the idea of being able to get in, even if the logic used to believe that it's likely is muzzy.

THE LAY OF THE LAND

You can't open a newspaper or magazine between January and April without reading about the college admissions frenzy—that there are more students, more qualified than ever before, applying now to fill the same number of slots at the most selective colleges and universities in the country. These are students who do everything right. They take advanced courses in which they work hard to earn good grades. They play three varsity sports, captain debate teams, edit newspapers and yearbooks, chair gay–straight alliances, go to math Olympiads and get certified as PADI scuba divers. They build habitats for humanity, and attend meetings of NYLC, AIME, SADD, FBLA, ASB, JROTC, JSA, YCC, and FCA. On weekends they go to Chinese school, or Hebrew school, or Bible study groups. They have hundreds of Facebook friends, and can use their thumbs with the speed and dexterity of plastic surgeons when they text each other. These are busy kids.

However, when it comes time to apply to colleges, their parents are able to find still more for them to do. Saturday mornings are filled with SAT prep courses. There are tutors for the academic areas in which they may not excel. There are summer enrichment programs at home and overseas, and there are private college counselors who will work with them to put together a compelling application.

Most parents want what is best for their children. This is good and natural, and to the benefit of the species. Many people believe that attending a selective college or university is a passport to financial security, an entry into the kind of social networks that ensure access to the upper echelons of our class-stratified society, and a way to meet appropriate life partners and friends. Whether or not this is true is something to which I will return later in this chapter.

It's become a rite of spring, a ritual as clichéd as the first rugged flowers pushing their way up through the hard earth, the appearance of florescent yellow marshmallow Peeps in the grocery stores, and the shift to daylight saving time: the annual article in the *New York Times* (and the other papers of record) announcing that this was the toughest year yet. This news has become a set-piece. In 2008, the *Times* ran the now-familiar headline: "Elite Colleges Reporting Record Lows in Admissions." And indeed, it was news in the single digits. Harvard, Yale, and Columbia each admitted fewer than 10 percent of their applicants. In order to make this entirely clear for its readership, the *Times* reporter explained that Harvard's 7.1 percent admit rate means that 93 out of every 100 applicants didn't get a fat envelope. Then there was the usual trend statement. Yale's dean of admissions was quoted as saying that the number of applicants rose to 22,813 this year, from fewer than 12,000 ten years ago. Next, there was the standard "it's not you, it's the pool" qualifier: "We love the people we admitted, but we also love a very large number of the people who we were not able to admit," said William R. Fitzsimmons, dean of admissions and financial aid at Harvard College. Finally, the "don't worry, be happy" rejoinder: "I know why it matters so much, and I also don't understand why it matters so much," said William M. Shain, dean of admissions and financial aid at Bowdoin. "Where we went to college does not set us up for success or keep us away from it." While that may be the case, it's not something that most people believe, especially not the families who want to continue—or begin—a legacy of attending elite schools. There are many parents who will do anything—and pay anything—to set their kids up for future success.

The truth is, given the huge numbers of college applicants, and that fact that many of them come from well-heeled families, the itch to make a buck in this market is getting scratched from all sorts of different places. The pre-college industry has been around for a long time, but new ventures are popping up like morels after a fire. The belief that it's possible to get an edge is propelling applicants and their parents into the clutches of old-fashioned snake oil salesman, well-intentioned mothers who, having been through the process with their own children, hang out a shingle to advise others, and MBAs who are looking to put technology and market-analysis to use.

THE OLD DAYS, THE OLD SCHOOL

It used to be there wasn't much need for private college counseling, since that was included in the price of admission to the selective private secondary schools. The deans of admissions at the "good" colleges would sit down with the college counselors at the "good" boarding and day schools, and would deal out their students: here's a Morgan for Princeton, a Stanley for Harvard, a Vanderbilt for Yale. Harvard could trade Yale a couple of Bushes for a Kennedy. It was a gentlemanly process, and character trumped all other concerns. Personal qualities were more important than academic accomplishment; the worst thing you could call someone at Yale was a "weenie," someone too interested in his studies.

In his book on the development and rise of the SAT, *The Big Test,* Nicholas Lemann writes that, in 1933–34, "Most of the students at Harvard College came from New England or New York and were graduates of private schools. As a group, these young men were not notably studious. Paying students were in short supply during the Depression, and to be admitted was not much of a feat if you had the money and the right background (unless you were Jewish, that is — all of the most prestigious private universities in America maintained informal but strict ceilings on the number of Jews they would admit, Harvard being unusual only in President Lowell's willingness to announce publicly that this was his policy)." Jerome Karabel's excellent study, *The Chosen,* takes this last parenthetical remark as his starting point, tracing the history of Jews at Harvard, Princeton, and Yale. Lemann uses a history of the SAT to track the cracks in the stranglehold the Episcopacy had on higher education; a standardized test seemed to be a more meritocratic basis for admission than who your father played squash with. Lemann shows how idealistic Harvard men like Henry Chauncey and James Conant Bryant went beyond seeking only the St. Grottlesex conglomeration of New England preppies and turned to midwestern public schools to recruit young lads to come and be educated in ivy-adorned buildings. The ability to assess the merits of these less refined boys was made possible by the SAT, and the idea that doing well on a test, regardless of what kind of shoes you wore, made the attainment of social and financial betterment by slipping through the gates of Harvard Yard an American dream.

So the SAT was a means of opening up the doors to meritocracy, and forward-thinking people like Kingman Brewster and his admissions man, "Inky" Clark, at Yale, were able to find talent and industry in rougher packages. A boy like Bud Trillin was able to attend school with people whose family names graced the products sold in his father's Kansas City grocery store, and as it turns out, these hardworking nonpreppies were outperforming the sons of power and privilege. Geoffrey Kabaservice traces this history in an article for the Yale Alumni magazine titled "The Birth of a New Institution": "By 1965, the Harvard Admissions Office was arguing that since somebody had to be in the bottom academic quarter, it was better to have a 'real' bottom quarter made up of students who are productive yet content to be there." Harvard proceeded to fill its "happy bottom quarter" with athletes, mediocre prep-school students, and alumni sons, and "sent glad tidings of this policy to the bottom quarter of the Andover senior class."

It didn't go unnoticed. As Trillin writes about Yale in *Remembering Denny*, "Most of us, I think, got the feeling that a lot of the rich Eastern people were at Yale because of some entitlement of family or class or money and that we were there because, in ways that were perhaps not immediately apparent, we somehow deserved to be. Many years after I left Yale, I realized that we had been bolstered by a belief that we would have never uttered out loud and may not even have articulated to ourselves: there was widespread circumstantial evidence that, on the whole, we were smarter than they were." *Plus ça change.*

STANLEY KAPLAN: THE MAN, THE COMPANY, THE EMPIRE

Once there was a test, and a means to get access, it was a natural progression to try to beat the test, or at least, to master it. One man revolutionized the way to approach a standardized test and created an industry. While long reviled by those who created the SAT, like Stanley Kaplan, Nicholas Lemann points out, loved the test: "He liked to call his test-prep course 'the poor man's private school.' He was helping hundreds of kids to go to fine colleges and enter professions that had been barred to them only a few years earlier, and he was proud of it."

Kaplan began by tutoring in specific subjects and then branched out into helping students prepare for the New York State Regents exam. He hit it big when he got into SAT coaching. He asked students to remember questions that had been asked on the test, and was able to build a bank of questions that helped test-takers know what to expect. Indeed, what started in the basement of his parents' Brooklyn home is now a gigantic, moneymaking machine. It is easy to learn on the Kaplan Web site how the business has expanded. In 1998, the company had annual revenues of $195 million. By 2007, that had increased to more than $2 billion. Test Prep and Admission is currently less than a quarter of the business; half of the Kaplan empire is now focused on for-profit education, with more than 70 campuses around the country and abroad, and test preparation has expanded to include coaching for professional licenses.

But the Kaplan name is still most closely associated with the SAT—and the alphabet soup of other standardized tests. I have experience with a whole bowlful of them myself. I taught Kaplan SAT prep classes at Kaplan Centers in Durham and Chapel Hill, North Carolina, and also in a private high school. I taught MCAT classes at Duke, and at East Carolina University. I've taught Kaplan GRE and GMAT classes, and even an LSAT class in Ithaca, New York. During times when I've been unemployed and working on a book, I have whored myself out for twenty dollars an hour. Because it's easy money, and because it's fun.

To get hired, I needed to have scored well on the test, either an actual SAT, GRE, or MCAT, or on one of Kaplan's making, and I had to audition by teaching a class in front of the manager. Since I first did this, in the late 1990s, it has become more like acting than teaching, since you get a script. You are given a gigantic notebook for each course, which has a minute-by-minute timeline for what you should be doing and saying in the class. If you could train a monkey to talk, she could teach an SAT prep class.

What the Kaplan Company, as well as its main rival, the Princeton Review, has done masterfully is to produce practice materials. The College Board, the body administering the SAT and other tests, has historically been Scroogey about releasing past versions, so the big test-prep companies, in the footsteps of Stanley Kaplan, created their own. You don't have to study many actual SATs to get a sense of the kinds of questions they ask, how they ask them, and what material you can expect to be covered. For content-based tests like the MCAT, the review books can be helpful study guides, with their Cliffs Notes-like versions of the greatest hits of organic chemistry or a top-10 list of physics principles, explained clearly and concisely.

When parents and students ask me if it's worth the money to take a test-prep course—it's now about a grand for a class that meets a couple of times a week for a couple of months—I usually say yes, unless the student is disciplined and motivated, in which case buying a book of sample tests and doing them conscientiously (and with a timer) and working hard to understand the principles behind the questions you get wrong, is just as effective. It's really a matter of becoming familiar with the test. It is, we've learned, a coachable test. I'm always shocked when students don't take the test officially more than once; as is the case with a marathon, you can usually expect to improve based on nothing more than having done it before, knowing you can go the distance.

Does it matter whether it's a Kaplan or Princeton Review course or book? The chance of getting a great teacher who will really help to explain the problems is a roll of the dice. What about classes offered by high schools? Again, this is a test that is beatable. The more opportunities to practice, the better. The thing about Kaplan is that it's like going to McDonalds. You know exactly what you're going to get, regardless if you're in Portland, Oregon, Portland, Maine, or Hong Kong, and while it's expensive, it's also seen as affordable.

Test prep was an obvious and lucrative way to help ease the path to selective colleges. But for a long time, it has been controlled first by Kaplan, and then a portion of the market share that went to the Princeton Review. There hasn't been much room for entrepreneurial innovation. This is where the college counselors come in.

HIGH PROFILE, HIGH PRICES: MICHELE AND KAT

Not long after I started working at the Duke University Office of Undergraduate Admissions, Michele Hernandez published her book, *A Is for Admission: The Insider's Guide to Getting into the Ivy League and Other Top Colleges*. I didn't pay too much attention, busy as I was, trying to learn the ropes. But I couldn't *not* hear the murmur of disdain that started whenever someone mentioned Hernandez's name. I thought it was related to the telling of tales out of school: She had worked at Dartmouth and had divulged "secrets." What I was learning is that being an admissions officer is less about counseling than about selling, explaining the process in a way that is honest and true can be useful. I may have skimmed her book at some point, but frankly, didn't find it compelling enough to read, though I think it's probably helpful and true. The fact that she got nearly half a million dollars as an advance was, to me, an indication of the belief in the widespread desperation of parents who wanted information on helping their kids get in.

While Hernandez's book may have ruffled some admissions feathers, it was her college counseling Web site that made people squawk. I remember a colleague running into my office at Duke, pulling up the site on my computer, and saying, "Can you believe it? She's charging $20 grand!" That was indeed shocking. What, we wondered, could she possibly offer that was worth that much money, especially given the fact that we knew, as she pointed out in her book, that the high school record was the most important part of the application?

More than a decade later, Michele Hernandez has turned herself into a brand. She now charges $40,000 for her services and has spun off a bunch of books, her own SAT tutoring program, and more remarkably, branded products that are handy versions of what you could find in a quick Google search. Hernandez sells a downloadable guide to summer opportunities for high school students for $249. A 60-page booklet listing contests and awards goes for $189. These seem like bargains compared to her premiere product, The Application Boot Camp, a "detailed multi-media kit," including access to "four phone-ins, one each day, to Dr. Michele Hernandez" and to her colleague. Parenthetically, you learn that these "phone-ins" are prerecorded mini-lectures, not live calls. All this for only $3,000, which she points out, is more than 65 percent off the price of admission to her live events. For admissions officers whose job it is to give out—or point students toward—this kind of information, the sticker shock is electrifying. How could her expertise possibly be worth this much?

Hernandez boasts that 95 percent of her clients are accepted to their first choice schools, but like the college counselors at the fancy private schools, she controls where her students apply. By telling a student that they have zero chance of getting into Harvard, she steers her clients toward more realistic goals and protects her outcome numbers. This is a typical way of cooking the books in college counseling offices, and also an obvious product of the self-selection that is inevitable whenever one is asking people to pay this much money for help. Hernandez's clients are likely to be targeted by the university development offices. If you can fork over a million bucks, you can buy your way into a lot of schools. What's an additional $20,000 to make your kid feel like she had something to do with her own admission? While the counseling process may help in some small ways, it's the advantages that bring these students to the attention of counselors that may, in the end, prove responsible for their ultimate success.

Hernandez worked in admissions and wrote a book that offered real insight into the process. When she found out about Katherine Cohen, made famous by a 2001 article in *New York* magazine called "The $28,995 Tutor," she raised her prices. Katherine Cohen worked as a first reader in Yale's admissions office when she was a graduate student. What first readers do is, essentially, clerical work. They transcribe test scores and grades, summarize teacher evaluations, and have no input into the admissions decisions. They do not argue for or against applicants and are generally not allowed into decision committee meetings. It took a lot of chutzpah to offer herself up as an admissions expert, but that's what Katherine Cohen did, with style and panache.

The *New York* article describes the plight of Anna, whose mother had sent her to a private school, spent thousands on individual tutors for the math and verbal portions of the SAT, and hired Kat Cohen: The article quotes her satisfied client: "'Katherine is very cool,' Anna attests. 'She's got great fashion sense. Her apartment is really cool. She started her own business. She cares about her clients. And she looks great in a bikini.'" The article quotes John Katzman, the head of Princeton Review and a friend of Cohen's, as saying "Guys lust after her and the girls want to be like her . . . She's only a couple of years older and much less parental."

Thus was born a megastar. Cohen wrote a book, *The Truth about Getting In,* and then wrote another book. She also had lots of friends in the right, groovy places. She was able to call on pals who worked in film and television to help out her clients—hey, can you give this kid an internship? That backfired in 2006 when it was discovered that one of her clients, Kaavya

Viswanathan, whom she had hooked up the William Morris Agency to handle her young adult novel, had in fact plagiarized big chunks of it.

Cohen's Ivywise college counseling business now has a staff of 15. While Hernandez may be sneered at, Cohen is hated. Surely she is aware of this. She wrote a defensive piece for *The Chronicle of Higher Education* called "Why Colleges Should Thank Private Admissions Counselors." She pointed out things that we all know, that college counselors have become ubiquitous in the process (there are now more than 4,000 members of the Independent Educational Consultants Association), though she attributes the reason for this growth to the rise of homeschooling. Now certainly, if you don't have a guidance counselor, an independent college counselor might be the best way to get information about making a school list or when to take standardized tests, and it is true that many counselors charge much more reasonable rates, but really? Homeschooling? These are the folks who are forking out $40,000 to get her help for their kids?

Cohen also cites international students applying to U.S. colleges and universities as a good portion of her market. Again, this is reasonable. I know from talking to applicants from the best English boarding schools that those students have no idea what the expectations of American admissions officers are, and they can use some tutelage in the vagaries of American culture in order to make themselves understandable, but the bulk of her article reads like an infomercial for her expensive services: "We teach students time-management skills and help them prioritize tasks. We counsel them on how to develop a strong sense of self-discipline, responsibility, commitment, and accountability; how to develop a mature response to setbacks; how to find the joy in scholarship; how to raise the level of classroom learning; and how to nurture their relationships with their teachers, peers, and high-school counselor(s)." In other words, Cohen is doing the job of parenting. This requires no experience with college admissions, just the ability to get the kids to listen to you. There's nothing wrong with helping a young person discover and then develop interests; it's a great thing to inculcate passion. It just seems weird pay for the prize of a nice car for what seems, really, to be parents' jobs.

As Cohen correctly notes, according to The Independent Educational Consultants Association, the number of private counselors has tripled since 1996. That's not counting a whole boatload of people (like me) who do counseling without a membership. Anyone can hang out a shingle and offer college counseling, and they can charge whatever they want. The right price, many of these counselors say, is what the market will bear. As we have seen, in a bull market, it will bear a lot.

There are many hard-working college admissions consultants. Why is there such hostility toward Michele and Kat (which, clearly, I share)? Part of it is surely the animus we harbor toward those who get a lot of attention. They seem to show up in every article about college admissions; they have, in ways, cornered the market and honestly, it's easy to be jealous of success. I think it's also about something else. Both of these women sniffed out the fear tinged with arrogance that lurks inside deep pockets. They preyed on a market segment that could afford to assuage its anxiety by throwing money at a problem. They made something that is neither complicated nor requiring of any real skill into a service beyond the reach of most people. They work only for the most privileged, for those who are least in need of this kind of help, and make the middle-class families who can't spend that kind of money feel like they are doing their own kids a disservice. Their insanely jacked-up prices imply that there's such a thing as quality in this business. Perhaps what I'm really irritated by is old-fashioned American enterprise, which, naively, I believe should not be applied to education.

I'm sure that plenty of kids are perfectly well served by white-haired grandmothers, knee-sock-wearing soccer moms, and tweedy academic men who have from zero to many years experience in the business, and offer their wisdom and advice about the admissions process for anywhere from what it's worth to a big fat check. It's hard to give really bad advice, since so much good information is readily available. Aside from a handholding component, there's not much value-added, except, of course, for the obvious benefit of having a calm person in the midst of a feeding frenzy. Should a student take Spanish or French? AP Art History or AP Statistics? Join the debate team or Future Farmers of America? Who cares except the kid and her parents? The admissions officers really don't. If someone telling you not to let your child drop Latin will soothe you, maybe it's worth the price. I'm not sure it can ever be worth what Michele Hernandez or Katherine Cohen charge, but then, I don't buy Prada bags or Manolos.

WHAT I DID LAST SUMMER

My own experience with the college admissions frenzy began during the summer between my junior and senior years of high school when I went on a trip. My parents had seen an article in the *New York Times* about a Franco-American project for high school and college students to work on the restoration of historic French chateaux. Knowing that if they had suggested it, I would have rejected the idea immediately, they simply left the paper open to the article. I found it, decided it was something I wanted to do, and they let me make my case.

I spent a summer lugging rocks around a dusty, falling-apart building, dancing to ABBA, and drinking wine that was less expensive than bottled water with kids who were panicking about their college applications, and making out with university students who intimidated the intellectual bejesus out of me. It was the first time I'd ever been in that kind of environment. In my mediocre public high school, most of my friends were expecting to go to one of the regional state universities, not caring much about which one. I had no idea who Stanley Kaplan was, had never heard of some of the colleges these sophisticated teens were dying to get into, and, when asked where I was applying, kept mum because I hadn't given it a moment's thought. I came home in a white-knuckle terror, afraid I'd already been left behind, and dying to go to Yale.

That summer was life-changing for me. During my time working in admissions, I read the applications of many students who wrote about similar experiences while attending geek camp. Sam wrote about finding his first love at the North Carolina Governor's School, a place where he learned that it can be hot to be smart. Other kids were able to be cool at All-State Band Camps; everyone was a band geek. I remember Julian, an academic standout at Duke, blushing while telling me about playing Spin the Bottle at the Telluride summer program located on Cornell's campus. Perhaps the most intellectually rigorous of all summer programs, the Telluride program, founded by Lucien Nunn along similar lines to the self-governing, student-centered ideals of his Deep Springs College, requires an intensive application process and is highly selective. Like Deep Springs, it is also completely free to the students.

Most summer programs, however, are not free. Some require nothing more than a check; others make a nod toward selectivity. Each summer, Duke's campus is filled with noisy children attending the Talent Identification Program. Duke's TIP program, like Johns Hopkins' Center for Talented Youth, does a kind of talent search, inviting young students to take the SAT or ACT and, if they score well, allowing them to come to campus to be recognized. For a number of years, I gave a talk on college admissions to seventh graders as part of TIP's Grand Recognition weekend celebration. When I was first asked to do this, I was horrified. I couldn't imagine fueling the flames of admissions anxiety for students (and their parents) at such a young age. Then I realized that this was exactly when I wanted to get to them: I could lay out the process by which they would be evaluated and they could make their choices, both curricular and extra-, from a better-informed perspective. Typically the questions the kids at these sections asked were better than the ones I got from roomfuls of high school juniors. They were serious about their studies and already had their eyes on glittering college prizes.

Some of them thought that being in the TIP program would help their chances of getting into the school. This wasn't true, but the students whose applications showed they had been recognized by Duke's TIP or Hopkins' CTY were usually strong. The same skills and focused attention that led them to do well on the SAT at a tender age generally showed up in other places in their record. Many of them had gone on to enroll in summer programs, taking courses on writing, political science, or physics, with the idea that they would be able to meet more kids like them (they would), have fun while living on a college campus (generally they did), and get a boost in their application to those schools (not). The programs, while offering some financial assistance, do not come cheap, but they offer an academic experience that can enrich the life of a student from a public high school who gets teased for being a dork because he's interested in chess or she wants to know more about physics.

There are math camps all over the country. There are camps for engineering, robotics, architecture, foreign language—you name it, universities have long been using their inter-semester vacated space to bring in paying students who are a couple of heads shorter than the average freshman. Sometimes the kids can get high school credit for their courses, sometimes even college credit.

Those who want to travel farther afield can take advantage of things like the Oxbridge Academic Programs, where American students can study in Oxford, Cambridge, Paris, and Barcelona. As is the case with the domestic summer study options, they won't be taught by professors. Instead, they'll get to work with graduate students who are, for the most part, already there and available. It's a good, safe experience of living in another country, and it can go a long way toward expanding provincial American worldviews, but it's not cheap.

In 1993, a company called Education Unlimited started offering college admissions camps. They offer 10-day boot camps that include SAT prep, writing workshops, and college counseling sessions. They recently added one at the Club Med Sand Piper Resort in Port St. Lucie, Florida. Fourteen days of SAT prep for just less than eight grand.

Granted, for students whose schools do not provide good college counseling (and this includes most public high schools), and for those who are more academically inclined than their peers, spending a summer this way can be useful, but generally those who can afford these programs have already received lots of help. The hysteria created by the highly competitive nature of the selection process is making parents desperate to do everything they can, and companies are sprouting to take advantage of this big market. This is not to say that it isn't a good thing, on its face, to go to geek camp, or to get focused instruction on the clarinet, or to be around a bunch of creative writers. These can be extraordinary opportunities, but to claim that this will better the chances of being admitted to a selective school is just bunk. They may make the student a more interesting person and push her to think harder, but from the admissions perspective, it looks like another incidence of buying advantage.

There are, however, cases when these experiences can make a big difference. There are a host of programs that fall within the pre-college category but outside of the entrepreneurial industry. For those smart, motivated kids from low-income families who somehow are able to find out about them, there are lots of great opportunities, not just for summer programs but for all sorts of academic options. Prep for Prep, A Better Chance, the Steppingstone Foundation, and Summer Search are just a few that are helping to change the world by providing access to the playing fields of privilege. For these students, who may in fact need the kind of "parenting" that people like Cohen and her cohort can provide, it can mean the difference not only of going to a fancy college, but to going to college at all. And that is, of course, a big difference.

HITTING THE ROAD

The horrors of the family road trip take on new dimensions when the destination is not Disneyworld or Cape Cod, but a whirlwind tour of colleges. The "if it's Tuesday this must be Williams" trip is a good way for kids and their parents to step foot on campus, but not necessarily the best way to suss out a good fit. If it's a crappy, rainy day, a first-choice school could be cut from the college list and family dynamics could be in shambles. There are companies like College Visits that, for a couple of grand, lets parents off the hook. You can ship the applicant off for a tour of collegiate campuses that all end up looking alike and making similar claims for great academics, great athletics, great food, and unsurpassed school spirit.

There are also, not surprisingly, specialized tours. You might choose to look only at the historically black colleges and universities on Black Student Tours, or you could put together your own group using College Tours and Educational Trips. This firm will create an itinerary, arrange the logistics, and then send you on your way.

How useful these visits are is another story. Seeing a deserted college campus in the summer is mostly a wasteful and expensive exercise. Attending monotone admissions information sessions, and following backward-walking, chirpy tour guides is probably not the best way to gain a good understanding of what the campus culture is really like. The sanitized view most students get of colleges while taking the tour may make some fall in love and turn others off, but they won't necessarily know if it's for good reasons.

While at some schools interviews are required and evaluative, at most they are nothing more than recruiting opportunities. The belief that an admissions officer "loved me" has led to more than one broken heart in April. However, families continue to pack up the dog and younger siblings and hit the road. The need to set foot on campus persists. "I just don't want to put my daughter at a disadvantage because of something I didn't do," a normally sane friend said to me, so off they went.

POST HOC ERGO PROPTER HOC

There's nothing like the arrogance of a kid who's been admitted to a fancy-pants college. She's been vetted, validated; she's on top of the world. The only thing she's really an expert in is being a college student, so she's happy to share her opinions with liberal good humor to anyone who asks. Younger siblings tend to be particular beneficiaries of this kind of attention. I know that my first experience as a college counselor came two years after I'd been admitted to Yale and began hounding my brother to get his applications done; I sent off for view books on his behalf and read and critiqued his application essay (it was about me). Web-based businesses have popped up in dorm rooms, set up by enterprising students who believe that, since they were admitted, they know what it takes to get in. They don't realize that it could be because they were from a school where the only other admissible applicant was an ill-qualified legacy, and that the committee decided to take someone on his coattails. Or that Dad decided to donate a million bucks anonymously. Or that the symphony was low on oboes that year. These students often make the sophomoric mistake of confusing causation with correlation and focus on the essay. I got in; therefore my essay must have been good. I know what a good essay is; I can help you.

Essay Edge was one of the first of these homegrown services, offering the services of current students and Ivy League graduates to read customers' essays and make suggestions. Begun in a dorm room at Harvard, it's now owned by Peterson's. There are plenty of others. Some will even write the essay for you. For a mere $300, students can use the Model Admission Essay Development service at admissionsessays.com which, for example, "provides you with an actual model essay drafted from scratch, completely tailored to your own personal facts. Through our proprietary Biography™ process, our experienced writers gather all your pertinent personal facts, and turn them into a completely unique, one-of-a-kind model essay or personal statement." If this is too expensive, for an order of magnitude less money, the Rapid Revision function of declaregood.com will "ask questions, highlight readability problems, and make concluding comments."

This firm promises 24-hour turnaround for $30. If you're willing to wait two days, it's only $15. They will also "improve" a letter of recommendation. Of course, the sites don't list the names and background of the "fresh" eyes that will be giving the work a once-over. All they say is that they're graduates of the nation's top colleges and universities.

Perhaps the most amusing—and frightening—of all the college counseling enterprises are the open forums. In ghettoes of the Princeton Review and College Confidential sites are discussion boards where advice is given for free. I guess in an age when parents kill their children's cheerleading rivals, and impersonate hot boys online to lure lonely girls into suicidal depression, it should come as no surprise that parents post as frequently—and as immaturely—on these sites as teenagers. They can whip each other into paranoid second-guessing and blithely pass along information that is not only wrong, but also can be damaging. They focus on "stats" and ask for comments on "what are my (or my child's) chances at___?" And kids, and their parents, answer them.

CROSSING OVER TO THE DARK SIDE

It was with great reluctance that I became a college counselor. I had quit my job in admissions and had written a book about the process. I knew that if I wanted to get rich and sell a lot of copies, I should write the "this is what you have to do to get into Harvard" version. Instead, I wanted to lay bare the way admissions decisions are made so that applicants and their parents could go into the ordeal knowledgeable, and aware that there was no way to beat the system. Jonathan Swift wrote, "Last week I saw a woman flayed, and you will not believe how much it altered her appearance for the worse." My book did not do much for reassuring anxious applicants. One of my friends told me that I had to call her daughter *right now!* to talk her down from the ledge of fear she had climbed after reading my book.

"I'm the bad-news girl," I would tell people. I claimed that admissions officers, almost uniformly nice, were not always the sharpest tools in the shed; that the majority of applicants looked the same and 80 percent could succeed if admitted, so that it was hard to make a "bad" decision; and that yes, you could buy your way in. A few years later, Dan Golden, in his smart book *The Price of Admission,* showed exactly how true this is. The information in my book was not what any parent really wanted to hear, though I believed it was important. I had my say and was finished, I thought, with the whole business.

I was also out of a job and working on my second book, a memoir. I'd gotten a modest advance for it, enough to support me—if I ate mostly popcorn for dinner—for a year. A couple of years had gone by. A good friend had a son who was in his junior year at a good private school. She peppered me with questions and then finally got straight to it. "We're going to hire someone to help him," she said. A few years before they had hired a consultant to work with their daughter. The consultant, she said, was an idiot. They had set up a fund for the kids' education (her ex-husband had heaps of money). They were going to pay someone, and no one could do a better job than me, my friend said. No one, she pointed out, needed the money more than I did.

I said no a few times. She persisted, trying to convince me that all the nasty things I had thought (and said, and wrote) about college counselors didn't have to be true. "You can do it in whatever way makes you feel comfortable," she said. "Just be you." I protested that nothing I could do was going to make that much of a difference. "It will make a difference to him," she said.

When finally I met with her and her ex-husband to talk business, I was clear and confident about exactly what I could and would do, and the fact that it probably wouldn't matter at all in terms of the outcome. "Don't worry about that," her ex said, "I'll make sure he gets in." As I said, he had big piles of money, and a long history of giving to similar institutions; he was likely right in assuming the strings he pulled would be connected to the right places. "Just do whatever you want to do," the dad said.

"Okay," I replied, and then he got out his checkbook and asked me how much I wanted to be paid. I froze. I panicked. I freaked the hell out. It had never occurred to me to set a number. I didn't know what the right number was. I told him to decide. He had obviously thought about it and handed over the biggest check I had ever held in my little popcorn-for-dinner hands. It was a pittance by the standards of Michele and Kat, but still, I stuttered. He assured. I sputtered. He reassured. I took it.

My first client was a bright and precocious kid. He was well and broadly read, and dripped with the sophistication that comes with entitlement. He had the confidence of one who was well loved, and he worked hard. He wanted to write his personal statement on film; being arty and all, he wanted to show off his artiness. That could work, I said, but I was more intrigued by the way his mother said he described himself, as a "deformed Jewish fag from Maine." Turns out, due to a congenital problem, one of his ears never developed; it was a little nubbin on the side of his head that was useless in terms of its original anatomical purpose. His mother told me a story about how her young son had researched surgeries and found that he could get a prosthetic ear that would allow him to look "normal." They met with the surgeons, were all set to go ahead, and then he changed his mind. He decided he liked his funny little ear. It was part of him, part of who he was.

That, I said, was his essay. But this is no big deal, he said. He honestly thought a pseudo-intellectual analysis of the films of Tarkovsky or Kurosawa or whomever would show him in a better light. I convinced him to try.

The essay was beautiful: smart, funny, poignant, and all him. I pushed him to be more specific when his language waxed vague, admonished him for unnecessary adverbs, and did little more than a light line edit.

We spent a lot of time that fall on the phone. I visited him and we'd sit in the kitchen for hours, talking first about his schoolwork and teachers, then about his essays, and then, after we'd covered all that ground, about life, about his expectations, about managing those of his parents. He seemed to think that wherever he ended up would be fine. Everything would be okay, he told me. Sometimes, though, he did call in moments of panic. He was a normal kid, after all.

He got in to his first choice via Early Decision. I'm not sure what, exactly, his father did, how much coin he spread around, but I do know that after he was admitted, his mother, my friend, was very chummy with the university's development staff. She was put on the Parent's Committee, jargon for "Big Honking Donors," and got cozy with the dean. She was invited on international trips with other donors and some token faculty members. In short, two things seem clear to me: the kid was a terrific applicant who put together a strong application, though his grades and test scores may have been a little subpar, and his father lubricated the way. The part that I played was minimal in terms of how he looked as an applicant; his mother said it was crucial in helping to keep his self-esteem (remember: "deformed Jewish fag") from being flushed down the toilet.

I was surprised by how much I liked doing this work—being an academic mentor—so when Kaplan started up a college counseling business, I checked it out and was hired. The Kaplan package was, as you would imagine, corporate and organized. I was given lots of forms to fill out, and lots of forms to have the clients fill out. Parents had to prepay for packages; the rate, naturally, came down as they bought more hours. Most of my clients ended up not using most of their hours. They were a hodgepodge of high-achieving kids (whom I loved working with) and others who needed deadlines and nagging (which I did not like).

After a while, I quit. There was too much paperwork and I wasn't the right match for certain kinds of clients (a homeschooled religious fundamentalist applicant nearly did me in), but then people started tracking me down and asking if I did college counseling. I never went into business for myself, it just happened. I've never set rates. Instead, I ask parents to decide an hourly rate that they think is fair and reasonable. When they ask for guidance, I tell them that Kaplan charges about $150 an hour. I have never drawn up a contract, and I have never asked for money up front. I keep track of my time in quarter hour increments and send out an itemized invoice at the end of the month (if I remember).

I tell potential clients that what I do adds absolutely no value to the college application. I'm not in a position to travel to college campuses to know, precisely, which would be the best fits for different kids. I can suggest tools (like Princeton Review's free Counselor-o-matic function on its Web site that generates school suggestions), but I'm not good at helping students come up with a list. That is up to the student. Nor do I have anything to do with the recommendations, except to suggest that students write a "Dear Teacher" letter to whomever they want to ask, reminding the teacher of what they did in her class. This is something I ask of my own students when they want me to write on their behalf; it helps me to write a good, not merely positive, letter. I don't help anyone prepare for the SAT, and if they want to know when they should sit for the test, they have to look up the dates on their own. I didn't set deadlines and I don't nag. This is their chance to get ready for college; that means being on top of schedules.

I am available to answer questions (*No, you don't have to do an on-campus interview; Yes, you do have to keep taking science*), but really, the only thing I work on is the essay, yet in the big picture of college admissions, the essay is a pixel. In terms of the final decision, it carries almost no weight. The only thing I can do, I tell parents, is help their child become a better writer—to understand what is required when writing in the first person, to uncover their tics and bad habits, to explain what makes for good writing and why most of what they put on the page is vague, generic, and typical, and to show them how they can do better. Even the best essay in the world isn't going to compensate for mediocre grades. My credentials include a dozen years as a university press editor, authorship of three books, and two regular columns in national publications. I can teach their kids a thing or two about writing, which will serve them well in college and beyond, but it won't do much to get them in.

There are people I won't work with. I talked to one man from Singapore, a CEO type, who told me how things were going to go. I told him I wasn't the right person for him. A mom from Los Angeles had already paid someone, a first reader at University of California, Santa Barbara, $300 an hour to help her daughter write essays that, she said, "sucked." When I told her that I didn't care where my clients ended up in school, that all I cared about was that they became better writers, she apparently hadn't been listening and said, "Why can't you just write the essays for her?" In general, my clients end up at top schools, often their top choices, but that's mostly because I select students who have done well enough to get into top schools, not because of the work I do with them.

The truth is, it's an enormous pleasure to discuss the films of Truffaut or the intricacies of Milton's poetry with a wicked smart 17-year-old. I love recommending *The Dancing Wu Li Masters* to my science geeks and *Flatland* to the math-heads. Generally, my teen clients work far harder on their essays than my creative writing graduate students do. They are more ambitious. It's fun to have them challenge me, and a privilege to be the cool grownup in their lives at a time when their parents are losing their minds, but is it worth what I'm being paid? I can't say that it is.

"WHAT ABOUT HAVING FUN?"

The person who signs my university paychecks wanted to have lunch with me. As it turned out, she was seeking my advice about college admissions for her daughter who was just about to start ninth grade. This self-possessed young woman had already decided that she wanted to go to Columbia or Dartmouth.

I gave them my spiel. Take the hardest courses available at your school, and ace them all; it doesn't hurt to nail the standardized tests either. Then, your teachers need to say that you're the best student they've had in 30 years of teaching. That's what is necessary, but it's still not sufficient. A majority of the students who are applying have exactly these same qualifications, so you have to stand out from that big, overachieving (exhausted) pack. You have to do extracurricular activities on a national level—you know, like write a novel or discover a protein. Finally, you have to produce an essay that makes a weary, bleary-eyed admissions officer, who may be reading the application at 3 A.M. after slogging through 50 others, fall in love with you. That's what it takes.

The girl listened, nodded, and gulped. Her mother, on the other hand, was not pleased. I've had this conversation many times. Sometimes it's been over the telephone; sometimes during a run. People ask me questions about this stuff, and I always give the same answers, because those are the right answers. The response is almost always the same: The mothers want to kill me. What about having fun? What about hanging out with your friends? What about being a good person? The woman who signs my paychecks was upset by the expensive free advice I was giving her.

That's all fine, I explained, and important, but there are a lot of fun-loving, friend-rich, good people who are applying to Columbia and Dartmouth. It's just not enough. Think about the numbers. This year, many of the fancy schools had admission rates in the single digits. She can have fun, but if she doesn't do the work, she's not going to get into an elite school.

And you know what? Maybe that's just as well.

THE GLITTERING PRIZE

I published a piece in *The Chronicle of Higher Education* in response to an essay in *The American Scholar* by William Deresiewiez on the disadvantages of an elite education. We agreed that there are disadvantages; we just didn't agree on what they are. I called my essay "God and Jerk at Yale." Deresiewicz starts by claiming that his time as a student at Columbia and a teacher at Yale left him incapable of having a conversation with a plumber who came to fix his pipes. (I am not making this up.) What Deresiewicz saw in his students was an air of entitlement, anti-intellectualism, and careerism—charges that have been leveled at the students of Harvard, Princeton, and Yale for at least a century—and a lack of diversity beyond the superficial. (He says, essentially, that while students may have different skin pigments, they all wear the color of money.) My take is different. Having read thousands of applications from students exactly like his, I know that they come into these colleges much more different from each other than they are when they graduate. Sure, there are plenty who are privileged, but the top schools are all looking hard for the rural valedictorians, for the students of color from disadvantaged backgrounds who have been thoroughly prepared for the Ivy League by programs like Prep for Prep and A Better Chance. There are also still a few kids like me—standouts at crappy public high schools whose academic ambitions outstrip their parents' resources.

But once they get to campus, they (we) adapt to the dominant culture. They learn how to appear cynical and sophisticated (they sometimes believe these traits go together like chocolate and peanut butter). They learn to fake it, whatever it is they need to fake to fit in. Some of them become cultural elitists. They change their names—Vicki becomes Victoria—revise their backgrounds, and forget how to talk to plumbers. Some live in fear that they will be exposed as frauds.

Because Deresiewicz came off as so unlikable in his essay, people were quick to pounce on him (he made himself, I confess, an easy and irresistible target). His smart piece generated a big response, as did mine. Both were picked up on the Arts and Letters Daily Web site, as was an essay by a man named John Summers, who wrote about the horrors of having to teach Harvard undergraduates. I had a momentary fantasy of Yale and Harvard, in an attempt to offer their matriculating students a kind of informed consent, sending these essays out and saying: *This is what the people who will be teaching you think of you. Still wanna come?*

If students can get through four years never talking to a professor and not knowing how much they are disdained by the faculty, it's also the case that, unless you went to one of these places, you can't really understand what it's like. This is because even those who were there can't figure out how to parse the experience. Fifty years later, Calvin Trillin is still trying to make sense of his time at Yale. Alumni have their memories, clouded by the comforting haze of nostalgia. Current students, like new-car buyers, tend to be emotionally invested in defending their school. It will be decades before they can speak honestly about things more challenging than trying to drink a lot of beer in a very short time, or pranks during the Harvard-Yale game. It takes a long time for the ivy dust to settle.

I started and ended my book, *Admissions Confidential,* with a question: How much does it matter where you go to college? To the thousands of students (and their parents) clamoring to get into the small number of schools at the top, it seems to matter a great deal, and the pre-college industrial complex has been set up to mine for gold.

There is a received belief that where you go to college will make a difference in how successful you are in life. A thick envelop from an Ivy League school is seen as passport to the upper levels of the American class system. You meet the friends and make the connections that will help you scramble beyond your original station. In some cases, of course, an Ivy education is still merely a continuation of privileges that have been granted by birth. A recent year-long study by PayScale, Inc., reported in the *Wall Street Journal,* showed that graduates of elite colleges make more money in starting pay and that the disparity continues over lifelong earnings. This isn't going to surprise anyone, since that's what most would expect.

So people clearly think it matters where you go, and I agree, but I would argue that it matters in ways far different from what is captured by the popular imagination. It matters in terms of who you become, how you see yourself, and, finally, how scarred you are by the experience. In some ways, attending an elite college is like choosing, blindfolded, a new identity. You may not like the one you end up with. And it may take years — even decades — to shed it.

As has been well documented, changes in Ivy League admissions policies opened up perceived gates to the meritocracy starting in the late 1950s. The top of the funnel broadened, and allowed admissions offices to create a Noah's Ark array of exotics — a couple of Catholics, some North Dakotans, and lots of Jews. Later, Chinese-American students whose parents emigrated through Taiwan, Asian Indians, and Iowan valedictorians were able to come to this crucible and mix in a rich, multicultural, multiclass environment where they not only received the best education money (or financial aid) can buy, but had a chance to rub shoulders, noses, and naughty bits with the best and the brightest. Being there, they were able to enter a world that gave them access to the networks of power of the ruling class.

As word got out that the elite schools were a possibility, the scramble to get in intensified. It is because of the great promise: This is the path to American success. If you can make it here, you can make it anywhere. Sure you'll have to take some classes, but (as we've learned in recent presidential elections) grades are immaterial in terms of future success. You will go to Master's Teas and meet famous and accomplished alumni. Your classmates will take you home with them to the country estates, or countries, owned by their families. You will spend summers working in firms or industries you once didn't know existed, but that everyone in this new environment seems to value. You will meet your best friends. You will be set for life.

This is the fantasy, this is what feeds the popular imagination and fuels the frenzy to get in, but what really happens during those four years? While the professors may demean the seriousness of the students, may chastise them for not being intellectual enough, and may even be jealous of what they perceive as huge class differences, I would argue that the experience of being at a place like Harvard or Yale can be devastating for many kids, and not just those lower-middle-class public schoolers who get to campus never having heard of Milton or Heisenberg. The sense of being a fraud, of having been admitted by dint of someone having made a mistake, is pervasive. My sense is that very few people feel at home at places like Yale. I know I didn't. I have to ask: With so many people with their eyes fixed so firmly on the prize, is it time to look at what the prize really is and if it's worth having?

If we start questioning the value of an elite education, will that lead us to shift away from the intense pressure to be admitted? Perhaps, in a worsening economy, parents will start to think of what will best serve their children, rather than what will be most helpful in getting them in. Perhaps state universities will come to be appreciated for the great values that they are and it will become a source of pride not to spend a fortune on fancy stickers for the back window of the car; people will sport Target circles instead of Prada triangles.

I taught in the honors division of the University of Montana, and I would put my students up against those from the finest colleges in the country. These terrific students, who stood out academically from their peers (while, at the same time, skiing, fly-fishing, and hiking with them), were cherished by the faculty and got the kind of one-on-one attention that you couldn't buy for all the tuition in the world. None of them had parents who would pay for private counselors, fancy summer programs, or Club Med SAT prep classes. They worked hard, they enjoyed learning, they had loads of fun, and they made great friendships. Shouldn't that be the goal when applying to college?

WORKS CONSULTED

Accepted Admissions Almanac—Ivy League Edge? Blog. http://blog.accepted.com/acceptedcom_blog/2008/8/1/ivy-league-edge.html.
Kaplan. About Kaplan. http://www.kaplan.com/aboutkaplan/.
Admissions.com. http://www.admissions.com/index.htm.
Berfield, Susan, and Anne Tergesen. 2007. "I Can Get Your Kid into an Ivy," *Business Week,* October 22, 2007, http://www.businessweek.com/print/magazine/content/07_43/b4055063.htm?chan=gl.
Black College Tours. http://www.blackcollegetours.com/.
BNET. No Day at the Beach? Education Unlimited Summer Program for Teens Teaches SAT Prep in Style. BNET. http://findarticles.com/p/articles/mi_m0EIN/is_/ai_n25124920.
CE Tours. College Tours and Educational Trips. http://www.cetours.com/.
Clindinst, Melissa. 2008. "NACAC: Admission Trends for 2008." *Recruitment & Retention in Higher Education* 22 (2008): 8.
College Confidential. College Admissions, Search, and Financial Aid Help. http://www.collegeconfidential.com/.
Confessore, Nicholas. 2004. "Independent Counsel." *Atlantic Monthly* 294: 135–40.
Dereseiwicz, William. 2008. "The Disadvantages of an Elite Education." *The American Scholar,* Summer): 20–31.
Edwards, Tamala M. 1999. "Guidance for Sale." *Time,* October 24, 1999, 68.
Essay Edge. Personal Statement, Application Essay, College Essay. http://www.essayedge.com/.
Fallows, James. 2003. "The New College Chaos." *Atlantic Monthly,* November: 106–14.
Finder, Alan. 2008. Elite Colleges Reporting Record Lows in Admission. *New York Times,* April 1, 2008, http://www.nytimes.com/2008/04/01/education/01admission.html?_r=1&oref=slogin.
Flanagan, Caitlin. 2001. "Confessions of a Prep School College Counselor." *Atlantic Monthly,* September, 53–61.
Gangemi, Jeffrey. 2003. "How to Buy Your Way into College." *Business Week Online* (10/03), http://www.businessweek.com/smallbiz/content/oct2006/sb20061003_685293.htm.

Gardner, Ralph J., Jr. "College Admissions Coach to the Stars Shares Secrets." Mainstreet. http://www.mainstreet.com/article/life-stages/educational-funding/college-admissions-coach-stars-shares-secrets.

Gardner, Ralph, Jr. 2001. "The $28,995 Tutor." *New York* magazine, April, 32.

Gladwell, Malcolm. 2001. "Examined Life." *The New Yorker*, December 17.

Golden, Daniel. 2003. So, Just How Much Do You Need to Donate to Get Your Kid In? *Wall Street Journal,* March 12, D1, Eastern edition.

Golden, Daniel. 2006. *The Price of Admission*. New York: Crown.

Gose, Ben. 1997. "Anxious Applicants to Top Colleges Seek an Edge by Hiring Consultants." *Chronicle of Higher Education,* January 24, A31–A32.

Gose, Ben. 1999. "Nationwide Chains May Shake up Admissions-Counseling Industry." *Chronicle of Higher Education,* July 2, A35.

Gose, Ben. 2000. "Kaplan Starts Online Course on College-Admissions Process. *Chronicle of Higher Education,* January 14, A53.

Graves, Lucia. 2007. "A Fight to Cap Those Apps." *U.S. News & World Report,* October 15. http://www.usnews.com/articles/education/2007/10/05/college-admissions.html.

Hernandez College Consulting Services. http://www.hernandezcollegeconsulting.com/services/tier3.html.

Hill, David. 1997. Counselor for hire. *Teacher Magazine,* 8: 12.

Hoover, Eric. 2007. "On the Road." *Chronicle of Higher Education,* October 12, A8.

Kingsbury, Alex. 2007. "Admittedly Unequal." *U.S. News & World Report,* June 25, 50–53.

Lemann, Nicholas. 1999. *The Big Test: The Secret History of the American Meritocracy*. New York: Farrar, Strauss, and Giroux.

Marcus, Amy Dockser. 1999. SAT coaches to offer help with admission. *Wall Street Journal,* June 28, B1, Eastern edition.

Mohn, Tanya. 2008. "If You Go . . ." *New York Times,* January 6, 8.

Needleman, Sarah E. 2008. "Ivy Leaguers' Big Edge: Starting Pay." *Wall Street Journal,* July 31, Eastern edition.

Oxbridge Programs. Summer schools in Oxford, Cambridge, Paris, Montpellier and Barcelona for Junior High and High School Students. http://www.oxbridgeprograms.com/index.php.

The Princeton Review. Test Prep: GMAT, GRE, LSAT, MCAT, SAT, ACT, and More. http://www.princetonreview.com/default.aspx?uid badge=$.

RapidRevision. College Application Essay Review Service. http://www.declaregood.com/.

Rimer, Sara. 2007. "Making a Hard-life Story Shine and Opening a Door to College." *New York Times,* July 27, A1–A21.
Salopek, Jennifer J. 2007. Special Delivery. *Currents* 33: 32–37.
Slatalla, Michelle. 2007. "The New Safeties." *New York Times,* July 29, 12–13.
Summer search. http://www.summersearch.org/.
Tergesen, Anne. 2006. "What Price College Admission?" *Business Week,* June 19, 82–83.
Terrell, Kenneth. 1998. "Are Consultants Worth the Cost?" *U.S. News & World Report,* August 31, 80.
Tonn, Jessica L. 2005. "A Leg Up." *Education Week,* August 10, 35–7.
Toor, Rachel. 2001. *Admissions Confidential: An Insider's Account of the Elite College Selection Process.* New York: St. Martin's.
Toor, Rachel. 2008. "God and Jerk at Yale." *The Chronicle of Higher Education,* August 15, B4.
Trillin, Calvin. 2005. *Remembering Denny.* New York: Farrar, Strauss, and Giroux.
Wang, Penelope. 2006. Steer Your Kids Clear of Rat Race U." *Money,* October. http://money.cnn.com/magazines/moneymag/moneymag_archive/2006/10/01/8387556/index.htm
Weinbach, Jon. 2007. "The Admissions Police." *Wall Street Journal,* April 6, W1-W10, Eastern edition.
Yale Alumni Magazine. 1999. "Birth of a New Institution." *Yale Alumni Magazine,* December. http://www.yalealumnimagazine.com/issues/99_12/admissions.html.

CHAPTER 9

The Importance of Business and Economic Models in Understanding the Historical Provision of Student Aid

Fred Galloway

For the past 60 years, the federal government, state governments, and institutions have played an active role in helping students finance their postsecondary education; during the 2007–08 academic year alone, more than $143 billion in financial aid was distributed to undergraduate and graduate students in the form of grants, federal loans, work study, and tax credits and deductions.[1] Although the exact amount (and type) of financial aid available changes every year as a result of legislative processes at the state and federal levels, one thing never changes—the intensity of the ongoing debate between those arguing for more need-based aid versus those arguing for a larger student share of costs. This debate, which is largely driven by the political and economic constraints faced by the major providers of financial aid, tends to produce solutions that appear to oscillate between the poles of equity and efficiency; however, to date no general theory has been developed to describe the way in which the three players—the federal government, state governments, and institutions—interact to produce this apparent back and forth movement in the need-based distribution of financial aid over time.

Although the development of such a theory is important for a number of reasons, perhaps the most important is also the most obvious: since institutions are clearly affected by the behavior and priorities of the states within which they operate, and since the behavior of states is also affected by the behavior of the federal government, the cost of not building these interactions into the business and economic models used by state governments and institutions is a less-than-optimal behavior. In other words, if a state ignores the actions of the federal government, then it may needlessly duplicate its behavior, resulting in a misalignment of state resources. For example, suppose that several states in the midst of a regional economic downturn are considering new revenue sources to maintain their previous level of need-based funding; however, if during the same period the federal government is also pursuing policies designed to increase the amount of need-based aid, then the state's actions could be viewed as duplicative and inefficient. While a similar story could be told about the potential for inefficient decision-making at individual colleges and universities, the take-away is still the same—the cost of *not incorporating* full information into the decision-making calculus of state governments and institutions is both real and costly.

In an effort to understand the motivations and decision calculus of those providing the assistance explicitly, and to help explain the 60-year pattern in the provision of financial aid, this chapter takes an historical look at the provision of financial aid from three different perspectives—federal, state, and institutional—and then uses these diverse perspectives to develop a theoretical framework that helps explain intertemporal patterns in the provision of financial aid. To accomplish this task, the chapter begins with a brief discussion of the importance of business and economic models for decision-making, paying particular attention to the economic principles underlying the models and their implications for both equity and efficiency. After establishing these basic principles, the discussion turns to the higher education landscape before the introduction of student loans and grants; this context will prove critically important in understanding the policy debate surrounding the creation of the Higher Education Act in 1965, as well as in understanding the basic motivations of stakeholders, which have changed surprisingly little over the last 50 years. These perspectives will then be used in a critical examination of three distinct time periods in the provision of student aid—the early years (1950s and 1960s), the formative years (1970s and 1980s), and the competitive years (1990s and 2000s). In the final part of the paper, the lessons learned from these distinct time periods will be distilled into a decision-making framework that helps explain why financial aid–funding patterns and policies seem to oscillate between the poles of need-based and non-need-based aid, or put another way, between the two extremes that define the efficiency/equity continuum.

THE IMPORTANCE OF THE BUSINESS/ECONOMIC MODELS IN THE PROVISION OF STUDENT AID

To understand the many ways in which models from business and economics can be applied to the provision of student financial aid, a necessary first step is to develop an understanding of exactly what these models have to say and, more importantly, why. As most students of introductory economics know, business and economic models are used to model optimal decision-making among consumers and producers; in this discussion, the focus is on the behavior of the institutions themselves, their operating constraints, and the implications of their behavior for themselves as well as others.

From the perspective of an institution, the application of business models requires only that institutions be able to identify measurable goals or objectives, align their resources with these objectives, and then actively pursue policies designed to achieve these goals. To model these processes, economists typically use optimization theory, which requires a measurable objective as well as the financial factors that may constrain decision-making. A relatively simple example of a model like this can be found in the areas of admissions and financial aid, where institutions often struggle in maximizing their yield, defined as the percentage of admitted students who actually enroll at their institution. This struggle occurs, of course, because the sizes of institutional financial aid budgets are limited; in other words, while institutions would like to offer every admitted student enough institutional aid to get them to enroll, they are clearly limited in their ability to do so.

For models of this type, where both the goals and financial constraints of the institution can be explicitly measured, several powerful analytical insights emerge. These insights, which are usually cast in the technical vernacular of first- and second-order conditions, describe exactly what decision rules should be used to optimize behavior. For the example given above, the decision rule might be that to maximize the number of students who actually enroll at the institution, admitted students should first be ordered by their likelihood of enrollment and then provided with just enough institutional grant aid to get them to enroll. In other words, if an extra $1,000 in institutional grant aid is just enough to turn a student from a nonenroller into an enroller, then the institution should not spend any additional monies on that student, since that would not be an efficient use of its limited financial resources.[2] This sort of efficient behavior can be easily contrasted with the behavior at institutions that are not attempting to solve *this particular* maximization problem; instead, perhaps the institution, in the name of fairness, attempts to minimize differences in the size of the institutional grants they provide to their students. Under this more equitable financial aid policy, the resulting decision rules from the model would suggest that admitted students all receive institutional grants of the same size, in addition to determining exactly what the size of this grant should be.

Another illustration of the way that business and economic models frame decision-making in the provision of financial aid involves the intertemporal behavior of state governments. For example, when sufficient funding is available (like during an economic expansion), state governments often maximize spending on their need-based state grant programs, which helps equalize outcomes for students within their state. However, during an economic contraction, funding for need-based programs is often reduced *and* tuition and fees are raised by enough to help cover the state budgetary shortfall; in both cases the outcome during the period of retrenchment is the same—students end up paying a greater overall share of the costs of providing their education, which from the perspective of state government is clearly more efficient.

Taken together, these examples illustrate an important behavioral insight: Although traditional business and economic models are often used to frame institutional decision-making, these optimizing models and their decision rules can be used to promote either equity or efficiency concerns, but rarely both. In fact, as long as decision-makers have the ability to identify measurable objectives and operating constraints, models like these can methodically guide decision-makers to their ultimate goal or objective. However, since the three key decision-makers in the provision of financial aid (the federal government, state governments, and institutions) often have their own set of competing objectives, not to mention that they each face a different set of political and economic constraints, the solutions that emerge are typically located along different parts of the equity/efficiency continuum. In fact, the main purpose of this paper is to use these models to construct a behavioral theory that explains how these decisions result in a long-run equilibrium that oscillates between the poles of need-based and non-need-based aid; this process begins with a look at the higher education landscape before the existence of student loans and grants.

THE HIGHER EDUCATION LANDSCAPE BEFORE STUDENT LOANS AND GRANTS

Although the origins of higher education in America can be traced back to the founding of Harvard College in 1636, the technological shocks and changes in knowledge that took place in the late 19th and early 20th centuries have led some researchers to refer to this time period (1890–1940) as the "formative years" in the development of higher education in the United States.[3] During this period, which was characterized by relative stability in the price of college and large increases in college attendance—at least for white males—most of the action was at the state and institutional levels, with the federal government only playing a decisive role from the mid/late 1940s onward. As such, this section begins with a discussion of the pre-WWII role of the federal government and then highlights important contributions made by the states and institutions during the formative years; the section concludes with a look at the two important contributions the federal government made during the mid/late 1940s—the G.I. Bill of Rights in 1944 and President Truman's Commission on Higher Education in 1947.

Despite the fact that the role of the federal government during this period may have been overshadowed by the states and institutions, the beginning of the period coincided with the second Morrill Act (1890), which increased the amount of federal funds available to land-grant colleges and universities and provided additional funds for the establishment of black institutions. This federal largess, which pushed society toward a more equitable distribution of educational outcomes, coincided with several broad societal shifts in the structure of knowledge, including the "application of science to industry, the growth of the scientific and experimental methods, and an increased awareness of social problems brought about by an increasing industrial and urban society."[4] Taken together, these large structural shifts in both what was known and how knowledge was packaged led to significant increases in both the scale and scope of many higher education institutions; as a result, an increasing number of subjects became subdivided with distinct specializations, and enrollment increased fivefold between 1880 and 1940.[5] Although this increase occurred at both private and public institutions, it was clearly the greatest in the public sector, where the fraction of students in publiclycontrolled institutions increased from about 22 percent in 1897 to about 50 percent in 1940, including junior colleges, and to about 45 percent excluding them.[6]

During this expansionary period for public institutions of higher education, the states played an increasingly important role. In contrast to the largely exogenous changes in the structure of knowledge that occurred in the earlier part of the period, large increases in the supply of high school graduates, especially in states that had well-functioning, public higher-education institutions, helped contribute to the growth in both the scale and scope of public institutions of higher education. However, when combined with the demise of independent professional institutions, a decline in independent schools of theology, and the rise of the modern (public) research university, this period was really a coming of age for public universities and the state governments that provided funding for them.[7] In fact, in the days before the explicit provision of student financial assistance, the setting of tuition and fees largely determined the affordability of public institutions, and while some state governments actively pursued policies designed to promote equity within their state, other states were clearly less enthusiastic.

To understand why some state governments were more active than others, it is important to realize that three factors played an important role: the extent to which their citizenry were already enrolled in public institutions of higher education within the state, the level and distribution of wealth within the state, and finally, the existence within the state of industries like agriculture, mining, and engineering that could capture the localized benefits of research at state institutions. Taken together, Goldin and Katz show how these factors helped explain the enormous variations that existed in state funding levels before the advent of the Great Depression; for example, in 1929, state and local spending on higher education per 1,000 inhabitants ranged from a low of $458 in New England to a high of $2,057 in the mountain states, while enrollments per 1,000 inhabitants ranged from .82 in New England to 6.04 in the mountain states.[8] Interestingly, many of these between-state differences still persist in 2008—those states with the longest history of private higher education and relatively low enrollments in their public sector typically provide the lowest per-capita level of support, while those with relatively shorter histories of private education and larger public sector enrollments typically provide the most. In fact, when using the year of statehood as a proxy for the strength of a state's relationships with private universities, Goldin and Katz found the cross-state correlation of public college enrollments per capita in 1994 with year of statehood is .70, and the 1994 level of in-state tuition at four-year public universities has a correlation of −.59 with year of statehood, revealing that many of the funding differences among states have persisted for decades.[9]

As the states struggled during this period with questions of how to fund their public four-year institutions, the institutions themselves were adapting to a significantly larger scope and scale of operations. For example, while in 1897 the median private institution had 128 students and the median public institution 242 students, by 1924 these numbers had increased to 359 students and 1,225 students, respectively. Put another way, the ratio of the public to private median size was 1.89 in 1897, 3.43 in 1924, and 4.02 in 1934, revealing that public institutions grew significantly faster than did private institutions during this period.[10] Of course, this growth occurred somewhat unevenly across the states, with the fastest growth occurring at those public institutions whose states were more generous in providing financial support, an early example of how some states were more concerned about issues of equity than others; when combined with the correlational work of Goldin and Katz, the evidence suggests that many of these state differences (and commitments to equity) still persist today.

For many private universities, this increase in scope and scale was both a blessing and a curse; it was a blessing in the sense of the reduced competition that resulted from the closing of many independent professional institutions (forced out by the rise of professional schools in universities), and a curse in terms of the increased competition from the rapidly expanding four-year public sector. Although the expansion of private universities was geographically uneven, the reputational quality of many of the older and established private institutions turned out to be especially important, as some of them transformed themselves during this period into modern research universities, increasing their market share by offering courses in fields such as medicine, law, and business.[11] In fact, the importance of these two factors—historical reputation and operating scale—have to this day continued to serve as effective deterrents for the entry of any new private research universities into the marketplace; as a result, the distribution of elite private research universities in the United States has remained essentially unchanged for the last hundred years.

While most of the action during the formative years was clearly at the state government and institutional levels, the last six years of this period saw two important interventions at the federal level: the 1944 G.I. Bill of Rights and President Truman's Commission on Higher Education in 1947. Although these interventions worked synergistically to expand access to higher education, the G.I. Bill is the best known and most publicized of the two. Passed in 1944 as part of the Servicemen's Readjustment Act, the bill subsidized tuition, books, and fees and provided living expenses for 7.8 million veterans, almost 98 percent of whom were men.[12] This massive infusion of federal dollars provided a huge boost to the economic fortunes of colleges and universities in the late 1940s and early 1950s as enrollment literally exploded, although many economists at the time considered it to be largely a solution to the problem of what to do with millions of out-of-work returning veterans. Regardless of purpose, however, the bill marked the federal government's entrance into the world of higher education finance, directly supporting returning veterans in their quest for higher education and, in the process, increasing both access to and equity in higher education.

As expected, the extraordinary success of the veterans furthered the expectation that some form of postsecondary education should be available to all, regardless of financial circumstance. However, before the federal government could respond, it needed proof that the return on another investment like this would pay big enough societal dividends to justify the large and recurring cost of providing such assistance. Fortunately, it found this evidence in the work of the Commission on Higher Education, formed by President Truman in 1947. Charged with examining "the functions of higher education in our democracy and the means by which they can best be performed," the Commission urged a major expansion of postsecondary schooling and argued that the ultimate educational goal was "an educational system in which at no level—high school, college, graduate school or professional school—will a qualified individual in any part of the country encounter an insuperable economic barrier to the attainment of the kind of education suited to his aptitude and interests."[13] Armed with both the report's recommendations and the undeniable successes of the veterans in the classroom, the federal government was now ready to begin its financial commitment to the equality of opportunity for all regarding postsecondary education—although it would still be almost a decade before it provided fellowships and loans to students through the National Defense Education Act.

IN THE BEGINNING—THE 1950s AND 1960s

As we have just seen, the 1950s ushered in a fundamentally new era in postsecondary education; a recently activist federal government had just scored a major policy success with the expansion of higher education through the G.I. Bill, while at the same time a Presidential Commission was calling for an even greater expansion of postsecondary opportunities. Meanwhile, enrollment at colleges and universities, especially public ones, increased significantly, and as institutions struggled with issues related to their newfound scope and size, state governments struggled as well with decisions regarding the extent to which students should pay the full cost of their within-state education. It was clearly a time of transition and change at multiple levels of society as equality of opportunity began to replace the notion that college was affordable only for those individuals blessed with significant financial resources.

At the federal level, much of the postsecondary policy thrust during the 1950s was driven by the increasing importance of the Cold War. For example, concerns about the United States' ability to compete technologically with the Soviet Union were reflected in the results of a 1956 study sponsored by the College Entrance Examination Board, *Encouraging Scientific Talent,* which concluded that math and science education at the secondary level in the United States needed significant improvement.[14] This was followed the next year by the launching of Sputnik, which helped focus many of the math and science adequacy concerns and led directly to the passage of the National Defense Education Act in 1958. This important legislative victory, which increased both the scope and level of federal involvement in postsecondary finance, provided fellowships and loans to college and postgraduate students working in areas deemed important to national defense like science, mathematics, and modern foreign languages.[15]

This expansion of the federal role in helping students pay for their education received a huge boost seven years later in 1965 with the passage of the Higher Education Act, which, among other things, embodied the first federal commitment to equalizing college opportunities for financially needy students. This explicit commitment to equity, which was expressed entirely in terms of need-based aid rather than merit-based aid, was made possible by the political leadership of President Johnson, who skillfully manipulated a supportive political and economic climate despite a series of other competing budget priorities. The finished product included needs-tested grants and monies for college work study, and required that colleges, as a condition for receiving the new basic Educational Opportunity Grants, make "vigorous" efforts to identify and recruit students with "exceptional financial need."[16] The Higher Education Act also created and provided funding for the Upward Bound and Talent Search programs, two programs designed to identify and foster access for low-income, college-able students. Perhaps more importantly, however, the Higher Education Act also created the guaranteed student loan program, which made subsidized loans available to students with financial need; in doing so, the federal government solved an important access to capital problem for students that had, ironically, been created by the very same business and economic models discussed earlier: Why would anyone loan money at below market rates to someone with no real job history, collateral, or guaranteed ability to repay the loan?

Taken together, the federal government's focus on equality of opportunity represented a real breakthrough for proponents of equity and need-based aid. Through the creation of need-based grants and the guaranteed student loan program, the federal government had made college more affordable for all, regardless of income, and in the process moved away from the traditional laissez-faire model of market behavior toward a more equitable, but less economically efficient set of higher education outcomes. As expected, the results were both powerful and swift; between 1950 and 1970, the percent of persons aged 25 to 29 who had completed four years of college more than doubled, from 7.7 percent to 16.4 percent.[17] Enrollment also surged during this period, with total enrollment in institutions of higher education more than tripling, from about 2.3 million in 1950 to about 8.6 million in 1970.[18] This increase in enrollment was not shared equally, however, and in the span of 20 years, public and private institutions went from splitting enrollment about equally in 1950 to a situation in 1970 where almost 75 percent of college and university students attended public institutions and only 25 percent attended private institutions.[19]

During this period of increasing federal involvement and financial largess, both state governments and institutions were also busy adjusting to their increased scope and size. At the institutional level, real tuitions were relatively flat among public colleges and universities, helping to drive the large enrollment increases in this sector.[20] However, real increases in tuition levels among private institutions, coupled with increased state support for public institutions, led to a significant loss of market share for private institutions of higher education.[21] (Interestingly, this loss in market share for the privates would never be regained, thanks in part to the continued expansion of the community college system.) However, to a large extent, the rising tide of both federal and state funding for higher education was able to make students and institutions significantly better off and, as a result, the 1960s ended with the United States on a path toward even greater equality of opportunity than ever before.

THE FORMATIVE YEARS—THE 1970s AND 1980s

The vigorous expansion of the federal government that occurred during the 1960s in the area of postsecondary finance resulted in a number of important societal changes. For example, one of the most important changes was a direct result of the need-based focus of the Higher Education Act, which clearly signaled a movement away from the traditional notion that higher education was only for those who could afford it, rather than for those who might benefit from it. The large enrollment increases that followed, which featured an increasingly diverse student population in terms of both race and gender, helped increase the demand for higher education even further, and even more importantly helped higher education be viewed and understood as a public good, one that all members of society could benefit from, regardless of whether or not they went to college.

This reframing of higher education as a public good was important in that, from at least the federal perspective, there was clearly more work to be done if this country was to achieve true equality of higher educational opportunity. The last major step to be taken in this direction occurred during the 1972 reauthorization of the Higher Education Act when Basic Grants (now called Pell Grants) were adopted. These grants, which have always been entirely need-based, were created in an effort to provide a foundation of financial support for undergraduates; in an interesting policy twist designed to harness the power of market forces, the grants were given directly to students rather than institutions, allowing students to take their federal aid to whatever institution they wanted, rather than letting institutions directly control the funds. After much debate, the grants were initially authorized at a maximum of $1,400, enough to provide a basic level of support for those entering four-year institutions; the hope among policymakers was that the campus-based programs would provide the additional support required to ensure institutional and programmatic choice for students.[22]

This continued activism by the federal government received an enormous boost during the 1970s from the relatively steady state tuition policies in place at most public and private institutions of higher education. For example, during the 1970s real average tuition actually fell by 10 percent at public institutions while increasing only 4 percent at private institutions.[23] As expected, these policies contributed significantly to the enrollment increases that continued throughout the decade—47 percent at public colleges and universities and 23 percent at private institutions of higher education.[24] Interestingly, much of this expansion came from the increased participation of women, who found support from the women's rights movement and the rapidly changing notions regarding the role of women in society. Taken together, these changes were enough that, by the mid-1970s, the participation of female students in higher education equaled that of males.[25]

In addition to the increasing participation of women, the decade of the 1970s also saw an increase in those students traditionally underrepresented in higher education—African Americans, Hispanics, and older students. For example, while about 15 percent of 18 to 24-year-old African Americans were enrolled in higher education in 1970, 20 percent were enrolled in 1980; among Hispanic students, about 12 percent were enrolled in 1972 (the first year that comparable data was available) and about 16 percent in 1980.[26] Interestingly, participation rates peaked during this decade for both African Americans and Hispanics in 1976, corresponding to the lowest net price (defined as tuition and fees minus aid received) recorded over the 20-year period; unfortunately, it would be another 10 years before African American participation rates reached their 1976 peak, and more than 15 years before Hispanic rates reached their earlier level.[27]

Although the impressive gains in equity during the 1970s would never have occurred without the financial intervention of the federal government, most institutions and state governments were engaged in highly complimentary policies—as evidenced by declining real tuitions at public colleges and universities and nominal increases at private colleges and universities. In addition, institutions also increased their spending during this period on scholarships and fellowships by a combined 128 percent, with the largest increase coming from private colleges and universities (152%) anxious to reverse the large shift in enrollment away from private institutions toward public ones.[28] As the 1970s came to a close, it seemed like all three institutional players in the area of postsecondary educational finance were finally pulling in the same direction—equity; however, the 1980s would find the three often going their own ways, driven by very different sets of operating constraints and concerns.

This directional change began at the top, when in 1980 the Republicans swept into power in both the White House and the Senate. The new direction was evident immediately as a number of social programs were eliminated or cut, and many recently liberalized rules for need-based aid were repealed. For example, in addition to reinstating need as a condition of eligibility for guaranteed loans (which had been repealed just two years earlier as part of the Middle Income Student Assistance Act), an origination fee of 5 percent was also imposed on borrowers as a cost-cutting measure.[29] Of course, these shifts in policy can be viewed from the federal perspective as a rational response to an economy suffering from double-digit inflation and sky-high interest rates; regardless, the federal government was signaling to all concerned that, with college participation rates at an all-time high and the economy in distress, the time for further federal largess had at least temporarily passed.

Not surprisingly, 1980 represented a high point for federal aid to postsecondary students; in real terms, federal assistance would not rise to this level again until the early 1990s. A powerful implication of this change in federal direction was that guaranteed loans, which of course need to be repaid, became a more popular form of assistance during this decade than need-based grants. For example, while new guaranteed loans in 1979 represented about 34 percent of the volume of total federal aid, by 1985 this share had climbed to 56 percent.[30] In addition, during this same time period the maximum Pell Grant as a share of the cost of attendance at public four-years declined significantly, from over 80 percent in 1979 to slightly less than 60 percent in 1985.[31] This historical shift from need-based grants to loans—which continues today and represents perhaps the most important structural shift in the last 40 years of postsecondary finance—has resulted in a contentious debate among stakeholders regarding the extent to which students should be subsidized by the government in paying for higher education.

This debate, which has traditionally pitted supporters of need-based grant aid against those who favor increased student borrowing, has its origins in the returns to education literature; specifically, proponents of debt financing feel that since students earn a large return on their investment in higher education, they should be more than willing to pay for it themselves through federallybacked loans. However, opponents argue that since both the private and social returns to education are high, federal and state governments should be encouraging participation in higher education through the issuance of need-based grants. Although the debate is, of course, still unresolved, it is important to note that the arguments on both sides can easily be recast into the language of equity and efficiency, with proponents of need-based grant aid pushing for a more equitable distribution of overall aid than supporters of increased lending, who argue that the high individual returns to education justify a more efficient financing mechanism, even if this means that some lower-income students would need to borrow more than their higher-income counterparts at private colleges and universities.

While this debate was playing out on the national scene in the 1980s, big changes were occurring at the institutional level. For example, beginning in 1982, tuition and fees at private colleges and universities literally exploded—increasing by 52 percent between 1982 and 1987.[32] Despite these large increases, enrollment continued to increase over this period by slightly more than 2 percent at private colleges and universities, suggesting that the returns on higher education were still high enough to justify an increasing student share of costs.[33] During this same period, tuition and fees at public four-year institutions increased by 44 percent, resulting in about a 5 percent increase in enrollment for ostensibly the same reason.[34] Fortunately, these increases in tuition were not enough to deter the increased participation of African American and Hispanic students, who still made small gains in participation.[35]

Meanwhile, while institutions were increasing their tuition and fees during the 1980s, state governments were busy struggling with the fallout from the political push to balance the federal budget, which had resulted in the devolution of federal programs to state and local governments. As many states struggled with their responsibility to provide increased funding for Medicaid, new prison construction, and K-12 education, not surprisingly, higher education fared poorly. In fact, state funding for public colleges and universities fell by almost 9 percent between 1980 and 1993 as states asked their students to shoulder a greater share of overall tuition and fees.[36] In other words, during this period, states moved away from their focus on equity and need-based aid to a more efficient solution—one in which students were asked to pay a greater, rather than lesser, share of their total costs—as respective state governments wrestled with their own fiscal crises.

THE COMPETITIVE YEARS—THE 1990s AND 2000s

The decade of the 1990s began with budget crises at both the federal and state level as governments struggled with a deepening recession in a significantly constrained fiscal environment. Not surprisingly, the debate over the federal provision of financial aid reflected these binding fiscal constraints, and as a result supporters of increased funding for need-based grants were forced to look elsewhere; this search eventually led them to support the creation of a more streamlined student loan program that, if implemented, would generate significant cost efficiencies in the provision of student loans. Since these efficiencies translated directly into monetary savings that could be used to support need-based grants, the newly elected President Clinton supported them enthusiastically; this led to the creation and implementation of the Direct Loan Program in 1994, which allowed the federal government to bypass banks and loan money directly to students. In addition to making it administratively easier for students and schools, the program also introduced the notion of income contingent repayment, which allowed borrowers with large student loan debt to enter relatively low-paying occupations thanks to a repayment program that allowed them to pay a fixed percentage of their income each month until their loans were paid off or until the passage of 25 years, at which time any remaining debt would be forgiven.

The introduction of the Direct Loan Program received tremendous scrutiny within the halls of Congress; in fact, the newly elected Republican majority in 1994 set their sites on the elimination of the program, claiming it was emblematic of "big government" and sure to suffer from all the traditional inefficiencies associated with any large, monolithic federal government program. However, with student borrowing increasing at double-digit annual rates during the mid-1990s and need-based grants playing an increasingly smaller role in the financing plans of students, the stakes were clearly high for supporters of need-based grants; after all, any budgetary savings that resulted from the successful implementation of the Direct Loan Program could be used to help fund their cause.[37] Although the result of this bitter partisan battle was ultimately a truce between the original guaranteed student loan program and the new direct loan program, with each program coexisting and sharing the market, it was a powerful example of how supporters of need-based aid were able to embrace business and economic models in their search for greater efficiencies that would free-up funds that could then be spent improving equity.

This search for savings in the student loan programs continues to this very day, and proponents of need-based aid have had several important victories; the most notable was the College Cost Reduction and Access Act of 2007, which redirected more than $11 billion over a five-year period away from lenders and toward Pell Grants. This work has been driven by a legitimate sense of urgency since, in 1986, the maximum Pell Grant covered 51 percent of average tuition and fees and board at public four-year colleges and universities and 21 percent at the average four-year private institution; however, 10 years later, in 1996, the figures had declined to 33 percent and 13 percent, respectively.[38] Even though the federal budget surpluses associated with the 1998–2001 period allowed for several years of real increases in the Pell Grant maximum award, the rest of the decade was characterized by little or no change; as a result, the respective shares covered by the maximum Pell Grant award slipped even further in 2006 to 32 percent and 13 percent, respectively.[39]

As expected, the decline that occurred during this period in the value of need-based federal grants was accompanied by large increases in student borrowing, both through the government-sponsored student loan programs and the largely unregulated private student loan market. And make no mistake—the increases that occurred were staggering: Among undergraduates, between 1996 and 2006 the number of subsidized student loan borrowers increased by 47 percent, the number of unsubsidized borrowers increased by 113 percent, and the number of individuals borrowing through the parental loan program increased by 92 percent; the corresponding numbers for graduate students were 66 and 110 percent, respectively.[40] Even more troubling, student borrowing outside of the federal loan programs has exploded in recent years; for example, 10 years ago, private loans represented only 5 percent of the total educational loan volume while today they represent 20 percent, with $17.3 billion in private loans issued in the 2005–06 academic year alone.[41]

This shift away from grants toward loans at the federal level comes as no real surprise, since the last 18 years have produced three significant national recessions and years of structural budget deficits. Taken together, these events have constrained the behavior of the federal government, and as programmatic budgets have been tightened or eliminated, students have been asked to share an increasingly larger burden of their educational expenses. Of course, state governments do have the ability to pursue policies designed to mitigate this sort of behavior, but for most of this period they were at least as financially strapped as the federal government, and as unfunded federal mandates combined with increased demands for expenditures on prisons, hospitals, and K-12 education, increased state support for higher education was effectively crowded out.[42] Although the extent of the problem varied among states, in the early 1990s real state appropriations for higher education actually fell for several years, before rebounding modestly; however, since the late 1990s a new and potentially disturbing trend has emerged in some states—the proliferation of non-need-based state aid, also known as merit aid.[43]

The growth in non-need-based state aid, which began with Georgia's Hope Scholarship program in 1993, represented the first example in this country of an entirely merit-based state scholarship program, one where a student's ability to pay for his own education was not a factor in determining whether or not he received the aid. Typical of many of the merit-based state programs that would follow (like the Bright Futures program in Florida and the Palmetto Fellows program in South Carolina), the goals of the original Hope Scholarship program were largely twofold: to offer academically superior students who would not otherwise be able to afford college the ability to attend, and to offer an incentive to academically superior students who can afford to attend college to remain in the state of Georgia.[44] The proliferation of programs such as these, many of which were designed to target limited state dollars on those thought to be "college ready and able" rather than risk supporting individuals with less proven track records, can again be viewed in the context of states struggling with very real budget constraints and limited funding opportunities. The growth in these programs, however, has been nothing less than remarkable; for example, the percentage of state grant aid to undergraduates based on something other than need increased from 9 percent in 1985 to 14 percent in 1995, and then to 28 percent in 2005.[45]

With the federal government and many state governments in retrenchment mode for much of this period, the need-based grant burden was placed squarely on the backs of the institutions themselves, who as it turns out were not really up to the job. Instead, both four-year public and private institutions were busy raising tuition and fees faster than the overall rate of inflation; for example, over the past decade, total charges for full-time students at private four-year colleges and universities have risen by an average of 5.3 percent per year—or 2.6 percent after inflation—while similar charges at four-year public colleges and universities have risen at an annual rate of 6.2 percent per year and 3.5 percent per year after adjusting for inflation.[46] Along with these hefty tuition increases came large increases in institutional aid, although at many colleges and universities most of this aid was merit, rather than need-based. In fact, for the first six years of this period, the size of the average institutional merit grant grew by 117 percent compared with the 47 percent growth in the size of the average institutional need-based grant.[47] This trend has continued over the last decade as institutional grants have grown by 79 percent in real terms; however, some of the wealthiest private institutions have been able to concentrate on both need- and merit-based grants, and a few select ones (Harvard, Yale, and Princeton) have completely eliminated need for low- and moderate- income students by replacing all their loans with need-based grants.[48]

Taken together, it seems that institutions were the only ones of the three during this period that had any real flexibility in helping students to finance their postsecondary education. Unfortunately, as the demand for higher education continued to increase dramatically even in the face of rapidly escalating costs, many institutions took the easy way out by providing institutional support to students who had already demonstrated academic prowess, rather than by concentrating their limited resources on those students with greater financial need. Although a number of explanations have been posited to explain this behavior, perhaps the leading hypothesis involves the revenue theory of costs first articulated by Howard Bowen, which states that, from the perspective of a college or university president, more revenues are always preferred to less since it allows all campus stakeholders to receive regular increases in funding from an ever-expanding pie, rather than the static shares that result from a zero-sum pie whose size never changes.[49] Regardless of the explanation, however, the truth is that some colleges and universities used their institutional aid to fill seats while others used it to diversify their class, suggesting that while some institutions had the luxury to concentrate on increasing equity within their class, others were primarily concerned with the efficiency of maximizing net tuition revenues.[50] As a result, during this period some institutions pushed back against the federal and state drift toward greater efficiency, while others exacerbated the move away from the equity pole on the continuum.

THE EQUITY/EFFICIENCY TRADEOFF REVISITED

As described in the introductory section of this chapter, the purpose of the preceding historical review was to examine the provision of financial aid from three different perspectives—the federal government, state governments, and institutions—and then to use these diverse perspectives to develop an understanding as to why the intertemporal provision of financial aid seems to oscillate between need-based and non-need-based concerns. The purpose of this particular section is to develop just that theoretical understanding; in doing so, special attention will be paid to the goals and objectives of each of the providers as well as the unique set of political and economic constraints that they face. In this manner, a theory can be developed that is not only consistent with the available empirical evidence but also offers insight into exactly how the providers interact to determine exactly where on the student aid equity/efficiency continuum society decides to locate.

The Importance of Who Goes First

The development of this theory begins with the actions of the federal government for at least three important reasons. First, although the federal government is not the largest of the three players in terms of the dollar value of its contributions, only the policies of the federal government have the potential to affect everyone enrolled in higher education, rather than just those enrolled in a particular state or institution. Second, even though these decisions are made through the interactions of multiple legislative and executive branch members, the federal government ultimately speaks with a single voice when it enacts policy—again unlike the 50 separate state governments and thousands of individual institutions of higher education. And finally, from both an economic and societal perspective, the largest interventions into the higher education enterprise during the last century—which include the G.I. Bill in 1944 and the passage of the Higher Education Act in 1965—were designed, implemented, and funded by the federal government; taken together these reasons suggest that everyone needs to pay close attention to the actions of the federal government before deciding on their own student aid policies.

For the reasons just discussed, it makes sense for policymakers involved at the state and institutional levels to pay close attention to the behavior of the federal government. For example, if Congress and the president decide to increase the amount of the maximum Pell Grant significantly, then this decision has implications for the behavior of institutions and state governments; the cost to them of not incorporating this information into their business and economic models is less than optimal behavior. In other words, policymakers need to incorporate the actions of the federal government into their optimization models because if they do not, the decision rules that flow from their models will be analytically flawed. In the earlier Pell Grant maximum example, this means that if the increase in federal funding occurred during a time of stable tuitions within the public sector, state governments might have then been able to concomitantly reduce their expenditures for need-based grants; of course, if this information was not incorporated into their models, then a more efficient solution to the problem would have been possible.

As discussed in the historical review, the ability of the federal government to alter the higher education policy landscape in a short period of time cannot be underestimated; however, the federal government also faces a continually evolving set of economic and political constraints that typically limits its ability to intervene. For example, it took both an overwhelming economic imperative and the political support of the executive and legislative branches of the federal government to make the Servicemen's

Readjustment Act of 1944 (also known as the G.I. Bill) happen; a less supportive economic and political environment would never have authorized the massive influx of capital required to support the higher education aspirations of millions of returning veterans. Similarly, the budget surpluses of 1956 and 1957 helped provide the federal government with the economic means necessary to fund the National Defense Education Act of 1958, while the launch of Sputnik earlier that year by the Soviet Union provided the necessary political capital. Passage of the landmark Higher Education Act in 1965 was also done in an incredibly supportive political environment under the leadership of President Johnson, and despite a number of competing budget priorities, the existence of a relatively balanced budget at the federal level provided the economic opportunity to fund such a massive federal investment in higher education.

Unfortunately, those occasions where the federal government is not constrained by either economics and/or politics are exceedingly rare; in fact, the majority of the time either one or both of the constraints appear binding. For example, while President Clinton enjoyed Democratic majorities in both the House and Senate during his first two years in office, he inherited a budget deficit so severe that he was unable to make the financial commitment toward need-based aid that he wanted until the nation's economic situation improved. However, several years later when the economy did improve and the federal budget was in surplus for four consecutive years (1998–2001), the political constraints loosened enough to provide a 22 percent real increase in total expenditures on Pell Grants for the 2001–02 academic year.[51]

What this means, of course, is that no matter what state governments and institutions are thinking about doing regarding the provision of student financial assistance, they first need to understand and account for the behavior of the federal government; as mentioned earlier, not incorporating this information into their economic models guarantees a less than optimal solution. Similarly, when institutions are faced with the decision about how their internal scholarship funds should be divided between need-based and merit-based aid, not taking into account the actions of both the federal government and their state government would also result in a suboptimal solution. An example of this might occur when the federal government is running a large budget deficit; depending on whether or not a particular state government is also in deficit may mean the difference between an institution focusing more on need-based aid rather than merit-based aid. In other words, if the institution only pays attention to the policies of the federal government and ignores the actions of state government, the institution runs the real risk of pursuing policies that needlessly conflict with those of the state.

The need for institutions to pay attention to the current policies of both federal and state governments holds for private institutions as well as public ones. Although the funding connection may not be as direct, if both the federal and state governments are expanding need-based aid significantly, then some private institutions may elect to rebalance their scholarship aid more in the merit direction, figuring that the action of both governmental bodies has moved the country in the direction of more equity. Similarly, if during an economic slowdown the federal government and state governments are pursuing policies designed to reduce the value of need-based aid, then some institutions may want to expand their need-based offerings in an effort to continue to attract a diverse group of students. Regardless of whether the institution is private or public, however, it makes economic sense to understand what the other players in the game are doing before acting.

Taken together, this suggests that a natural decision-making hierarchy exists, beginning with the actions of the federal government, followed by the actions of state governments, and then institutions. In other words, since the student financial assistance policies of the federal government affect all students enrolled in higher education in this country, its decisions must be incorporated into the models and policies of the states and institutions; similarly, since the policies of state governments affect all students within that particular state, their decisions must be incorporated into the models and policies of institutions within that state. This notion of nesting these models within each other makes analytical sense in that it allows an optimal solution to emerge at each stage of the problem, rather than building and solving models based on less-than-full information.

The Existence of the Oscillatory Equilibrium

Recognizing the existence of a natural ordering for such policy-related decision-making is critical for developing an understanding as to why the intertemporal provision of financial aid seems to oscillate between need-based and non-need-based concerns. What this means in practice is that by having the most money to spend and by going first, the federal government initially selects where our country will be along the equity/efficiency continuum. In the next stage of the policy process, state governments then try to react to where the federal government has positioned the country along the continuum, and, depending on the policy goals and objectives of the particular state, this may result in movement in the direction of greater equity or in the direction of greater efficiency. In the final stage of the process, institutions align their own strategic goals with the actions of the federal actors and their state government and, if needed, reposition themselves along the equity/efficiency continuum.

Not surprisingly, the largest movements along the continuum, which are typically in the direction of equity, are caused by the actions of the federal government operating in an unconstrained environment. However, during those times when the federal government is constrained either economically or politically, the absence of federal action usually moves society away from equity in the direction of efficiency, albeit at a slower pace. Historical evidence supports this view in that many of the largest single policy interventions occurred at the federal level during periods of economic expansion or during budget surpluses. This is also largely true at the state level, where the largest movements along the continuum in the direction of equity occur during periods of economic expansion, while the largest movements in the direction of efficiency typically occur during periods where the state governments are severely constrained economically.

Depending on the vantage point of the decision-maker, this pattern of behavior often produces an incremental series of opposing moves along the continuum. For example, economically constrained state governments may view an increase in federal support for need-based grants (which moves society in the direction of equity) as an opportunity for them to cut back on their own need-based spending, which represents a movement away from equity toward the efficiency pole of the continuum. Institutions watching this chain of events may feel the need to react as well, and if their decision is to rebalance the distribution of their own institutional aid toward more need-based funding and away from merit-based aid, then the familiar oscillatory pattern regarding the provision of student aid results. In other words, the federal government first moves society in the direction of equity, some states then move back in the direction of efficiency, and finally, institutions move society back in the direction of equity.

Of course, this pattern works in reverse as well; often times the policies of a severely constrained federal government are mitigated by more equitable policies at the state level, which can allow financially constrained institutions to concentrate less on need-based aid and more on merit-based aid. More importantly, this oscillatory pattern is not always on display, since sometimes the decisions made by all three players are mutually reinforcing; however, when this occurs, sooner or later one of the players will see an advantage in going against the grain and the oscillatory pattern will again begin to emerge. In fact, the existence of this oscillatory pattern can be used to understand both the decisions made by the players within a single year and the longer-run pattern of decision-making that is clearly linked to observable political and economic trends.

SUMMARY AND CONCLUSIONS

Given that the goal of this chapter was to develop a long-run economic framework that helped explain intertemporal patterns in the provision of financial aid, the discussion began with a look at how business and economic models are used by decision-makers involved in the provision of need-based and non-need-based aid. These models, which typically require users to specify a specific organizational goal or objective, have the mathematical ability to optimally align resources in a constrained environment; more importantly, the more information included in these models, the more general the solution. When these models were applied to the historic provision of student financial aid by the federal government, state governments, and institutions, it became clear that, for a number of reasons, there was a natural ordering to the decision-making process: the federal government goes first, followed by state governments, and then finally institutions.

A direct consequence of this natural decision-ordering is that the federal government is typically the first to position society along the equity/efficiency continuum, and its selection depends, of course, on the extent to which it is constrained economically or politically. During unconstrained times, for example, the federal government typically moves in the equity direction, while during politically or economically constrained times, the movement is often back in the other direction. State governments are next to play, and as they react to the actions of the federal government and their own constraints, they either push back against the direction of the federal government or in the same direction; often, however, their attempt to leverage federal actions and dollars means that they move in a direction opposite that of the federal government. Similarly, when the third and final player, public and private institutions, reacts to the decisions of their own state government, they too often push back in an effort to balance the actions of the two players that have come before them.

Taken together, this pushing and pulling among players often results in an oscillatory equilibrium of sorts, where one player moves in the equity direction and another player moves back in the direction of efficiency. This back and forth behavior can occur in the course of a single year, as players quickly align their own allocation decisions with any directional changes made at levels above them, or over the course of a number of years where, for example, all players may be moving in the same direction for awhile until one player realizes that they may have moved to far in that direction, and then the oscillatory pattern starts all over again. Regardless of the time period, however, the long-run path along the equity/efficiency continuum is still the same—a continual back and forth between the poles of need-based and non-need based, with movements along the continuum being driven either by shifting objectives or binding political or economic constraints.

NOTES

1. College Board, *Trends in Student Aid* (New York: The College Board, 2008), 2.

2. Linda Siefert and Fred Galloway, "A New Look at Solving the Undergraduate Yield Problem: The Importance of Estimating Individual Price Sensitivities," *College and University* 81, no. 3 (2006): 11–17.

3. Claudia Goldin and Lawrence Katz, "The Shaping of Higher Education: The Formative Years in the United States, 1890 to 1940," *National Bureau of Economic Research Working Paper 6537* (1998).

4. Ibid., 4.

5. Ibid., 8.

6. Ibid., 17.

7. Ibid., 12–16.

8. Ibid., 24.

9. Ibid., 29.

10. Ibid., 10–11.

11. Lawrence Veysey, *The Emergence of the American University* (Chicago: The University of Chicago Press, 1965), 121–79, 338.

12. Marvin Lazerson, *American Education in the Twentieth Century: A Documentary History* (New York: Teachers College Press, 1987), 132.

13. Ibid., 134.

14. Ibid., 140.

15. Lawrence Gladieux, "Federal Student Aid Policy: A History and an Assessment." *Financing Postsecondary Education: The Federal Role. Proceedings of the National Conference on the Best Ways for the Federal Government to Help Students and Families Finance Postsecondary Education* (Washington, DC: U.S. Department of Education, 1995), 39.

16. Lawrence Gladieux and Arthur Hauptman, *The College Aid Quandary* (Washington, DC: Brookings Institution, 1995), 15.

17. Ibid., 30.

18. National Center for Education Statistics, *Digest of Education Statistics* (Washington, DC: U.S. Department of Education, 1990), 167.

19. Ibid.

20. Ibid., 285.

21. Ibid., 168.

22. Gladieux and Hauptman, *The College Aid Quandary,* 16–17.

23. Maureen McLaughlin, "Trends in College Tuition and Student Aid since 1970," *Congressional Budget Office Staff Working Papers* (Washington, DC: Congressional Budget Service, 1988), 5.

24. National Center for Education Statistics, *Digest of Education Statistics* (Washington, DC: U.S. Department of Education, 1998), 196.

25. Patricia Gumport, Maria Iannozzi, Susan Shaman, and Robert Zemsky, "Trends in United States Higher Education from Massification to Post Massification," National Center for Postsecondary Improvement, 1997, 5.

26. Ibid., 6.

27. Ibid.

28. National Center for Education Statistics, *Digest of Education Statistics* (1990), 291.

29. Gladieux and Hauptman, *The College Aid Quandary*, 18.

30. Michael McPherson and Morton Shapiro, *Keeping College Affordable* (Washington, DC: Brookings Institution, 1991), 26.

31. Jacqueline King, *2000 Status Report on the Pell Grant Program* (Washington, DC: American Council on Education, 2000), 10.

32. College Board, *Trends in College Pricing* (New York: The College Board, 2007), 10.

33. National Center for Education Statistics, *Digest of Education Statistics* (1998), 196.

34. College Board, *Trends in College Pricing*, 10.

35. Gumport, Iannozzi, Shaman, and Zemsky, 6.

36. Ibid., 24.

37. College Board, *Trends in Student Aid*, 12.

38. King, 8.

39. College Board, *Trends in Student Aid*, 18.

40. Ibid., 11.

41. Project on Student Debt, "Improving Consumer Protections for Private Student Loans," http://www.projectonstudentdebt.org/files/pub/Private_Loan_Agenda.pdf (accessed December 1, 2008).

42. Steven Gold, "State Fiscal Problems and Policies," in *The Fiscal Crisis of the States: Lessons for the Future*, ed. Steven Gold (Washington, DC: Georgetown University Press, 1995), 25–27.

43. Patrick Callan, "Reframing Access and Opportunity: Problematic State and Federal Higher Education Policy in the 1990s," in *The States and Public Higher Education Policy: Affordability, Access, and Accountability*, ed. Don Heller (Baltimore, MD: Johns Hopkins University Press, 2001), 88.

44. Patricia McDonough, Shannon Calderone, and William Purdy, *State Grant Aid and Its Effects on Students' College Choices* (Boulder, CO: Western Interstate Commission for Higher Education, 2007), 14.

45. College Board, *Trends in Student Aid,* 17.
46. College Board, *Trends in College Pricing,* 11.
47. Donald Heller, "Merit and Need-Based Aid: Recent Changes in State and Institutional Policy," U.S. Department of Education, Advisory Committee on Student Financial Assistance, April 12, 2000, http://www.personal.psu.edu/deh29/papers/papers_index.html (accessed December 1, 2008).
48. College Board, *Trends in Student Aid,* 6.
49. William Lasher and Charlotte Sullivan, "Following the Money: The Changing World of Budgeting in Higher Education," in *Higher Education: Handbook of Theory and Practice, v. 19,* ed. John Smart (Dordrecht, The Netherlands: Kluwer Academic Publishers, 2004), 207.
50. David Breneman, *Liberal Arts Colleges: Thriving, Surviving, or Endangered?* (Washington, DC: Brookings Institution, 1994), 38.
51. College Board, *Trends in Student Aid,* 18.

CHAPTER 10

The Business of Intercollegiate Athletics

J. Douglas Toma

Intercollegiate athletics, as an industry, is not unlike other highly stratified spheres, where great wealth is concentrated at the very top and the environment there is quite dynamic—and everyone else is, essentially, pretty normal and even boring. College sports is akin to the income distribution in the United States, where the U.S. Census reports that the top quintile (20%) earns 50 percent of all income (with the top 5% taking 21% of that), and the other 50 percent is spread across the remaining 80 percent of the population, with the lowest two quintiles (40%) at about 12 percent.[1] Universities and colleges, as a sector, are arrayed similarly, with a relatively small percentage of institutions—the ones that garner nearly all of the attention—having significant resources at their disposal and the vast majority operating much more modestly and even anonymously. Even within institutions, some academic units have much more impressive budgets—say, the business school—than their neighbors across campus. This is the situation in college sports. At a relatively few institutions (around 5%), a couple of sports (mostly football) provide the capacity to generate revenues that enable the entire athletics department not only to operate, but to do so relatively comfortably and to be self-supporting. Everywhere else, athletics operates not unlike a typical unit within a university or college—one without much capacity to produce revenue, as through tuition or user fees. So, like student affairs or academic advising, there is just not much "business" to speak of.

In considering the business of intercollegiate athletics, I first explore the divide between these few revenue-generating programs and everyone else. There is an interesting line within the "everyone else"—the subsidized programs—with 50 or so programs that do not really generate revenue competing directly in certain respects with the 75 or so that do. In closing the first section, I consider why these institutions are willing to take a significant loss on intercollegiate athletics each year, as opposed to still sponsoring a program but doing so as modestly as possible, as do the vast majority of institutions nationally. I then explore revenues and expenditures in college sports, focusing mainly on the revenue-generating sector, which is where the action is in the business of college sports. In discussing ticket sales and private donations, television revenues and conference distributions, and sponsorships and royalties, the revenue-producing programs operate in a vibrant environment. The same is true on the expenditure side with salaries and benefits, as well as administration and operations, in which I include scholarships, academic support, recruiting, travel, and facilities and maintenance. I also address the fact that most of the revenue-generating programs are spending all that they earn. I conclude with a note about the challenges associated with maintaining the perception of amateurism necessary for essentially professional and commercial enterprises like football and men's basketball to retain their standing within the university—and the tax-exempt status that comes with it. I also discuss the difficulties that can accompany stratification within an industry, noting the possible antitrust trouble that could come from an action based on the interests of those athletics programs just outside of the revenue-generating group. Finally, I primarily employ sources throughout the chapter, including from the popular media, from within the past two or three years, given that the financial dynamics in college sports tend to evolve so rapidly.

REVENUE-GENERATING AND SUBSIDIZED PROGRAMS

Just as the resources available to different universities within a given sector—or across sectors—are significantly different, so are the revenues and expenditures of different athletics programs. For instance, the University of Michigan had $890 million in research expenditures and endowment assets of $5.3 billion in 2005, making it the national leader among public institutions in research (and second to Johns Hopkins' $1.4 billion and second to the University of Texas in endowment, (and eighth overall among public and private institutions). Virginia Tech, the institution ranked 50th among all institutions in research, had $290 million in expenditures—about one-third that of Michigan—and the University of Wisconsin, Milwaukee, ranking 200th nationally, was at $33 million (about 4% of Michigan). The institution with the 50th-largest endowment, the University of California, San Francisco, was at $1.2 billion—less than one-fourth of Michigan—and the University of Wyoming, at 200th overall, had an endowment of $260 million (about 5% of Michigan). (Michigan, on the other hand, trailed considerably the $29 billion endowment at Harvard.)[2]

Within Division I, the 330 or so institutions that compete at the most prominent level in collegiate athletics, there are programs such as Ohio State, Texas, and Michigan that generate and spend 30 times what the smallest programs in the division do, such as Nicholls State, Maryland-Eastern Shore, and North Carolina-Asheville. Division II and Division III institutions operate more like these smaller institutions, but there are still differences, as with greater spending at elite small colleges such as Williams. So, athletics is similar to higher education generally, where a relatively few institutions have revenues from tuition, appropriations, research, and endowments that far exceed most others. With these resources at universities and colleges come advantages in attracting the most accomplished students and most desired faculty, including through generous financial packages and impressive facilities. The same is true in athletics: with greater resources come better opportunities to make the investments needed, including in infrastructure, to recruit the most promising student athletes and to attract and retain the coaches and administrators in the greatest demand.

For athletic programs, what marks the divide between those rich in resources and everyone else is the ability to generate a budget independently—through ticket sales, private gifts, television revenues, and so on—versus being funded through subsidies from the institution. About 75 institutions with prominent football programs (or basketball teams as a surrogate) can generate sufficient revenue essentially within the program alone to support annual athletics budgets over $40 million—sometimes approaching twice that figure. (So, even within the elite group, like with research expenditures and endowment assets, there are among the "haves" a few programs that are "haves-plus.") Everyone else creates an annual budget for intercollegiate athletics primarily through student fees and institutional funds—transfers from the institution—thus marking a significant divide within intercollegiate athletics. The 50 or so other programs in the Football Bowl Subdivision (FBS; formerly Division I-A) and a few Football Championship Subdivision (FCS; formerly Division I-AA) departments have budgets in the $15 million range. In football, these institutions compete mostly with one another, but also a few times each year with the larger programs. The remainder of the roughly 330 Division I members compete in basketball, including in the early season against the larger programs, and are eligible for the annual NCAA tournament. About 90 institutions in Division I do not offer football, so the division is split roughly into thirds among FBS, FCS, and nonfootball programs.[3]

Like Division II (roughly 285 members) and Division III (about 450 members) institutions, smaller Division I programs have budgets below $10 million, often well below. Apart from the NCAA, there are nearly 300 members of the National Association of Intercollegiate Athletics (NAIA), which parallels Division II and III in scale. Again, the difference between these 1,200 or so (1,600, including community colleges) athletics programs and the 75 programs atop the FBS is that the latter can generate their own massive budgets while the former rely nearly entirely on institution subsidies to cover more modest expenditures. Orszag and Orszag summarized spending and revenue across NCAA Divisions I and II, concluding that in 2003 FBS institutions spent, on average, $29.4 million (and produced $27.2 million), and the other divisions averaged about the same in expenditures and revenues: $7.2 million in spending in the FCS, $6.2 million at non-football-playing Division I institutions, $2.6 million in Division II with football, and $1.7 million in Division II without football.[4] Operating expenses in 2003 for Division III institutions with football were $1.6 million and $900,000 for institutions that did not sponsor football.[5]

Revenue-Generating Programs

Atop the resources heap in college sports are the so-called BCS (Bowl Coalition Series) schools. These are the institutions with football teams within the six major conferences (the Atlantic Coast, Big East, Big Ten, Big Twelve, Pacific Ten, and Southeastern) and the University of Notre Dame. These 66 most prominent athletic programs have budgets ranging from $30 million to around $90 million. According to figures published in 2006 by the *Indianapolis Star* drawing on NCAA data for public universities (with a few not reporting),[6] 13 of these institutions had athletics revenues in excess of $60 million, with another 23 over $40 million.[7] Expenditures and revenues typically balanced within the group, but sometimes there were surpluses, as with Georgia spending $24 million less than the $69 million it had in revenues, or Berkeley taking an $8 million loss against $52 million in expenditures. There are also a few private institutions without football programs but with the capacity to generate revenue through men's basketball at the more modest end of this group—universities like Marquette, Xavier, or Georgetown.

These institutions tend to derive significant revenue from a few spectator sports. For instance, the largest athletics program nationally, Ohio State (OSU), earned nearly $90 million in 2006 according to the *Star* data, with football accounting for $52 million of this figure and men's basketball another $11.5 million—more than two-thirds of all revenue. Ohio State generated $34 million from ticket sales, mostly associated with football, and garnered $20 million in private support (about one-half associated with football); $7 million in royalties (as through licensed apparel), advertisements, and corporate sponsorships; $5 million in concessions and parking, $3 million from summer sports camps; and $2 million from media rights sales beyond those by the NCAA or conference (as with local radio broadcasts). $11.5 million of the Ohio State budget came from NCAA or Big Ten distributions generated from sources such as football bowl games and basketball tournaments (about one-half from each). The athletics department also generated almost $2 million annually from its endowment and investments. OSU athletics does not receive state support, student fees, or institutional support. For instance, the athletics department does not receive funds for tuition waivers or the use of university staff such as counsel or maintenance workers. Ohio State spent all that it raised, including $26 million on football, about one-half of what it generated from it. Among these football expenditures were $2 million on student aid, $4 million on coaches' salaries, $3 million on travel, and $13 million on facilities and maintenance. Overall, the athletics department spent $10.5 million on student aid, $14 million on coaches' salaries, $11 million on support staff, $5 million on travel, $3 million on games, $1.5 million each on sports camps and promotion, $26 million on facilities and maintenance, $2.5 million on medical services, and $10 million on other operating expenses.[8]

Forbes magazine estimated the market value for the major NCAA athletics programs—what they might be worth if, like professional teams, they were sold on the open market—releasing the rankings for the top 20.[9] Notre Dame has the highest estimated value, at $101 million and estimated net revenue of $46 million, with Texas and Georgia football making a similar profit and Michigan, Florida, LSU, Tennessee, Auburn, and Alabama (ranked four through nine by *Forbes*), as well as Penn State, in the $35 million range. The value of the leading 13 programs (including Ohio State, Oklahoma, South Carolina, and Penn State, at 10 through 13 in the rankings) is over $70 million, with the last seven (Southern California, Arkansas, Texas A&M, Washington, Nebraska, Michigan State, and Wisconsin) in the $50 million range in value and around $18 million in net revenue.[10] (Six of the top nine programs are in the SEC, with two more in the top 20; five are from the Big Ten, four the Big Twelve, two from the

Pacific Ten, and Notre Dame is an independent.) In producing revenue, especially in increasing the margin, winning matters. Florida, after winning the 2006 national championship, increased its football-related revenue by $11 million, to $59 million.[11] Finally, Notre Dame athletics contributes $21 million to the academic side, which is as much as the next five institutions combined.[12] Despite the popular notion, athletics programs rarely contribute to the broader university and are at all but the largest institutions nearly fully subsidized by them.

Not every institution participating in the six major football conferences has the resources—or expenditures—of the top institutions in the *Forbes* ranking, but each institution can generally produce revenue in the same several categories as those illustrated by Ohio State above—ticket sales, private contributions, royalties, and sponsorships, NCAA and conference payments, and so on—sufficient to support a program that can compete evenly (or, at least, relatively so) with Ohio State. In addition, BCS institutions tend to draw and spend their budgets in roughly the same proportions as Ohio State. For instance, UCLA, which ranks 29th in revenue among the Division I public institutions in the 2006 *Indianapolis Star* data (about at the median of BCS institutions), has a $46 million annual budget. It raises, for instance, $15 million through ticket sales (and another $1 million through road football games)—or about one-third of its budget, a bit less than OSU. However, UCLA earns $6.5 million of its budget from selling local media rights, much greater than Ohio State, and about the same in advertisement and sponsorships as OSU, even though its budget is one-half that of the other program. Similarly, UCLA spends $13 million on football, or about the same proportion of its budget as Ohio State.

Again, the parallel here is with universities and colleges generally. Institutions within the same classification typically do not have access to identical resources, but they can compete relatively evenly with one another. Just as Virginia Tech (or even UW-Milwaukee) will not be foreclosed by Michigan from receiving research grants or attracting the most desirable graduate students, Ohio State does not have a particular advantage over UCLA in athletics. Another parallel is with professional sports, where some teams, such as the Yankees in Major League baseball, make and spend six or seven times the teams, such as the Marlins, with the most modest budgets, but the Marlins won the World Series in 1997 and 2003. The Yankees, like Michigan in research and Ohio State in football, just have a more comfortable margin, including for error.

It is also important to note that, even within the 10 percent or so of programs across intercollegiate athletics that generate their own resources, only a couple (or perhaps a few) sports earn any revenue at all—and even fewer produce net revenue. Only football and men's basketball teams at each institution typically draw the broad attention, especially from those outside of the university, needed for them to have commercial potential, as with attracting tens of thousands of spectators and millions of television viewers. (They also have liabilities associated with having to pay head coaches salaries competitive with the National Football League [NFL] or National Basketball Association [NBA].) There are other sports at some institutions that earn some revenue—women's basketball at Connecticut, men's hockey at Wisconsin, women's gymnastics at Georgia, and baseball at Louisiana State, for example—but it is modest in relative terms. Sports such as swimming and diving or track and field—and even football and men's basketball outside of Division I—are essentially student activities, generating minimal interest and having the personal development of those students participating as a paramount goal.[13]

Among the revenue-generating athletics programs, it is the net revenue from football, mostly, but sometimes men's basketball, that supports the entire enterprise. In 2006, football produced $40 million in net revenue at Texas and Georgia, according to the *Indianapolis Star* data, and the median BCS institution cleared around $8 million from the sport. Basketball contributes about $2 million in net revenue at the typical revenue-generating institution, but the figure is as high as $13 million at Louisville and Arizona.[14] The bottom line is that the resources generated by a couple of sports at a relatively few institutions can support an entire athletics program—a comprehensive one at that.

Subsidized Programs

Apart from these institutions is everyone else. One category is the other Football Bowl Subdivision (formerly Division I-A) conferences (Conference USA, the Mid-American, Mountain West, Sun Belt, and Western Athletic), which have budgets in the $10 million to $25 million range. Some public institutions in the Football Championship Subdivision (formerly Division I-AA) have similar budgets, with James Madison the largest at $22 million. What separates these institutions from those in the BCS conferences is the need to derive revenue through transfers from the institution, whether through student fees, state funds, or institutional support. Alesia reports that nationally ranked athletic programs at Division I public universities and colleges receive over $1 billion per year in institutional transfers, including student fees.[15] He adds that only 15 programs out of 164 the *Indianapolis Star* surveyed (having made 215 requests for information) would have broken even without subsidies, with a resulting average deficit of $5.7 million.

Eastern Michigan provides an example. EMU has a $20 million annual budget, covering $7 million from student fees, $2 million from state funds, and $8 million in institution support, both direct and indirect. (Direct support is in the form of tuition waivers or actual transfers, while indirect support involves the use of universities' facilities and staff.) It generates minimal funds through tickets sales, contributions from individuals, conference distributions, and the other sources that contribute to enriching an athletics department like Ohio State's. These non-BCS Division I institutions—and especially those with more modest means—will typically take "guarantee" games to generate revenue, visiting a BCS school for a football game in exchange for what can approach $1 million (but which is usually closer to $400,000). In 2008, Texas paid Florida Atlantic $900,000 for a game, Alabama-Birmingham went to South Carolina for $750,000, and Chattanooga earned $935,000 for games at Oklahoma and Florida State.[16] At Western Carolina, which has a $7 million athletics budget and competes in the FCS, about one-tenth of that comes from guarantees involving the football and men's basketball teams.[17]

On the expense side, Eastern Michigan had costs for student aid similar to the BCS schools, $7.5 million, as it offers generally the same number of sports and provides scholarships for most students competing. Salaries for coaches are lower—considerably so in the spectator sports—requiring $3 million of the budget (with another $2 million for support staff). So are other operating expenses. So, EMU competes in two areas. Against other "mid-majors," especially their compatriots in the Mid-American Conference (MAC), they are relatively similarly situated, with the 10 institutions reporting budget data between $20 million and $14 million. When Eastern competes with Michigan State and Maryland, as they did in football in 2008, they are going against programs with operating budgets for the sport of $14 million and $9 million, respectively, as opposed to $4.5 million at EMU. It is a challenge similar to what Eastern Michigan University would have in competing for students or faculty with Michigan State—the two simply do not have the same resources at their disposal.

A second category of subsidized programs is smaller Division I institutions that have budgets as small as $3 million, along with Division II and III athletics departments that have expenditures of even less than that. The University of Maryland, Eastern Shore is among the smallest Division I programs, not competing in football and operating in many ways like a Division II institution (or Division III one, except that it provides athletics scholarships). Eastern Shore receives $1.2 million of its budget from state support, $1 million from student fees, and $350,000 in direct institutional support—nearly all of its budget. The program generates its other revenue essentially from $150,000 each from ticket sales for men's and women's basketball and $150,000 from NCAA distributions (mostly for having a conference team compete in the tournament each year with an automatic bid). UMES spends about one-sixth of its budget on its basketball program, $500,000, and allocates $900,000 to student aid and $1.2 million to salaries (about one-half to coaches), and keeps travel costs to $350,000 and equipment and game expenses to $150,000 and $100,000, respectively. The key difference between UMES and the larger subsidized programs is in size. At Western Carolina, for instance, most of its $7 million budget comes from student fees ($2.5 million) and direct and indirect institutional support ($2.4 million)—and Eastern Michigan generates three-quarters of its $20 million budget from these sources.

Although receiving funding through institutional transfers provides a critical difference from the BCS conference schools, other aspects of how athletics programs in both sectors are organized are similar. Both are likely to have roughly similar organizational charts headed by an athletic director with several associate athletic directors or unit heads charged with areas such as academic support, administration, compliance, equipment, event management, facilities, finance and business, fund-raising, marketing and promotions, media relations, tickets, and training. There is also the coach in charge of each sport and the various assistant coaches. Larger programs have deeper staffing, with several people often assigned to each unit, while smaller programs may have only a single person involved with each. Again, picture the difference between the research administration or development offices at Michigan and UW-Milwaukee, both research universities. Also, whether they are revenue-generating or subsidized, all athletics programs are subject to NCAA oversight. As is typical in higher education (and especially in accreditation), institutions themselves, in combination with one another, regulate intercollegiate athletics. What is unusual in athletics is the degree of power and influence the NCAA has—far more than any accrediting agency could ever imagine holding. The NCAA, particularly over the past several decades, has developed a detailed set of rules essentially attempting to prevent corruption in the recruiting and retention of athletes—and the ability to enforce them through significant penalties on institutions found to be in violation.

The NCAA also requires that institutions exercise control over their athletics department. Typically, subsidized athletics programs are similar to other institutional units, including in financial matters. Revenue-generating programs tend to operate more autonomously within the university. Sometimes, the most apt comparison is to auxiliary units like housing or dining that are expected to operate without subsidy and perhaps even produce some revenue for the institution to capture, but the largest athletics programs are more separate than that, connected to institutions more tangentially. There are practical and symbolic connections to the university. For instance, athletic directors report to presidents; there are faculty representatives on athletic association boards; and athletes must be properly admitted and enrolled as students, but athletic associations have considerably more flexibility, including in their financial and other operations. (Just one example: football coaches commonly hire their sons or brothers to be assistants—finding an example of a dean or department chair doing the same would be unusual.) Perhaps Geiger has it right when he suggests that both athletics and academic medical centers occupy separate fiscal and organizational compartments within the university.[18]

There is an interesting analogy here with faculty at elite institutions or those with independent resource bases. Institutions have much less leverage over these faculty than, say, those at a comprehensive institution, community college, or less selective liberal arts college.[19] In a statement that could be applied rather equally to higher education generally, the Knight Commission framed the situation in Division I athletics: "competitive balance is crumbling as the gap between the haves and the have-nots widens. While a relative few programs flourish, many others have chosen to discontinue sports other than football or basketball to make ends meet. Even some of the "haves" react to intense financial pressure to control costs by dropping so-called minor sports."[20] Oriard contends that occasional forays into the Bowl Championship Series, the four leading bowl games plus the annual national championship context, by non-BCS institutions is misleading: "The occasional upset and rogue title contender shouldn't obscure the fact that mostly, the same schools contend for the championship each year . . . These outliers break through one at a time, then promptly lose their coach to a major BCS power temporarily fallen on hard times (or lose their star quarterback to the NFL) and once again take their proper places in the food chain."[21]

Another potential similarity between athletics programs of both types is their sensitivity to economic declines. Subsidized programs, like other departments with a university or college, are not immune to institutional budget cuts.[22] So, with a 10 percent cut in a state-appropriated budget across a university, there is likely to be a significant cut in athletics. If nothing else, athletic programs are commonly subject to the argument that funds expended there would be better allocated to academic pursuits[23]—and these only promise to become louder as budgets become more challenging.

At private institutions also, including the most elite, budget problems can extend into athletics. In January 2009, Stanford University suspended $1.3 billion worth of construction projects, having already cut executive pay, frozen most salaries, and laid off staff, in response to a 20–30 percent decline in its endowment, which was $17 billion in 2008. For 2010, the institution projects a $63 million cut in its $800 million general-funds budget, which covers most faculty and staff salaries, core administrative operations, and other nonresearch expenses.[24] Stanford, unusually, has built an endowment for athletics of over $500 million, yielding almost $18 million in operating revenue from it in fiscal year 2007. (By way of context, the University of Oregon is ranked 150th in the 2007 NACUBO endowment report, at $456 million.)[25] The decline in the value of the endowment, as well as likely cuts in the annual $9.5 million subsidy Stanford athletics receives from the university, will likely prompt cuts in staff and perhaps sports, Cross suggests.[26]

There is also some difference across intercollegiate athletics in the number of sports offered within an overall program, although not necessarily between revenue-generating and subsidized programs. The Ivy League, which generates minimal revenue and thus subsidizes athletics, sponsors competition in 33 sports, while the Big Ten has 25 championships—with Harvard fielding 41 teams and Ohio State 39 (20 for women and 19 for men) to lead their respective conferences. The SEC, the conference that generates the most net revenue from football, has only 17 sports, avoiding expensive teams such as ice hockey and rowing. So, the net revenue from football of $40 million or so at Georgia is explained, in part, by spreading its resources among fewer non-revenue-producing sports. Ohio State makes as much as Georgia on football, but has twice as many sports to fund.[27] Also, the Mid-American Conference, which includes Eastern Michigan, sponsors nearly as many championships, 23, as does the Big Ten, even thought budgets in the MAC are one-half or one-third of the other conference. So, MAC schools need to budget more carefully, paying head coaches less, for instance—especially in football—and watching travel expenses.

Why do institutions subsidize athletics programs? Universities and colleges commonly subsidize activities associated with the personal development of their students—and athletics, apart from what draws significant external interest, fits neatly here. So, volleyball and tennis at a BCS institution and football in Division II and III (and even some of Division I) are more about the students participating than the enterprise itself. (Remember: almost all participation in intercollegiate athletics occurs here—Alabama football and North Carolina basketball are essentially outliers when looking at the whole of college sports.) Subsidies here are as reasonable as they are for a student leadership initiative, study abroad programs, or even a fitness center. The same is not true of football and men's basketball (and occasionally selected other sports) in most of Division I. These sports are more commercial and professional than they are participatory and amateur. For instance, a coach in a so-called nonrevenue or Olympic sport at an institution could likely finish with a .500 record—winning as many games as he or she loses—over several years and retain his or her job, especially if his or her students were solid academically. In Division I football and men's basketball, a coach who graduated all of his players on time, sending several off to graduate or professional school or promising positions in business or public service, would eventually—and often quickly—be out of work if his win–loss record was even in the range of .500. So, decisions about college sports, including business decisions, depend upon whether a sport is commercial or participatory in nature.

The line here is not between revenue-generating and subsidized programs, but instead between programs that aspire to be revenue generating and then enjoy the perceived institutional benefits of having a prominent football or men's basketball program. Subsidizing programs, like the non-BCS institutions in the Football Bowl Subdivision, cannot be justified as furthering student development. Instead, it is universities investing as they do elsewhere in external relations, building the image and extending the reach of the institution.[28] Institutions are willing to take a loss on intercollegiate athletics in the hopes that they, too, will someday be able have the advantages associated with athletics prominence.[29] These include the ability to more readily connect with alumni and potential donors, having a more concrete national identity and higher profile among local constituents, and fitting more neatly within the popular conception of a major American university.[30] Several institutions have enhanced their commitment to athletics in search of such ends. Doing so is no different, of course, than the strategic direction of seemingly every moderately selective U.S. university or college, attempting to "move to the next level" of prestige through investments in attracting more accomplished students and notable faculty, as well as in facilities (often impressive and even luxurious ones) such as student residences, dining commons, fitness centers, and commercial districts. Therefore, when the most recent example, Western Kentucky, includes moving to FBS (Division I-A) football in its overall strategy to be more competitive with the University of Kentucky, it makes sense—nationally prominent athletics is part of being the type of institution that Kentucky is and Western wishes to become.[31]

The challenge here is that breaking into the revenue-producing group is particularly difficult, so institutions seeking to do so often commit to losses over decades. But there is psychological value in being an FBS program. The institutions in the Mid-American Conference are unlikely to ever break away from subsidies for athletics, significant ones at that, but none would likely want to no longer be grouped with the leading programs. The same is true with classifications of institutions. It is important to institutions to be within the research universities designation, say in the former Carnegie classifications, even though they may be doing a small fraction of the research of institutions at the top of the category. So, categories tend to expand to the point that they lose their meaning—Michigan and UW-Milwaukee are both research universities. But to criticize subsidies for athletics for aspirational ends misses an important point. Part of what makes American higher education so dynamic is that institutions are so ambitious—everyone is constantly seeking that next level of stature. Also, spectator sports are important in raising the profile of an institution and making it fit within the popular conception of a university. Developing a football program is not unlike the other tools that institutions are employing in positioning for greater standing.[32]

Also, there are occasional success stories of an athletics program emerging into prominence. In men's basketball, the University of Alabama at Birmingham (UAB) became a force in the 1980s, shortly after moving to Division I. There have also been smaller programs that have reached the Final Four, most recently George Mason in 2007. In football, South Florida entered the Big East conference before the 2005 season and briefly was number two in the polls during the 2007 season. Writing in the *New York Times Magazine,* Michael Sokolove noted the desire of USF to draw attention to itself by developing the markers of a traditional campus, including residential students—and football.[33] He also underscores the many possible downsides of spectator sports, including the need for institutional subsidies and the ever-present potential for embarrassment when corruption is uncovered or a prominent athlete runs afoul of the law. There is also the likely need to stretch admissions standards to accommodate recruited athletes in the spectator sports. The *Atlanta Journal Constitution* concluded that, at 54 public institutions, including the members of the BCS and other institutions that finished in the top 25 in football or men's basketball in 2007–08, football players had scored 220 points lower on the SAT than students on average (at Florida, the difference was 346, the highest nationally).[34] In addition, more likely than the on-field success at South Florida is the situation of the teams in the Sun Belt Conference, most of which "went Division I" as some point in the 1990s or 2000s. These teams play multiple guarantee games to generate needed revenue, are on television rarely and only in its more obscure corners, and struggle to fill even small (by Division I standards) stadiums—and still take a meaningful financial loss each year with their football programs. Nevertheless, these institutions get the psychological advantages of being in the same classification as the leading institutions nationally.

Finally, at smaller, tuition-driven colleges, there is a trend toward strategic investments in athletics, primarily to boost enrollments. These institutions, which regularly struggle to fill their first-year classes and combat a high attrition rate, have found that offering the opportunity to compete in intercollegiate athletics is a competitive advantage in attracting and retaining students. So, an institution with 800 students might have 100 football players and 300 or 400 athletes generally on campus. These institutions are already discounting their tuition, sometimes rather dramatically, so directing what they can frame as "partial scholarships" to athletes is not a stretch. The difference is stark between using athletics to fill a first-year class at a financially fragile institution and a nationally televised game on football Saturday from Gainesville, State College, Norman, or Eugene. But it underscores that the business of intercollegiate athletics occurs very much in two worlds, one revenue-generating where the athletics department can separate itself (including financially but also culturally in many ways) from the rest of the university, and the other subsidized in the same way most units are, including academic ones.

REVENUES AND EXPENDITURES

The revenue-generating programs have focused on enhancing revenues over the past several years, investing in stadium improvements, such as constructing luxury boxes and stadium clubs, and continuing to leverage broadcasting contracts and sponsorship possibilities. Schwartz notes that 10 college football programs generated $45 million in revenue in 2006—with none having done so just five years earlier.[35] Costs at these institutions have continued to increase—and most of these athletics programs spend each year what they produce in revenue. Salaries and benefits, especially for football coaches, continue to increase, as do investments in various other arms races, including in having the impressive facilities that those in athletics and across institutions perceive to be so connected to successful recruiting. Subsidized programs continue to be dependent upon their institutions for budgets—and increases have become rare given financial pressures across higher education. Orszag and Orszag offer the reminder that the average FCS (Division I-AA) program loses $408,000 per year in football and the average Division II program $149,000.[36] So, it is, once again, the relatively few larger programs that can generate revenue.

Institutions are also generating more revenue, even with declines in government funding and effective limits on their ability to increase tuition and fees, especially seeking new revenues at their peripheries through satellite academic programs and various auxiliary programs, as well as through enhanced fund-raising efforts, but they are also spending more, given not only increases in basic services like health care, technology, and energy, but also arms races in attracting the most accomplished students and noteworthy faculty, including through building impressive facilities.

Meanwhile, they are attempting to cut compensation by shifting more to part-time faculty and outsourcing what services they can.[37] Revenue-generating athletics programs are responding similarly, especially in producing what revenue they can and spending what they feel they must to remain competitive nationally.

Finally, athletics budgets have expanded markedly over the past two decades. Padilla and Baumer analyzed the budgets of the major 35 eastern athletics programs and concluded that the average revenue in the early 1990s was $10.4 million, with expenditures slightly higher, with a high of $18.3 million and low of $4.4 million.[38] Median revenue in 2006, according to Fulks, was closer to $35 million, with a high of over $100 million. Just in the past two years, revenue has increased markedly.[39] Fulks reports that the median FBS football program generated $10.6 million in 2006 revenues, an increase from $8.3 million two years earlier, with expenses of $8.5 million (up by $1 million from 2004).[40] In men's basketball, the median program generated $4 million and had $2.7 million in expenses, an increase from $3.2 million in revenue and $2.5 million in expenses from 2004. Women's basketball had median expenses of $1.5 million and revenue of less than $200,000 in 2006.[41]

REVENUES

The main sources of revenue in intercollegiate athletics are through ticket sales and charitable contributions, television and distributions, sponsorships and royalties, and fees and transfers. Ticket sales and charitable contributions are linked to spectator sports, with the latter often motivated by perks such as priority in purchasing tickets and determining their location. Television contracts with conferences yield another increasingly important source of revenue, and athletic programs receive annual payments from the NCAA and conferences from tournament revenue. Corporations are direct sponsors of athletics programs, and institutions earn royalties from merchandizing the name and image of their teams. Finally, subsidized programs receive transfers from student fees collected by institutions to support intercollegiate athletics and direct payments from institutions or governments.

Tickets and Contributions

Fulks reports that ticket sales and various contributions constitute over 60 percent of revenue generated by FBS programs, with tickets accounting for 28 percent of generated revenue and 23 percent of total revenue and contributions as 31 percent of generated and 25 percent of all revenue.[42] In the FCS, tickets sales are 5 percent on all revenues and fund-raising is 8 percent, a much less robust source of budgets.[43] Ohio State, as an example (once again), earns almost $30 million from football ticket sales, the highest nationally according to the *Indianapolis Star* data, with the other top 25 programs having sales above $10 million. But these figures fall off quickly, with the program ranked 50th selling only $4 million in tickets, the 70th program below $1 million, and the 100th program closer to $200,000. Overall, Ohio State again leads in ticket sales at $34 million, with the top 25 programs above $13.3 million, the top 50 programs above $6.5 million, and programs near 100 at around $500,000 per year. Most of the larger institutions also collect $1 million or so in guarantees, according to the *Star* data.[44]

The *Atlanta Journal-Constitution* estimates that each of the six Georgia football games every year produces $7 million, including over $2 million from tickets to 93,000-seat Sanford Stadium (60,000 season tickets, 18,000 student tickets, 10,000 tickets for visiting fans, and faculty, staff, and guest tickets), and another almost $4 million in ticket priority payments ($26 million total in fiscal year 2007). In addition, the 77 suites at the stadium earned $400,000 per game (or $3 million per year), and stadium concessions and advertising yielded $300,000 each.[45] That $42 million does not include the split with Florida of the revenue earned from the annual game in Jacksonville. Also, Georgia keeps football ticket prices relatively low, at around $40 each, choosing to generate revenues through ticket priority. Texas, in contrast, prices its tickets differently based on how desirable a game is, with the 2008 Florida Atlantic game at $65 and the Texas A&M game in Austin at $90.

In another example from a leading revenue-generating institution, Michigan nets $35 million annually in ticket revenue (after paying guarantees), about $30 million from football and the remainder about evenly from basketball and hockey. So, even without any luxury seating, which will open at Michigan Stadium in 2010, Michigan generates almost one-half of its $80 million budget through ticket sales alone. Therefore, playing as many home games as is possible is lucrative for larger programs, given their ability to generate ticket revenue. For instance, adding an eighth home game increased the value at LSU estimated by *Forbes* by 11 percent, to $76 million.[46] Also, adding seats to stadiums, especially premium ones, is attractive. It is one difference between revenue-generating and subsidized programs. The average stadium size in 2004 was almost 70,000 among the six major conferences and Notre Dame, with the other five conferences below 45,000; capacity averaged 88 percent in the former but only 55 percent in the latter.[47]

Like other larger programs, Georgia, Michigan, and Texas have a formula for determining what is called ticket priority, with larger cumulative and annual giving totals to athletics yielding initial access to tickets and then more desirable seats and various other perks, like access to conference championship and bowl game tickets. According to the 2006 *Indianapolis Star* data, Georgia, Virginia, and Florida each raised around $27 million in contributions, much of it associated with ticket priority, to lead the nation, with 27 programs with over $10 million in giving and the top 75 Division I programs with over $2 million. These figures have increased dramatically in the past decade at several institutions, including being up from the $3 million in nonendowment athletic donations Virginia raised as recently as 2000. There is even an art to knowing how to give to athletics. In 2008, it took over $10,000 in giving simply to earn the right to purchase Georgia football tickets for the first time.[48] Furthermore, 80 percent of these donations to Georgia are tax deductible. So, keeping its tax exempt status is critical for athletics departments. Alesia argues that if $714 million in donations to the 164 athletics programs in the *Indianapolis Star* survey were taxed, they would generate $100 million in federal revenue—and donations, if taxed, would likely decrease markedly.[49] Palaima suggests that this would not matter to many donors, noting luxury suites at Texas costing between $50,000 and $80,000 annually continue to be so popular as to be scarce.[50]

Apart from ticket priority, which is akin to an annual fund, athletics departments also have major and planning gifts programs that parallel those at universities and colleges generally, including in their increased emphases. There have also been massive gifts, such as the $250 million by T. Boone Pickens to Oklahoma State and the $100 million by Phil Knight to Oregon. Also, athletics departments nationally are seeking to endow coaching positions and athletes' scholarships, as Stanford has done so successfully. Georgia Tech, for instance, is seeking to endow 222 scholarships at $500,000 each (or $111 million total), a "full ride" costing $15,000 annually for an in-state student and twice that for out-of-state students.[51] As is common across higher education, athletics donors receive increasing levels of recognition—and, in athletics, direct perks, such as ticket priority—for contributing larger sums. There are questions about whether such donations distract from giving to academic pursuits, as well as about the influence gained by those making massive gifts. These questions are not unlike those common in higher education development generally.

In response to the potential to realize significant revenue through ticket sales and priority payments, institutions have made significant investments in stadiums through expansion and renovations. Schwartz reports that 16 of the 20 programs on the *Forbes* most valuable list have done so, with three others in the planning stage.[52] Premium seating has emerged over the past decade as an important revenue source. Texas, for instance, raised $12 million annually from its previous premier seating in 2006—before adding 44 additional luxury suites and 2,000 club seats in one end zone of Royal-Memorial Stadium in anticipation of the 2008 football season.[53] Michigan is adding 83 luxury and 3,200 club seats to its 110,000-seat stadium for the 2010 season at an estimated cost of $226 million—an expense it expects to recoup through added revenue. Even without these seats, Michigan football had an $85 million value and $36 million profit in 2006 (fourth behind Notre Dame, Texas, and Georgia) according to *Forbes*. Tennessee has added 10,000 seats and 78 suites to Neyland Stadium over the past decade. Indeed, just about every revenue-generating program has made some investment in adding premium seating, with many able to raise funds to help underwrite expenses. (Such gifts are fully tax deductable.)

Even sales on game days, including concessions and parking, are another related revenue source and part of the business of college sports. Wisconsin, for instance, earned $6.6 million in 2006, with the top 10 programs all over $2 million and the top 30 over $1 million.[54] Finally, prominent football programs contribute to the local economy through game days. The largest programs, such as Notre Dame and Texas, inject $10 million per game into the local county economy (with Arkansas, for instance, at $7.5 million), and Auburn home games are worth $50 million to rural Lee County, Alabama, each year.[55]

Television and Distributions

The larger programs also capture significant revenue by selling broadcast rights. The Big Ten launched its own cable television network in 2007, reaching 30 million homes and charging $1 per subscriber. The SEC went in a different direction. With the prospect of beginning an SEC network on the table, it entered into 15-year broadcast rights contracts with CBS for $55 million annually and ESPN for $150 million annually, with institutions able to negotiate their own local packages.[56] Florida, for instance, has its own deal with Sun Sports for 10 years and $100 million.[57] Several institutions can already attract significant fees from selling local media rights, led nationally by Alabama and Tennessee at around $7.5 million, with 13 institutions over $2.5 million and the top 30 all over about $1 million.[58]

Even without local rights, the proportion per institution of the overall SEC package exceeds the $9 million that Notre Dame realizes from its current contract with NBC to broadcast Fighting Irish football games. In

2007, the SEC shared $127 million among its 12 members (an increase from $16 million in 1990), with $51 million from television rights for regular-season football—a figure that will increase dramatically with the new contracts.[59] Writing on his blog for the *Orlando Sentinel,* Stevens argues that coverage of SEC events employing the Internet is likely to increase, and that smaller conferences such as Conference USA and the Sun Belt may find their leverage diminished in pursuing broadcasting deals, with their games shifted even more to the middle of the week or even to the Internet.[60] He also contends that because CBS and ESPN will only hold rights for home games, there will be less incentive for SEC teams to play road football or basketball games and more desire to pay even higher guarantees to attract opponents for contests at home.

The NCAA also has an impressive television contract, having signed a $6.2-billion, 11-year contract in 1999 with CBS to broadcast the annual Division I men's basketball tournament. The NCAA generates over 90 percent of its operating budget through the tournament, almost all through the television deal.[61] In 2010, the NCAA is scheduled to receive more than $600 million from the tournament.[62] The NCAA transfers much of the television money to member institutions, distributing $780,000 for each win in the tournament.[63] In 2002–03, the 62 BCS conference institutions received $124 million in NCAA distributions (and a similar amount in net income from football bowl games), while the other FBS conferences earned $6 million from football and $46 million from basketball.[64] Overall, the NCAA reported that it allocated over $420 million (69% of its budget) to Division I institutions in 2007–08, with 3 percent going to Division III and 4 percent to Division II.[65] Conferences tend to collect these funds and distribute them evenly among their members.

The football bowl games operate under a different model, one apart from the NCAA—a product of the 1984 U.S. Supreme Court decision deregulating college football broadcasting.[66] The Bowl Coalition Series, a partnership of the six largest conferences and Notre Dame established in 1996, arranges broadcast contracts for the four largest bowl games, plus the annual BCS championship game (with the Rose Bowl negotiating its own package with ABC-ESPN). The most recent contract, signed between the BCS and ABC-ESPN in late 2008, is worth $500 million over four years to broadcast the Orange, Fiesta, and Sugar Bowls and the BCS Championship Game. (The previous four-year package with Fox was worth $320 million and excluded the Rose Bowl.[67]) Each bowl game provides the competing teams with a payout, which was $17 million per team for the five BCS bowls in 2008. For the 29 other bowls, payouts range from $4.5 million for the Capital One Bowl and $3 million for the Cotton and Outback Bowls to less than $1 million for several games involving teams from the smaller FBS conferences, such as the GMAC Bowl in Mobile and the Armed Forces Bowl in Fort Worth. Each conference has agreements, called tie-ins, with certain bowls to send a representative each year. For instance, the SEC and Big Ten each send teams to the Capital One and Outback Bowls, who can choose from teams not in the BCS games.

Conferences like the Big Ten pool the payouts from all of its teams, distributing them evenly among all of the conference teams—about $2 million each after the participating teams take their travel expenses, usually $1 to $2 million, off of the top. Iowa and Purdue led the nation in distributions with over $15 million each in 2006, with the top 20, all members of BCS conferences, all over $10 million. The figures fall to around $2 million for institutions just in the top 60 such as Southern Mississippi.[68] Furthermore, the bowls require teams to sell a certain amount of tickets, which is generally easy for larger programs. For smaller programs participating in smaller bowls, much of the payout is often consumed by the delegation traveling to the game and other expenses, such that they can lose money on the enterprise. Still, there has been an explosion in the number of bowl games, as smaller programs are seeking a way in and larger programs and conferences want to ensure their annual revenue and exposure. In 1996, there were only 18 bowl games.[69] In another aspect of the business of college sports, each of the bowl games has a corporate sponsor.

Television revenue and bowl distributions were an important cause in the significant realignment in conference affiliations that occurred about a decade ago, when the ACC added three teams from the Big East. Another factor was the ability to add a conference championship game, which required a 12-team conference under NCAA rules. So, as an SEC member, Georgia earned $1 million from the annual football playoff game in Atlanta, in addition to $2 million in bowl revenue, $1.5 million in men's basketball tournament distributions, and $4 million from television.[70] The Georgia radio contract was worth $3 million. Michigan makes about $10.5 million in distributions, about $6 million from television contracts for football and basketball, $2 million in bowl games, and $2.5 million in NCAA distributions. Sandbrook notes that television ratings have been higher most years, over 35 percent in 2003 and 2004, for the BCS championship game than for the final game of the NCAA men's basketball tournament (although advertising rates remain higher for the tournament game).[71]

Finally, there is also a robust competition among football and men's basketball programs, particularly among those outside of the elite, to secure nationally televised games. There is now a televised college basketball game each day of the week, with ESPN alone typically broadcasting several games per night across its four channels and teams willing to play at unusual times to accommodate television. In college football, not only are there games broadcast from noon until well after midnight on Saturday, but also those other than the traditional powers have shown a willingness to play on Thursdays and just about every other night of the week to gain national television exposure. For teams in the Mid-American, Conference USA, Sun Belt, Western Athletic, and Mountain West conferences, the choice is to play at an unusual time to get a once-a-season national audience or not be televised. Even for major conference teams, like Louisville in the Big East, weekday games have become a staple—the only way they can squeeze past traditional powers to get national notice. Also, ESPN and the other networks commonly broker made-for-television nonconference games. Television also has a role in the increase in bowl games—each of which is broadcast, most by ABC-ESPN—from 18 in 1991, to 25 in 2001, to 35 by 2008.[72]

Sponsorship and Royalties

Another source of revenues comes from relationships between athletics programs and corporations. Michigan led all programs with almost $10 million in what the *Indianapolis Star* terms advertisements, with the top 30 programs all over $2.5 million and the top 55 programs over $1 million.[73] In 2007, Michigan and Adidas signed a deal worth $7.5 million annually, Michigan having been with Nike since entering a path-breaking $1 million per year agreement in 1994. So, the present $10 million figure at Michigan will increase in subsequent years. As another example, Pepsi is in its third year of a 10-year, $27-million sponsorship deal with the University of Florida.[74] Institutions are also increasingly selling the naming rights to their stadiums. Louisville recently opened Papa John's Cardinal Stadium, Maryland basketball now plays in the Comcast Center, and Minnesota is building the TCF Bank Stadium to bring Gopher football games back on campus. Doing so is certainly consistent with the trend of selling bowl game name sponsorships to corporations. (The NCAA does not allow advertising in its tournament venues, but does sell official sponsorships that firms can identify during commercials during broadcasts.) Finally, another source of revenue is royalty income from merchandising. Such income to the University of Texas athletics program doubled to $8 million following their 2005 football national championship.[75]

SUBSIDIES

Among the 166 programs in the *Indianapolis Star* survey, 138 collected student fees. James Madison, an FCS institution, collects the most, at almost $18 million, with Central Florida next, at nearly $12 million. Student fees for intercollegiate athletics are as high as almost $1,200 annually at James Madison, and the average student at Miami of Ohio pays $635, with Ball State at $412.[76] (Even with the subsidy, JMU cut 10 sports in 2007.) The top 25 programs are all members of the FCS or non-BCS institutions, with the exception of Maryland, which receives $7.2 million and ranks 16th. Even financial powerhouses like Georgia collect $3 million in fees, ranking 65th. For football alone, Florida International collects $3.7 million in student fees, with Akron and Miami of Ohio approaching $3 million.

There are several other sources of subsidies. Seventeen institutions receive over $1 million in government support, led by Massachusetts at $7.5 million and UNLV at $5.4 million, with only 27 institutions, mostly FCS institutions, receiving more than $100,000 in such aid.[77] As for direct institutional transfers, Rutgers leads the country at $14.6 million, with the top 25 receiving over $4.5 million. Most of these are FCS institutions, like Rhode Island and Maine at around $7 million, but some are FBS programs and even BCS conference schools, such as Minnesota at $7.5 million to rank seventh. One hundred eight institutions received over $1 million, according to the *Indianapolis Star* data, with only 25 of 166 programs not having any direct transfer from the institution, many of these among the leading revenue-generating programs. Thirty-two programs received indirect support from institutions of over $1 million, led by Tennessee at $5.2 million, with a mix of subsidized and revenue-generating programs.

Transfers, including student fees, have commonly been omitted in various reports, just as capital expenditures and long-term bonded debt have also not always been captured. In a report to the NCAA calling for the new data-reporting requirements, a panel of presidents underscored as problematic the increased importance of "allocated funds," defined as those coming from the institution, student fees, or governments.[78] The most recent NCAA data now better captures allocated (internal) and generated (external) revenue. With allocated revenue discounted, Fulks reports, only 19 FBS athletics programs were in the black in the 2006 fiscal year, averaging $4.3 million—and the other 100 Division I programs had a median deficit of $8.9 million, the gap between the "haves" and others having grown by $2 million from the 2004 numbers. In the FCS, generated revenues are only 27 percent of all revenues.[79]

Finally, endowment income is important, with Georgia Tech reporting $9.4 million to lead the 166 public institutions in the *Indianapolis Star* survey, with the top 10 over $2 million and 28 institutions over $1 million.

EXPENDITURES

According to reports commissioned by the NCAA, expenditures on athletics represented 3.8 percent of total higher education spending at FBS institutions in 2003 (up from 3.3% in 2001);[80] resources became increasingly inequitable between leading and other athletics programs in the 1990s when looking at football and men's basketball; and there was a reasonable amount of movement by programs in rankings of revenues and expenditures over the period.[81] Despite the increase in athletics spending, Orszag and Orszag conclude that: "operating athletic expenditures in the aggregate are a relatively small share of total higher education spending for Division I-A [FBS] schools."[82] Nevertheless, expenditures have increased steadily across athletics, exceeding increases in revenues in the Football Bowl Subdivision.[83] In the FCS, the challenge is even more acute, with negative net-generated revenue at $7.1 million in 2006, worsening from $6.2 million and $5.9 million in the two previous years, with no institution reporting positive net-generated revenue. Nonfootball Division I program medians were similar to the FCS, with a median net loss of $6.6 million. The average expense per athlete in the FBS is $66,000, compared to $23,000 in the FCS and $29,000 at the nonfootball Division I institutions.[84]

Salaries and Benefits

Fulks reports that salaries and grants-in-aid marked two of the largest growth areas in spending. The top 50 programs spent over $5 million in coaches' salaries, with Ohio State, Texas, Tennessee, and Texas A&M all over $10 million and the top 25 over $7 million.[85] Salaries in the FBS accounted for 32 percent of total expenditures in 2006, with that divided roughly between compensation for coaches and compensation for others in athletics.[86] The median salary for FBS head football coaches increased by 47 percent in the two years before 2006—from $582,000 to $856,000 annually—with men's basketball increasing by 15 percent to $612,000, and women's basketball increasing from $202,000 to $242,000. Fulks concludes that these increases were fairly consistent across program types.[87] The median FBS institution spent an additional $1.5 million on salaries and benefits for assistant coaches in 2004, an increase of 23 percent since 2004. These increases in spending are market-driven, so when one institution decides to raise the ceiling on what it is willing to pay to attract or retain a coach, other institutions are compelled to follow or risk falling behind. For instance, with Tennessee agreeing to pay NFL assistant Monte Kiffin $1.2 million to be an assistant coach under his son, the market for such assistants has entered a new era.

The American Association of University Professors compared football head coaches' salaries with those of full professors and presidents, noting the average full professor makes $102,000 and the average president makes $417,000, while the average of 107 of 119 Football Bowl Subdivision coaches makes $918,000, or 9.4 times the professors and 2.4 times the presidents.[88] At Oklahoma, where Bob Stoops made $3.5 million annually, the highest salary nationally, the ratio was 36:1 between the coach and faculty. At Miami of Ohio, the ratio was lowest, with the head football coach making 1.5 times the average of the full professors and essentially the same as the president. Alabama attracted Nick Saban from the Miami Dolphins of the NFL with a $4 million average annual contract—the largest in college football (but still less by about $500,000 than he was making in Miami).[89]

USA Today compiled a database of FBS football coaches' salaries based on data current through late 2006.[90] Of Stoops's $3.5 million in total compensation was a $950,000 base, $2.5 million in other income, and $745,000 in possible bonuses. Totaling over $2 million were the coaches at Iowa, Southern California, Texas, Auburn, Tennessee, Ohio State, Texas A&M, and Virginia Tech. Several coaches who were soon fired for poor performance, such as John L. Smith of Michigan State, Bill Callahan of Nebraska, and Mike Shula of Alabama, made the top 20 in salary (more than $1.5 million). Others, such as Florida head coach Urban Meyer, who was just in the top 20, would soon enjoy massive increases based on success in the BCS championship game. Still others, like Kirk Ferenz of Iowa, second in the survey at almost $3 million, were rewarded for early success that has not been repeated. Coaches in the smaller conferences like the Mid American and Sun Belt were more likely to make in the $200,000 range, with the median for those institutions included in the survey around $1 million.

The arms race in salaries is not limited to football. Writing in the *New York Times,* Rhoden describes how the University of Tennessee is doing "whatever it takes" to retain Bruce Pearl, the basketball coach who quickly thrust the Volunteers into national prominence, signing him for six seasons at an annual average of $2.3 million—an increase of $1 million from the previous year.[91] Doing so is a preventive measure, discouraging him from moving to another program, such as Indiana, which hired the Marquette coach, Tom Crean, as Tennessee was negotiating with Pearl. Like other high-salary coaches, Pearl draws his compensation from a variety of sources. His new package is a combination of annual salary, including a base salary of $350,000, $500,000 for media commitments, a $500,000 equipment fee, and a $250,000 endorsement fee, and various bonuses, including some based on performance, such as $100,000 for appearing in a final four or $250,000 for winning a national championship.[92]

Tennessee can justify the new contract based on a spike in revenue coinciding with the Vols finishing 31–5 in 2007–08, winning their first outright SEC title since 1967, and reaching the NCAA tournament regional round (the sweet 16) for the second consecutive year. For instance, average crowds for men's games have increased from 13,000 to 20,000, with concessions revenue increasing from $200,000 to $1.1 million over four years. Moreover, Rhoden reports, before it hired Pearl from the University of Wisconsin, Milwaukee, Tennessee had planned to renovate Thompson-Boling Arena, paying for the work by adding 26 luxury suites. It also planned to construct a basketball practice facility. As Pearl arrived, Tennessee had sold five of the suites and had $2 million pledged for the facility. With the men's basketball team's rapid emergence as a national power, including reaching the top spot in the polls for a week in late February 2008, not only were the remaining suites quickly sold, but Tennessee also added 12 more, and the funds pledged for the practice facility increased to $24 million.[93]

Finally, when Stoops or Pearl is fired, as most coaches one day are, their contracts will likely include a buyout, sometimes of several million dollars, to compensate for years left on the agreement. These buyouts are another expense associated with running an athletic program, particularly a larger one.

Administration and Operations

There are several administrative and operational expenses associated with an athletic program. Grants-in-aid to athletes were 16 percent of total expenditures in the FBS in 2006, according to NCAA data.[94] Both Michigan and Ohio State spent over $10.5 million to lead public institutions in spending on athletics student aid, with those programs ranking between 5th and 73rd in spending between $8 and $4 million and even the smallest programs spending over $1 million.

Tutoring is also an increasing expense for athletics programs, the Associated Press found in a survey of the BCS institutions.[95] For instance, the University of Mississippi retains 14 full-time tutors dedicated to student-athletes; larger programs are spending upwards of $2 million per year on academic support; and program after program is constructing an academic support facility for athletics, with Mississippi State spending $10 million and South Carolina planning to spend $13 million. Critics of these programs point to equity concerns, as they are not available to all students, and suggest that they exacerbate the practice of clustering athletes in a preferred major where they are perceived to have the best opportunity for academic success. Oriard discusses the decided disadvantage that non-BCS conference institutions (and even some in the group) have in areas like academic support, citing the new $15 million academic support center at LSU and wondering how schools without the potential to generate excess revenue can compete.[96] He notes that all are subject to the same standard in the Academic Progress Rate (APR) legislation from the NCAA, which measures student-athletes maintaining their academic eligibility to compete and ultimately their retention, penalizing teams for falling below a certain threshold.

Furthermore, 10 programs had recruiting budgets of over $1 million, and the top 50 were over $500,000.[97] Wisconsin spent $6.3 million on team travel to lead the nation, with the top 10 programs all spending over $4 million and the top 55 programs over $2 million. A smaller program such as Ohio University, ranked 90th, spends $1 million. (The NCAA covers travel expenses for championships, providing a considerable cost saving, especially for smaller programs.) Thirty-four programs spent over $1 million in equipment, with seven schools over $2 million, led by Alabama at $4.8 million and Illinois at $2.9 million.[98] Twenty-one programs spend over $1 million on game expenses, with Georgia, Houston, and Connecticut over $2 million. Oregon State reported promotion expenses of over $5.6 million, with the top 17 public institutions over $2 million and the program ranked 42nd, Central Florida, at $1 million. Ohio State reported $26 million in facilities and maintenance expenses, with 14 programs over $10 million and 32 programs over $5 million. Facilities maintenance constitutes 14 percent of total expenses for athletics departments.[99] Other programs report expenditures for payments to institutions for administrative and facilities support, such as $5.2 million at Tennessee and $3.6 million at Binghamton, which has an otherwise modest athletic budget. Medical expenses are as high as $2.3 million at Ohio State and over $1 million at 11 institutions and over $500,000 at 36 programs.[100]

There is also an arms race not only related to stadiums and salaries, but also for other facilities. Capital expenditures in athletics increased 250 percent in the seven years prior to a 2001 Knight Commission report—and have clearly continued to increase in the 2000s.[101] Institutions are building practice facilities, such as the $30 million one recently completed at Georgia for basketball and gymnastics, as well as competition venues, as for softball and tennis.

Finally, offering one last expenditure issue, Thelin argues that needing to reach compliance with Title IX gender equity requirements has not precipitated athletic programs dropping men's nonrevenue sports, but that departments had long been doing so.[102] Also, women's programs, when added, are of relatively low cost, given disparities in budgets between them and parallel men's programs.

CONCLUDING THOUGHTS

Atwell argues that the fundamental challenge in intercollegiate athletics is that it is impossible to deemphasize given investments, both financial and emotional, in programs, but to professionalize them would require compensating athletes and paying taxes—and a divide in the athletics department between professional and other programs (which would perhaps have to be funded by the university budget).[103] Indeed, there is always the risk given that intercollegiate athletics are such a business that legislation would treat it like any other industry. In a December 2006 editorial in the *NCAA News*, I remind readers that the significant commercial and professional aspects of football as played at the most prominent level have existed since the beginning of the modern game nearly a century ago.[104] There is little really new about the corporate sponsorships, races to build impressive facilities that go well beyond function toward opulence, salaries for coaches far in excess of others on campus, and so on that define contemporary college football, but these commercial and professional traits have become increasingly conspicuous, with major donations to the athletic foundation required for access to good seats and television asserting ever more influence over scheduling, arranging games on practically every night of the week, particularly for institutions that do not receive significant exposure on Saturdays.

Such attributes connect college football as much with commerce as with higher education, and perhaps more so. Institutions have, by necessity and over time, exhibited great skill in framing football as amateur in character. After all, maintaining a plausible connection to the accepted missions of universities, including developing character in students through extracurricular activities, enables the enterprise itself. It is what allows college football, even with its commercial and professional nature, to fit within the university. As such, college football is deemed, like the rest of the university, to have value to society such that it is exempt from federal and local taxation. The present bowl system, as just one example of the business of college sports, with its prominent corporate connections and advantages for more prominent conferences and programs, risks both its traditional tax exemption and running afoul of the antitrust laws. Either result would lead to severe challenges for football, athletics departments, universities, and conferences alike.

Tax-exempt status is central to the significant and increasing reliance upon private donations of athletics programs—revenue often connected with priority football season ticket seating. Priority seating, when pursued aggressively by athletics departments, shades toward the commercial and away from the philanthropic intent on which tax benefits are founded.

Legislation or rulemaking abolishing or even curtailing the nonprofit tax exemption for revenue sports would not only require that athletics departments pay taxes, but would also remove the incentive under the tax code for those who make charitable gifts. Furthermore, as commercial activity increases and fund-raising becomes ever more important across institutions, particularly research universities, such a precedent could prove to be dangerous outside of college sports. Should universities be so brazen here, essentially flaunting significant corporate connections while claiming an exemption from taxation as amateurs?

The present bowl system is also questionable under antitrust laws, which apply to intercollegiate sports and weigh procompetitive benefits against anticompetitive effects when looking at monopolistic practices. Currently, there is token access for deserving teams from smaller conferences to a BCS slot, but the vast amount of revenue from the bowls as a whole goes to the six major conferences and ultimately the institutions within them (as well as Notre Dame). If challenged in court by a class of perceived Division I FBS outsiders, as was threatened a few years ago, the question would become whether the anticompetitive effects of the BCS system within the FBS, given its relative exclusivity, outweigh the procompetitive impacts. Legislation could have the same impact of applying the antitrust laws to the bowl system. The business of intercollegiate athletics, as expressed in the bowl system, could be treated as what it is.

ACKNOWLEDGMENT

Thank you to Dennis Kramer II, who, in his first act as a doctoral student at the Institute of Higher Education, impressively built the bibliography at the core of this chapter, doing so in record time.

NOTES

1. Carmen DeNavas-Walt, Bernadette D. Proctor, and Jessica C. Smith, "Income, Poverty, and Health Insurance Coverage in the United States: 2007," U.S. Census Bureau, 2008, http://www.census.gov.

2. John V. Lombardi, Elizabeth D. Capaldi, and Craig W. Abbey, "The Top American Research Universities: 2007 Annual Report," The Center for Measuring University Performance, 2007, http://mup.asu.edu.

3. Division II and III athletics programs are part of the overall budget of the institution, and students can receive athletics scholarships, within limits, in Division II, which is the main difference between Divisions II and III. The NCAA requires 16 sports in Division I, 12 in Division II, and 14 in Division III (five sports each for men and women and two each for

men and women). Some Division II and III institutions compete in Division I hockey (such as Wayne State and Clarkston, respectively) or lacrosse (such as Division III Johns Hopkins and Hobart). Finally, athletics programs at most community colleges are governed by the National Junior College Athletics Association, which has 436 members.

4. J. Michael Orszag and Peter R. Orszag, *Empirical Effects of Division II Intercollegiate Athletics* (Indianapolis, IN: National Collegiate Athletic Association/Competition Policy Associates, 2006).

5. NCAA, "Division III Facts and Figures," *NCAA Division III Management Council, Supplement No. 30* (2007), http://www.ncaa.org.

6. Indianapolis Star, "NCAA Financial Reports Database," *Indianapolis Star*, http://www2.indystar.com/NCAA_financial_reports (accessed November 1, 2008).

7. Among the BCS football conferences, there are 10 private institutions: Duke, Boston College, Miami, and Wake Forest (ACC); Syracuse (Big East); Northwestern (Big Ten); Baylor (Big Twelve); Stanford and Southern California (Pac Ten); and Vanderbilt (SEC). The *Indianapolis Star* does not include data from these schools or from Penn State, Pittsburgh, or Oklahoma. It also includes only about one-half of the smallest Division I institutions. The *Star* built its database from freedom-of-information requests for the academic year 2004–05 budget reports required to be submitted to the NCAA, collecting data from three-quarters of the 215 public Division I institutions.

8. It is important to remember that financial data related to intercollegiate athletics are somewhat imprecise, often not considering the full costs of capital expenditures, debt service, and various indirect program costs. Knight Commission on Intercollegiate Athletics, "A Call to Action: Reconnecting College Sports and Higher Education," John S. and James L. Knight Foundation, 2001, http://www.knightcomission.org, 17. Goff provides insight into various accounting challenges, including capturing in general university accounts revenue or expenditures associated with athletics, as well as difficulties in the true incremental cost of athletic scholarships to universities. See Brian Goff, "Effects of University Athletics on the University: A Review and Extension of Empirical Assessment," *Journal of Sports Management* 14 (2000): 85–104.

9. *Forbes* based its ranking on what the football programs contribute to: (1) the university (the value of contributions from football to the institution for academic purposes, including scholarship payments for football players); (2) the athletic department (the net profit generated by the football program ultimately retained by the department); (3) the conference (the distribution of bowl game revenue); and (4) the local community (incremental spending in the county during home-game weekends).

The magazine weighted these in declining order. Peter J. Schwartz, "The Most Valuable College Football Teams," *Forbes* November 20, 2007. http://www.forbes.com/2007/11/20/notre-dame-fooball-biz-sports-cx_ps_1120collegeball.html (accessed February 20, 2009).

10. Despite these impressive figures, professional teams are of much greater current value. In comparison, the value of franchises in the NBA ranged from the Knicks and Lakers at around $600 million to the 10 least valuable of the 30 league franchises in the $300 million range. See Kurt Badenhausen, Michael K. Ozanian, and Christina Settimi, "The Most Valuable Basketball Teams," *Forbes,* December 3, 2008, http://www.forbes.com/2008/12/03/business-basketball-nba-biz-sports-nba08-cz_kb_mo_cs_1203nba_land.html (accessed February 20, 2009). In the NFL, the range was $1.6 billion for the Cowboys and Redskins to around $900 million for the 12 least valuable of the 32 league franchises. See Kurt Badenhausen, Michael K. Ozanian, and Christina Settimi, "The Most Valuable Football Teams," *Forbes,* September 10, 2008. http://www.forbes.com/2008/09/10/nfl-team-valuations-biz-sports-nfl08_cz_kb_mo_0910nfl_land.html (accessed February 20, 2009). In professional baseball, it was from $1.3 billion for the Yankees, around $5 billion for the teams ranked from 6 through 13, and closer to $300 million for the 8 teams at the bottom of the 30-team league; see Kurt Badenhausen, Michael K. Ozanian, and Christina Settimi, "The Most Valuable Baseball Teams," *Forbes,* April 10, 2008. http://www.forbes.com/lists/2008/33/biz_baseball08_The-Business-Of-Baseball_Rank.html (accessed February 20, 2009). Manchester United had a greater current value than any franchise worldwide, at $1.8 million, with Real Madrid, Arsenal, and Liverpool also over $1 billion, and the top 14 franchises over $400 million in value; see Jack Gage and Paul Maidment, "The Most Valuable Soccer Teams," *Forbes,* April 30, 2008. http://www.forbes.com/2008/04/30/valuable-soccer-teams-biz-soccer08-cx_jg_pm_0430soccer_land.html (accessed February 20, 2009). There is also scholarly literature on the valuation of professional sports franchises, see Scott Rosner and Kenneth Shropshire, *The Business of Sports* (Boston: Jones and Bartlett, 2004); John E. Kane, "Sports Team Valuation and Venue Flexibility," in *The Handbook of Advanced Business Evaluation,* ed. Robert F. Reilly and Robert P. Schweihs (New York: McGraw-Hill, 1990), 367–96; and the economic impact of teams and stadiums on a community, see Ian Hudson, "The Use and Misuse of Economic Impact Analysis," *Journal of Sport and Social Issues* 25 (2001): 20–39; John Siegfried and Andrew Zimbalist, "The Economics of Sports Facilities and Their Communities," *Journal of Economic Perspectives* 14 (2000): 95–114; Roger G. Noll and Andrew Zimbalist, *Sports, Jobs, and Taxes: The Economic Impact of Sports Teams and Stadiums* (Washington, DC: Brookings Institution Press, 1997).

11. Schwartz, "The Most Valuable College Football Teams."
12. Ibid.
13. J. Douglas Toma, *Football U: Spectator Sports in the Life of the American University* (Ann Arbor: University of Michigan Press, 2003).
14. Only U-Conn produced in excess of $1 million in net revenue in women's basketball, at $1.5 million, and only three other institutions made more than $100,000 per year—and Tennessee $1.7 million in the red.
15. Mark Alesia, "Colleges Play, Public Pays $1 Billion: That's How Much Universities and Students Contributed to Athletic Departments Last Year," *Indianapolis Star,* March 30, 2006, A1.
16. Steve Megargee, "Guarantee Games Don't Always Go as Planned," Yahoo.com/Rivals.com, August 26, 2008. http://collegefootball.rivals.com (accessed February 20, 2009).
17. Indianapolis Star, *NCAA Financial Reports Database.*
18. Roger L. Geiger, "Review Essay: The Commercialization of the University," *American Journal of Education* 110 (2004): 389–99.
19. Sheila Slaughter and Gary Rhoades, *Academic Capitalism and the New Economy: Markets, State, and Higher Education* (Baltimore, MD: Johns Hopkins University Press, 2004); Robert Birnbaum, *How Colleges Work: The Cybernetics of Academic Organization and Leadership* (San Francisco: Jossey-Bass, 1988).
20. Knight Commission on Intercollegiate Athletics, *A Call to Action*, 17.
21. Michael Oriard, "Bowling for Dollars: Why College Football Is More Cutthroat and Competitive than the NFL," *Slate,* November 6, 2008, http://www.slate.com (accessed February 20, 2009).
22. Libby Sander, "As Athletics Officials Meet, Talk Keeps Turning to the Economy," *Chronicle of Higher Education,* January 16, 2009.
23. Alesia, "Colleges Play, Public Pays $1 Billion."
24. Lloyd M. Krieger, "Stanford Suspends $1.3 Billion in Construction Projects as Endowment Plunges," *San Jose Mercury News,* January 23, 2009, www.mercurynews.com (accessed February 20, 2009).
25. NACUBO, *2007 NACUBO Endowment Study* (Washington, DC: National Association of College and University Business Officers, 2008).
26. Michael Cross, "Stanford Budget Announcement Suggests Trouble on the Horizon," *Ultimate Sports Insider,* January 22, 2009, http://www.ultimatesportsinsider.com/2009/01/stanford-budget-announcement-suggests.html (accessed February 20, 2009). With $72 million in annual revenues and expenditures, Stanford has one of the largest athletics budgets nationally. The subsidy and endowment account for almost 40 percent of the Stanford athletics budget (with another $12 million in expendable gifts annually), with the remainder looking not unlike other Pac Ten programs.

See Stanford University, "Home of Champions: Stanford Athletics Annual Report, 06/07," 2007, 1-36, http://grfx.cstv.com/pho tos/schools/stan/genrel/auto_pdf/2007-Annual-Report.pdf.

27. Georgia offers 17 sports beyond football: baseball, basketball, cross-country, golf, swimming and diving, and tennis for men, and, for women, basketball, cross-country, equestrian, golf, gymnastics, soccer, softball, swimming and diving, tennis, track and field, and volleyball. Ohio State offers, additionally, for men: cheerleading, fencing, gymnastics, ice hockey, lacrosse, pistol, rifle, soccer, volleyball, and wrestling. For women, there are teams in: cheerleading, fencing, field hockey, ice hockey, lacrosse, pistol, rifle, rowing, and synchronized swimming.

28. Toma, *Football U*.

29. The concept of taking a loss is not entirely clear. Both Sheehan and Goff argue that athletics are more profitable than often portrayed—and there are significant intangible benefits also. Richard G. Sheehan, *Keeping Score: The Economics of Big-Time Sports* (South Bend, IN: Diamond Communications, 1996); Goff, "Effects of University Athletics on the University."

30. Toma, *Football U*. One recent study focusing on Louisiana State even found a link between athletics success—the 2005 national football championship—and more positive perceptions among Louisiana citizens, especially the less well-educated ones, about the academic quality of the institution. See Robert Kirby Goidel and John Maxwell Hamilton, "Strengthening Higher Education through Gridiron Success? Public Perceptions of the Impact of National Football Championships on Academic Quality," *Social Science Quarterly* 8, no. 4 (2006): 851–62. There is also a literature connecting athletics success with alumni giving, applications received, entering standardized test scores, and graduation rates, with some studies finding it matters and others concluding that it does not. For a synthesis of this research, see Robert H. Frank, *Challenging the Myth: A Review of the Links among College Athletic Success, Student Quality, and Donation* (Miami, FL: John S. and James L. Knight Foundation, 2004). http://www.knightfoundation.org/dotAsset/131763.pdf (accessed February 20, 2009).

31. J. Douglas Toma, "Positioning for Prestige in American Higher Education: Case Studies of Strategies at Four Public Institutions Toward 'Getting to the Next Level'" (paper presented at the Association for the Study of Higher Education annual meeting, Jacksonville, FL, November 5–8, 2008). A few institutions dropped Division I-A football in the 1990s, including Pacific, Cal State Fullerton, and Long Beach State, but institutions moving into the division since 1990 include Central Florida, Florida Atlantic, Florida International, and South Florida, as well as

Alabama-Birmingham, Arkansas State, Boise State, Buffalo, Idaho, Louisiana-Monroe, Louisiana-Lafayette, Marshall, Middle Tennessee, Nevada, Troy, and Western Kentucky.

32. There is a significant amount of literature attacking spectator sports in higher education as an affront to academic values. See, for example, William G. Bowen and Simon A. Levin, *Reclaiming the Game: College Sports and Educational Values* (Princeton, NJ: Princeton University Press, 2003); James Lawrence Shulman and William G. Bowen, *The Game of Life: College Sports and Educational Values* (Princeton, NJ: Princeton University Press, 2001); Murray A. Sperber, *Beer and Circus: How Big-Time College Sports is Crippling Undergraduate Education* (New York: Henry Holt, 2000); Andrew Zimbalist, *Unpaid Professionals: Commercialism and Conflict in Big-Time College Sports* (Princeton, NJ: Princeton University Press, 2001). There have also been prominent efforts to reform the excesses associated with the more commercial and professional side of college athletics, most recently by the Knight Commission on Intercollegiate Athletics. These have been somewhat successful in combating the exploitation of athletes and corruption in their recruitment and retention. But there has been little done to restrain spending and prevent athletic departments from operating as "independent subsidiaries of the university," although there have been successful initiatives to increase financial transparency. See Knight Commission on Intercollegiate Athletics, *Reports of the Knight Commission on Intercollegiate Athletics* (Miami, FL: John S. and James L. Knight Foundation, 1999). http://www.knightcommission.org/index.php?option=com_content&task=view&id=69 (accessed February 20, 2009).

33. Michael Sokolove, "Football Is a Sucker's Game," *New York Times Magazine,* December 22, 2002. http://www.nytimes.com/2002/12/22/magazine/football-is-a-sucker-s-game.html (accessed February 20, 2009).

34. Mike Knobler, "AJC Investigation: Many Athletes Lag Far Behind on SAT Scores," *Atlanta Journal-Constitution,* December 28, 2008. http://www.ajc.com/gwinnett/content/sports/stories/2008/12/28/acadmain_1228_3DOT.html?cxntlid=inform_artr (accessed February 20, 2009).

35. Schwartz, "The Most Valuable College Football Teams."

36. Orszag and Orszag, *Empirical Effects of Division II Intercollegiate Athletics.*

37. J. Douglas Toma, "Expanding Peripheral Activities, Increasing Accountability Demands, and Reconsidering Governance in U.S. Higher Education," *Higher Education Research and Development* 26 (2007): 57–72.

38. Arthur Padilla and David Baumer, "Big-time College Sports: Management and Economic Issues," *Journal of Sports and Social Issues* 18 (2004): 123–43. The *Chronicle of Higher Education* reported average Division I-A (the FBS) revenues in 1997, including institutional support,

of $17.7 million and a surplus of less than $500,000 including subsidies and a deficit of over $800,000 excluding institutional support. In Division I-AA (the FCS), without institutional support, revenues were $3 million with a deficit of almost $2 million, with Division II (with football) having revenues of $500,000 and deficits approaching $1 million. In each of the categories, expenditures increased at a greater rate than did revenues between 1995 and 1997. See Joshua Rolnick, "Finances of Big-time College Sports Take a Sharp Turn for the Worse: NCAA Study Finds That Expenditures Grew at a Faster Rate than Revenues," *Chronicle of Higher Education,* October 23, 1998, A59.

39. Daniel L. Fulks, "2004–06 NCAA Revenues and Expenses of Division I Intercollegiate Athletics Programs Report," National Collegiate Athletic Association. http://www.ncaapub lications.com/Uploads/ PDF/ NCAA_Revenues_Expenses.pdf798f201d-c 82a-4cb3-9b05-e845a3cf24 ec.pdf (accessed February 20, 2009).

40. Ibid.

41. In his biennial report, Fulks offers the advantage of reporting data for all 330 NCAA Division I teams, divided among FBS (119), FCS (118), and Division I without football (93). The disadvantage is that his conclusions report medians, which is problematic given the vast difference between the top and bottom institution in each group, although he does report deciles, providing a sense of the range of revenues and expenditures between and among programs. For instance, in the FBS, some programs have budgets in the $80 million range and others are closer to $10 million, according to the *Indianapolis Star* data. Fulks offers an even greater range. The median FBS institution in the Fulks data has a budget of around $39 million.

42. Ibid.

43. Ibid.

44. *Indianapolis Star,* NCAA Financial Reports Database.

45. Tim Tucker, "Game Day at UGA Rakes in $7 million," *Atlanta Journal-Constitution,* November 8, 2007. http://en.newspeg.com/Game-day-at-UGA-rakes-in-$7-million-4638211.html (accessed February 20, 2009).

46. Schwartz, "The Most Valuable College Football Teams."

47. John Sandbrook, "Division I Postseason Football: History and Status," Knight Commission on Intercollegiate Athletics, 2004, http://www.knightfoundation.org.

48. Lee Shearer, "Football Pays Off Big at UGA: Athletic Association Could Take in as Much as $82M," *Athens Banner-Herald,* September 1. 2008, http://www.onlineathens.com/stories/090108/foo_325963373.shtml (accessed February 20, 2009).

49. Alesia, "Colleges Play, Public Pays $1 Billion."

50. Thomas G. Palaima, "The Real Price of College Sports," *Chronicle of Higher Education* 53, no. 13 (2006): B-12. Sigelman and Bookheimer concluded over two decades ago that, while studies connecting winning in football with giving to annual funds are mixed, success on the field does appear to be the best predictor of contributions directly to athletics. See Lee Sigelman and Samuel Bookheimer, "Is It whether You Win or Lose? Voluntary Contributions to Big-time College Athletic Programs," *Social Science Quarterly* 64 (1983): 347–59. In studying elite institutions, Turner, Meserve, and Bowen find no connection between winning and general giving; see Sarah E. Turner, Lauren A. Meserve, and William G. Bowen, "Winning and Giving: Football Results and Alumni Giving at Selective Private Colleges and Universities," *Social Science Quarterly* 82 (2001): 812–26.

51. Georgia Tech, "Scholarship Endowment," Georgia Tech Athletic Association, 2009. http://www.development.gatech.edu/priorities-needs/assets/Athletics-Endowment.pdf (accessed February 20, 2009).

52. Schwartz, "The Most Valuable College Football Teams."

53. Ibid.

54. *Indianapolis Star*, NCAA Financial Reports Database.

55. Schwartz, "The Most Valuable College Football Teams."

56. In comparison, the television deal between ESPN-ABC and the Atlantic Coast Conference, renegotiated in 2004, is for $258 million and runs through 2010. See Tony Barnhart, "SEC, CBS Extend TV Deal to 2023," *Atlanta Journal-Constitution,* August 15, 2008, http://www.ajc.com/ajccars/content/shared/sports/stories/2008/08/FBC_SEC_CBS_0815_COX.html (accessed February 20, 2009). The NFL splits $4 billion in television revenue annually among its 32 franchises (Oriard, "Bowling for Dollars").

57. Tim Stevens, "Winners and Losers in SEC Television Deals," *Orlando Sentinel,* August 28, 2008. http://blogs.orlandosentinel.com/sports_college/2008/08/winners-and-los.html (accessed February 20, 2009).

58. *Indianapolis Star,* NCAA Financial Reports Database.

59. Barnhart, "SEC, CBS Extend TV Deal to 2023."

60. Stevens, "Winners and Losers in SEC television Deals."

61. Knight Commission on Intercollegiate Athletics, "A Call to Action."

62. Sandbrook, "Division I Postseason Football."

63. Knight Commission on Intercollegiate Athletics, "A Call to Action."

64. Sandbrook, "Division I Postseason Football."

65. NCAA, "2007–08 NCAA Budgeted Expenses," National Collegiate Athletic Association 2008, http://www.ncaa.org.

66. Ibid.

67. Diane Pucin, "ESPN and BCS Confirm Agreement on Four-Year Deal," *Los Angeles Times,* November 19, 2008, http://articles.latimes.com/2008/nov/19/sports/sp-espn19 (accessed February 20, 2009).
68. *Indianapolis Star,* NCAA Financial Reports Database.
69. Sandbrook, "Division I Postseason Football."
70. Shearer, "Football Pays Off Big at UGA."
71. Sandbrook, "Division I Postseason Football."
72. Knight Commission on Intercollegiate Athletics, *A Call to Action.*
73. *Indianapolis Star,* NCAA Financial Reports Database.
74. Schwartz, "The Most Valuable College Football Teams."
75. Ibid.
76. Alesia, "Colleges Play, Public Pays $1 Billion."
77. *Indianapolis Star,* NCAA Financial Reports Database.
78. NCAA, "The Second Century Imperatives: Presidential Leadership—Institutional Accountability," National Collegiate Athletic Association 2006, http://www.epi.elps.vt.edu/Perspectives/NCAAfinal2006.pdf, 1–63 (accessed February 20, 2009).
79. Fulks, "2004–06 NCAA Revenues and Expenses of Division I Intercollegiate Athletics Programs Report."
80. Fulks puts 2006 athletics spending at around 5 percent of total institutional spending at the median FBS university.
81. Orszag and Orszag, *Empirical Effects of Division II Intercollegiate Athletics*; see also Robert E. Litan, Jonathan M. Orszag, and Peter R. Orszag, *The Empirical Effects of Collegiate Athletics: An Interim Report* (Indianapolis, IN: National Collegiate Athletic Association/Sebago Associates, 2003). The reports could not confirm connections between expenditures and alumni giving or academic quality, but did conclude that spending does not increase net revenue or winning percentages.
82. Orszag and Orszag, *Empirical Effects of Division II Intercollegiate Athletics,* 3.
83. Fulks, "2004–06 NCAA Revenues and Expenses of Division I Intercollegiate Athletics Programs Report."
84. Ibid.
85. *Indianapolis Star,* NCAA Financial Reports Database.
86. Fulks, "2004–06 NCAA Revenues and Expenses of Division I Intercollegiate Athletics Programs Report."
87. Ibid.
88. American Association of University Professors, "Financial Inequality in Higher Education: The Annual Report of the Economic Status of the Profession, 2006–07," American Association of University Professors 2007, http://www.aaup.org/AAUP/comm/rep/Z/ecstat report2006-07/

survey2006-07.htm (accessed February 20, 2009). Averages here can be misleading, given the stratification in higher education. For instance, the salaries of full professors in the FBS study ranged from Duke, at over $136,000 to Marshall, at $63,000, and presidents varied from $768,000 at Southern California to Memphis at $228,000. Even Stoops's salary is contrasted with the Louisiana-Monroe coach making a $130,000 base. Also, faculty salaries increased only 5 percent in the decade before 2005–06, while presidents' salaries increased by 35 percent.

89. Schwartz, "The Most Valuable College Football Teams." The AAUP (2007) noted that the entire needs-based financial budget in the state of Alabama in 2004–05 was $3.35 million.

90. USA Today, *Compensation for Div. I-A College Football Coaches Database, USA Today,* http://www.usatoday.com/sports/graphics/coaches_contracts/flash.htm (accessed November 2, 2008).

91. William C. Rhoden, "A Coach's Value: Wins, Losses, Dollars Raised," *New York Times,* March 28, 2008, http://www.nytimes.com/2008/03/28/sports/ncaabasketball/28rhoden.html?fta=y (accessed February 20, 2009).

92. Associated Press, "Pearl Gets New Contract at Tennessee for Average of $2.3M," *USA Today,* July 2, 2008, http://www.usatoday.com/sports/college/mensbasketball/sec/2008-07-02-tennessee-pearl_N.htm (accessed February 20, 2009). Legendary women's coach Pat Summitt is scheduled to make $1.3 million under her present contract.

93. Rhoden, "A Coach's Value."

94. Fulks, "2004–06 NCAA Revenues and Expenses of Division I Intercollegiate Athletics Programs Report."

95. Associated Press, "Schools Spending Big Money to Help Athletes Reach Graduation," *Athens Banner Herald,* December 31, 2008, http://www.onlineathens.com/stories/010109/foo_372935023.shtml (accessed February 20, 2009).

96. Oriard, "Bowling for Dollars."

97. *Indianapolis Star,* NCAA Financial Reports Database.

98. Ibid.

99. Fulks, "2004–06 NCAA Revenues and Expenses of Division I Intercollegiate Athletics Programs Report."

100. *Indianapolis Star,* NCAA Financial Reports Database.

101. Budig argues that there is another arms race in the high schools, with some schools leveraging pride within communities and competitiveness among them to construct new facilities and attract and retain what are becoming celebrity coaches. See Gene A. Budig, "An Athletic Arms Race," *Phi Delta Kappan* 89 (2007): 283–84.

102. John R. Thelin, "Good Sports? Historical Perspective on the Political Economy of Intercollegiate Athletics in the Era of Title IX, 1972–1997," *Journal of Higher Education* 71 (2000): 391–410.

103. Robert Atwell, "The Only Way to Reform College Sports Is to Embrace Commercialism," *The Chronicle Review, Chronicle of Higher Education,* July 13, 2001, http://chronicle.com/article/The-Only-Way-to-Reform-Coll/36140/.

104. J. Douglas Toma, "Playoff Would Temper Taxation Concern," *NCAA News,* December 18, 2006, http://www.wwwncaa.com/wps/ncaa?key=/ncaa/ncaa/ncaa+news/ncaa+news+online/2006/editorial/playoff+would+temper+taxation+concern+-+12-18-06+ncaa+news (accessed December 18, 2006).

CHAPTER 11

College Rankings Reformed: The Case for a New Order in Higher Education

Kevin Carey

In August 2006, the news magazine *U.S. News & World Report* published new lists of "America's Best Colleges," as it has every summer since it launched its college and university rankings in 1983. If past editions are a measure, the magazine will sell millions of copies of the latest report to students and parents eager to find the best possible place to pursue a higher education in a world where economic opportunity is increasingly defined by the learning that students obtain beyond high school. Today, more than two-thirds of new high-school graduates go directly to college, compared to fewer than half in the early 1970s.

Many other ranking reports and often-bulky guides to college admissions, including those from *Barron's, Peterson's,* and the *Princeton Review*, crowd bookshelves and magazine racks. But *U.S. News* dominates the market for higher-education information. Applications and alumni donations rise and fall with the magazine's ratings, and many colleges and universities work assiduously to move up the *U.S. News* ranking ladders.

The *U.S. News* rankings have become the nation's *de facto* higher education accountability system—evaluating colleges and universities on a common scale and creating strong incentives for institutions to do things that raise their ratings.

But the *U.S. News* ranking system is deeply flawed. Instead of focusing on the fundamental issues of how well colleges and universities educate their students and how well they prepare them to be successful after college, the magazine's rankings are almost entirely a function of three factors: fame, wealth, and exclusivity. They directly or indirectly account for 95 percent of a school's ranking, as Table 11.1 reveals.

As a result, the influential rankings have led colleges and universities to focus their energies on becoming wealthier, more famous, and more exclusive, often at the expense of what matters most—educating their students well. College rankings have increasingly defined the terms of the marketplace in higher education and the message from the market is clear: wealth, fame, and exclusivity are what gets colleges and universities ahead today.

Gary Randsell, the president of Western Kentucky University (WKU), is well aware of that fact. While the lion's share of public attention to higher education is focused on elite colleges and major research universities, institutions like WKU—public, regional, masters-granting institutions—are actually far more representative of higher education today. Along with community colleges, the WKUs of the world are where most college students actually go to college.

By today's standards, Randsell has been an unusually successful president, rapidly growing WKU's applicant pool, enrollment and endowment, recruiting new faculty and building new university facilities. "I want nationally competitive faculty," he says. "I want nationally competitive students. I want facilities that are national or world-class in terms of technology. I want a campus that is second-to-none in beautification. You've got to compete, you've got to work hard, you've got to be doing things that continue to improve your quality, or you're going to get passed in a hurry in this business. . . . We're going to compete in that arms race and we're going to win."[1]

President Randsell's comments illustrate just how fiercely successful leaders will compete on whatever terms the marketplace demands—and they suggest how little the terms of today's marketplace have to do with how well students are taught, how much they learn, whether they graduate, and whether they succeed in their future lives.

Because today's rankings reward institutions for wealth, many college presidents are no longer national intellectual leaders but narrowly focused fund-raisers-in-chief. Because rankings reward institutions for their "scholarly" reputations, colleges recruit faculty who are distinguished in research even if their teaching skills are subpar. Because the current rankings reward colleges for selective admissions and high freshman SAT scores, more scholarships are going to wealthy, high-achieving applicants, instead of the lower-income students who need financial aid the most.

The failure of the *U.S. News* rankings to provide colleges with incentives to improve the quality of their teaching is one reason why studies have found that many American collegians aren't learning what they need

Table 11.1 Components of the *U.S. News & World Report* College Rankings

Measure	Percentage of Ranking	Measured Characteristic	Total
Peer assessment	25%	Fame	25%
Percentage of classes with fewer than 20 students	6%	Wealth	
Percentage of classes with more than 50 students	2%	Wealth	
Average faculty salary	7%	Wealth	
Percentage of professors with highest degree in field	3%	Wealth	30%
Student/faculty ratio	1%	Wealth	
Percentage of faculty who are full time	1%	Wealth	
Spending per student	10%	Wealth	
Percentage of students in top 10 percent of high school class	6%	Exclusivity	
Student SAT scores	7.5%	Exclusivity	
Acceptance rate	1.5%	Exclusivity	40%
Graduation rate	16%	Exclusivity	
Retention rate	4%	Exclusivity	
Alumni giving rate	5%	Exclusivity	
Graduation rate performance (predicted versus actual)	5%	Quality	5%

An analysis of the latest *U.S. News & World Report* college rankings shows that university scores are, directly or indirectly, almost entirely a function of three factors: fame, wealth, and exclusivity.

Forty percent of the rankings are based in various ways on exclusivity. While conventional wisdom is that colleges can drive up their *U.S. News* rankings by inducing

(Continued)

Table 11.1 Components of the *U.S. News & World Report* College Rankings (*Continued*)

Twenty-five percent of the *U.S. News* rankings are based on a survey of college presidents, provosts, and deans of admissions, who are asked to rate other institutions' academic programs on a scale from 1 to 5. How college leaders are supposed to accurately make such judgments about scores of competitors is unclear; most are challenged to get good information about their *own* institutions. Inevitably, they rely on past reputations, heavily influenced by previous *U.S. News* surveys. To the extent that judgments are based on firsthand knowledge, they tend to focus on scholarly or research reputations, not success in educating students. This is basically a self-reinforcing measure of fame and renown. As one college president said about the college he ranked first, "I don't know anything about [the college]. I've never been there. But they are at the top. So they must be good, right?"[3]

Thirty percent of the rankings are based directly or indirectly on wealth. Direct measures include spending per student; indirect measures include faculty salaries, class size, faculty credentials, and other things that cost money to buy.

many students to apply and then rejecting them, acceptance rates only make up 1.5 percent of the rankings. But items like average freshman SAT scores and the percentage of freshmen from the top 10 percent of their high school class serve a similar function, since those are the students the most exclusive institutions recruit and enroll. Graduation and retention rates seem at first like real measures of quality, but statistical analyses show that they're strongly correlated with other measures of exclusivity, like SAT scores.[4]

Five percent of the rankings are based on the percentage of alumni who give money, working mostly to the advantage of small, private, exclusive institutions with fewer, wealthier alumni to solicit for donations.* That leaves 5 percent for the one real quality measure in the mix—the difference between an institution's statistically *predicted* graduation rate, based on SAT scores and other factors, and its *actual* graduation rate.

Five percent for the only measure that speaks to how well institutions work to help their students succeed. And that measure is used only for national universities and liberal arts colleges—for Master's-granting universities and comprehensive colleges, *U.S. News* uses no quality measure at all.

---

*For example, 9 institutions were ranked by *U.S. News* among the top 50 national universities despite not ranking in the top 100 in terms of their alumni giving rates. Eight of nine were large, public universities.

Source: *America's Best Colleges: 2007 Edition*, U.S. News & World Report LP, 2006.

to know. In a recent report on college-student literacy, for example, the Washington, DC-based American Institutes for Research revealed that only 38 percent of graduating seniors could successfully perform tasks like comparing viewpoints in two newspaper editorials.[2]

What the *U.S. News* rankings do, in effect, is confirm the status of colleges and universities that by virtue of their prestige are valuable to students irrespective of the quality of the education they provide. Students could get a rotten education at Harvard and Yale and they would still be ahead of the game because Ivy League degrees have so much cachet.

But the vast majority of college students—almost 90 percent—don't attend selective colleges and universities. They attend institutions that don't have the status to open doors for their graduates on the basis of name alone. Instead, what matters to these students is the quality of the education that they receive.

Reinforcing the status of the nation's wealthiest, most famous, and most exclusive institutions has been lucrative for *U.S. News* and other organizations that rank colleges and universities. But they have not deliberately excluded measures that shed light on the quality of college teaching and learning. Rather, they exclude such measures because information that answers questions that would be most helpful to the most students—Where are students taught the best? Where do students learn the most? Where do students have the best chance of earning a degree? Where are students best prepared to succeed in their lives and careers?—simply hasn't been available.

Until now. New research and advances in technology in the last several years have led to a host of new metrics and data sources that together offer an unprecedented opportunity to measure how well colleges and universities are preparing their undergraduate students. The new measures provide information about a range of important factors like teaching quality, student learning, graduation rates, and success after college. Many of them are eye-opening, suggesting that existing rankings badly mislead students and parents about the "best" colleges and universities. Some institutions currently mired in the lower reaches of the *U.S. News* rankings show outstanding results, while some of the exclusive institutions so prized by striving students don't live up to their reputations for excellence.

The wealth of valuable new information provides the possibility of replacing existing college rankings with a vastly improved ranking system. This report explains what the new measures can show, how those measures can be combined into new college rankings, and why the new rankings would benefit both students and colleges.

The new rankings would give students and their parents far more useful information for choosing colleges. They would create strong incentives for colleges and universities to take steps to improve their undergraduate instruction and reward institutions that have excelled at that task. They would bring two-year institutions more fully into the mainstream conversation about higher education quality. And they would even help address the problem of rising college costs.

In the long run, higher education would greatly benefit from the new rankings. They would give colleges and universities fair terms under which to compete and excel. They would help justify new public investments in higher education. And they would create a more dynamic, efficient market by giving students the ability to pick and choose the institutions that will actually serve them best.

ATTENTION TO TEACHING

In 1998, Russ Edgerton saw an opportunity. Then the director of education programs for the Pew Charitable Trusts and a former president of the American Association for Higher Education, he called a meeting of some of the best minds in higher education to discuss the absence of information about the quality of undergraduate teaching in U.S. colleges. The gathering included people like Alexander (Sandy) Astin, director of the Higher Education Research Institute at UCLA, and Arthur Chickering, coauthor of the seminal publication, "Seven Principles for Good Practice in Undergraduate Education." They focused on one source of information—students themselves.

From that meeting came a survey, one that would ask students a wide range of questions designed to uncover the quality of undergraduate education at individual campuses. Indiana University, which was already working with a well-respected survey instrument called the "College Student Experiences Questionnaire," and which also housed a professional survey research unit, was chosen over a number of other competitors to administer what became known as the "National Survey of Student Engagement," or NSSE.

NSSE (pronounced "Nessie") was launched in 2000 to provide institutions with confidential data about how well they teach and engage their students. Students are given an 80-question survey about their college experiences focusing on the teaching practices and university environments that, research shows, usually lead to learning. Years of study have found that the more time and effort students spend researching papers, interacting with faculty, and studying with classmates, the more they learn.

To measure how much students are challenged academically, a sample of freshmen and seniors are asked about things like the number of books assigned, lengthy papers written, and time spent preparing for class.

Students are also asked about how much of their coursework is focused on synthesizing complex ideas and applying theories to practical problems. Other questions focus on "active and collaborative learning" (i.e., how often students ask questions in class, work with other students, and participate in community-based projects).

Because student-faculty interaction is a key element of effective teaching, students are asked how often their professors provide prompt feedback on performance and how many times they discuss ideas with faculty outside of class. NSSE also documents "enriching educational experiences," such as interaction with students of different economic, social and racial backgrounds, study abroad, and the availability of culminating senior experiences.

Institutions receive detailed reports comparing them to the average results at groups of peer institutions and regional competitors. Some groups of institutions have formed consortia to share results for research purposes. It is not an expensive enterprise: Web-based surveys are used to gather information from thousands of students per institution for as little as $1.50 a head.

Edgerton had originally wanted NSSE results to be public, to serve as an alternative to *U.S. News*'s rankings. But he also wanted NSSE to be broadly used and financially self-sustaining. That meant getting a lot of institutions to both agree to participate and pay for the privilege. Many were willing on one condition: the results would be kept confidential and not released to the public. Institutions didn't know how they would fare on the survey and were afraid of bad publicity. Said Peter Ewell, Vice President of the nonprofit National Center for Higher Education Management Systems and one of the main architects of NSSE: "People won't pay for the gun that shoots them in the head."[5]

NSSE quickly exceeded its creators' most optimistic projections. As NSSE staff worked to continuously refine and improve the survey, the number of institutions participating grew rapidly to more than 560 per year by 2006. Pew invested nearly $4 million in research and development and operational support in the initial years, but by 2003 NSSE was completely financially self-sufficient.

As Figure 11.1 shows, NSSE results vary significantly between institutions, and even more among different students within institutions. NSSE also confirmed the suspicions of Edgerton and others that many institutions simply don't ask as much of their students as they could. Thirty percent of students nationwide reported being assigned four or fewer books to read in their entire senior year, while half were assigned *zero* written papers of 20 pages or more. Half of all freshmen spend 10 or fewer hours per week doing homework and preparing for class.

Figure 11.1 Level of Student-Faculty Interaction: First-Year Students at 12 Liberal Arts Institutions

[Chart showing Student-Faculty Interaction Score (0–100) across 12 Liberal Arts Institutions, with 90th Percentile, 50th Percentile, and 10th Percentile Student Response lines.]

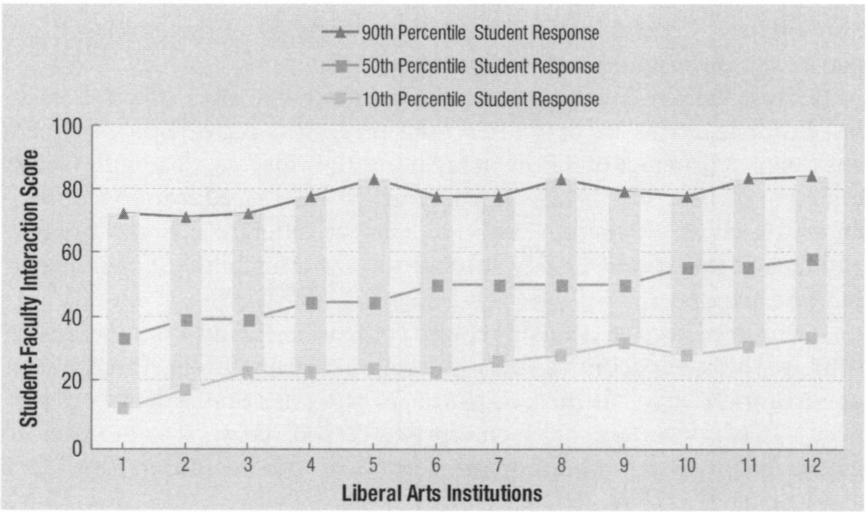

Source: National Survey of Student Engagement.

Figure 11.1 shows a group of liberal arts colleges. Each line shows the range of combined student responses to NSSE questions about student faculty-interaction at a single institution, converted to a 100-point scale. A score of 100 would represent the highest level of student-faculty interaction. The top of each bar shows the 90th percentile response, while the bottom shows the 10th percentile response. The middle mark shows the median response. The highest median score among these colleges is half again as large as the lowest, with an even larger spread *within* each college. Clearly, not all colleges are equally successful in engaging students.

NSSE data also show little or no relationship between having a respected brand name and teaching students well. The 2005 NSSE annual report found no statistically significant relationship between any of NSSE's benchmarks of effective educational practices and institutional selectivity, as measured by the popular *Barron's Guide to Colleges*. Teaching at big-name schools wasn't any better than at lesser-known colleges and universities. A similar comparison to the components of the *U.S. News* rankings found correlations for some elements but not others. The *U.S. News* peer evaluation of "academic reputation"—the single largest component of the rankings—had no correlation with whether an institution was successful or unsuccessful in promoting active learning, student-faculty interaction, or a supportive campus environment, the NSSE study found.

That suggests that some low-ranked institutions are being unfairly maligned, and some high-ranked schools don't deserve their peers' esteem. Consider Miles College in Alabama and Jackson State University in Mississippi, both historically black institutions. Both serve predominantly lower-income students who don't score high on the SAT and ACT and spend relatively low amounts of money per student. As a result, both languish in the *U.S. News* rankings: Jackson State is in the bottom tier among national research universities, while Miles College is the third tier (out of four) among Southern "Comprehensive" colleges, which are less prestigious than those in the "Liberal Arts" college category.

Most schools don't make their NSSE results public, but Miles and Jackson State do and, as Table 11.2 shows, both institutions score above—sometimes *far* above—the national average on a range of NSSE measures. Their students are more likely than their peers nationwide to be engaged with their peers, to receive prompt feedback from professors, to be assigned lengthy papers to write and to work on projects in the community. Conventional measures rank Miles and Jackson State below par; NSSE tells exactly the opposite story. But because NSSE results aren't public for most institutions, the data aren't part of existing rankings, and institutions like Miles and Jackson State don't get the credit they seemingly deserve.

While the number of institutions reporting NSSE data to the public is slowly increasing, there appears to be little chance that simply asking institutions to provide the data voluntarily will result in students having comprehensive, comparable information for all colleges and universities. Less than 15 percent of colleges ranked by *U.S. News* provided NSSE data to the magazine when asked, and *none* of the top-tier national universities released results. The newsmagazine *Maclean's,* which ranks Canada's 47 universities, recently used freedom of information requests to pry NSSE data out of Canadian public university hands (the results mirrored those reported by U.S. schools: many Canadian universities are doing a poor job of engaging students). But it would be an immense legal challenge to use this approach for the many hundreds of U.S. public universities, and private colleges wouldn't have to comply.

By 2006, NSSE had become an unqualified success, having worked with nearly 1,100 different institutions and more than 3 million students in the United States and Canada, staffed by 35 full- and part-time employees, and spawning related surveys for community colleges (CCSSE), faculty (FSSE), law schools (LSSSE), and high schools (HSSSE). After two years of field testing, a survey for beginning college students (BCSSE) will be

Table 11.2 Percentage of Students Who Answered "Very Often" When Asked by the National Survey of Student Engagement About College Experiences in 2004

	National Average	Miles College	Jackson State University
Asked questions in class or contributed to discussions	43%	65%	43%
Worked with classmates outside of class to prepare assignments	22%	39%	39%
Participated in a community-based project as part of a regular course	7%	25%	21%
Discussed ideas from readings or classes with faculty outside of class	8%	28%	18%
Received prompt feedback from faculty on academic performance	21%	36%	23%
Wrote 11 or more papers between 5 and 19 pages in length during the current school year	18%	26%	25%
Wrote five or more papers of 20 pages or more during the current school year	16%	41%	30%

Source: http://www.usnews.com/usnews/edu/college/rankings/ranknsse_brief.php.

launched in 2007. Concluded Edgerton in the introduction to the 2005 NSSE annual report:

> Colleges that become more selective are rewarded with rising rankings in *U.S. News*. But colleges that become more effective in contributing to student learning are largely ignored ... excellence in higher education is still largely defined as having resources others don't have—like students with high SAT scores and faculty with national reputations as scholars. Institutions that aspire to be "the best" are encouraged to become more exclusive. What America needs instead are colleges that are inclusive, and excellent, too. I do not believe that the traditional order will ever be overthrown. There will always be a race to be like Harvard, or what people perceive it to be. But the pursuit of prestige need not be the only game in town.

WHAT STUDENTS NEED TO KNOW AND BE ABLE TO DO

Making NSSE data available for all institutions would be a major advancement. But evidence of good teaching is still one step removed from evidence of actual student learning. K–12 schools attempt to measure learning with standardized tests in core subjects like reading and math. It might seem impossible to do the same in higher education. Elementary and secondary students are at least expected to complete similar courses, to learn the same rules of punctuation and applications of the Pythagorean Theorem. Undergraduate studies are far more diverse: Some students choose to spend four years immersed in Ovid, others in organic chemistry.

But there turns out to be an answer: Instead of testing discrete pieces of knowledge, test the high-order critical thinking, analysis, and communications skills that all college students should learn (and which employers value most). The Collegiate Learning Assessment (CLA), recently developed by a former subsidiary of the RAND Corporation called the Council for Aid to Education (CAE), does exactly that. Instead of filling in bubbles with a No. 2 pencil, students who take the CLA at hundreds of participating colleges and universities are writing lengthy essays, analyzing documents, and critiquing arguments. In making this process standardized and affordable, the CAE has met a goal that higher education has been reaching toward for the better part of a century.

The roots of this important work date back nearly eight decades to 1928. That year, the Carnegie Foundation for the Advancement of Teaching administered a comprehensive test of knowledge to 4,580 Pennsylvania college seniors. Today's seniors who complain about the length and difficulty of modern-day tests like the GRE and LSAT should be thankful they didn't matriculate in that era—the first version of the Pennsylvania test had 3,200 questions and lasted for 12 hours. Later versions were shorter but still covered English, math, foreign literature, fine arts, history, science, and social studies, including questions such as "True or false: The slow movements of Beethoven's symphonies are somewhat inferior to the rest of those compositions," and "[Which] of Corneille's plays, 1 *Polyeucte*, 2 *Horace*, 3 *Cinna*, 4 *Le Cid*, shows least the influence of classical restraint?"[6]

In the late 1930s, the designers of the Pennsylvania study went on to help found a new organization, ETS, where they developed what became the most widely used general test of college graduates: the GRE. ETS struggled to manage one of the main shortcomings of the Pennsylvania exam, the high cost of paying people to hand-score such a lengthy test. Their solution was to use new machine-scoring technology developed by a growing company called International Business Machines. By the 1950s, the GRE had evolved away from testing specific knowledge to become a test of general language and math abilities, leaving Beethoven and Corneille far behind.

The GRE thus did little to assess the advanced knowledge and higher-order thinking skills that are the hallmarks of higher education.

The University of Chicago worked to develop a better test in the 1950s and gave all undergraduates an exam with open-ended questions designed to assess the ability to apply principles to explain phenomena, interpret works of art, and interpret and synthesize information from texts. In the 1970s, ACT—maker of the college entrance exam of the same name—developed an assessment using a combination of multiple choice, short answer, essay, and oral response questions to assess students' ability to communicate, solve problems, and analyze information. Similar task-based assessments were piloted by the state of New Jersey in the 1970s and 1980s.

But these efforts ultimately foundered for the same reason ETS chose to partner with IBM—complicated tests required real people to administer and score, and thus were simply too expensive to administer widely. They couldn't compete with the massive economies of scale-driving tests scored by machines.

CAE has used the latest advances in technology to solve that cost/benefit dilemma. Like NSSE, the CLA is administered to a sample of freshmen and seniors at a given college or university. Students write lengthy analytic essays "making" or "breaking" a certain argument or proposition. They also tackle "performance tasks" that require analyzing a series of documents, synthesizing written and quantitative information, forming conclusions, and making recommendations.

The CLA is administered online, cutting administrative costs. And while the performance tasks are scored by trained personnel, the essays are scored by computer programs using holistic scoring rubrics. While some efforts to score essays with computers have been problematic, CAE has validated its system by having a sample of essays scored by both computers and humans and finding the two methods to be equally reliable and consistent.

The cost-reducing power of technology—combined with early financial backing from some of the same nonprofit foundations that supported NSSE—has made the CLA an attractive, relatively inexpensive source of new information about student learning. First piloted in the 2002–03 academic year, the test was given at 121 colleges and universities to more than 30,000 students in 2004–05. Double that number will participate in 2006. Like NSSE, the CLA doesn't cost very much: for $6,300 per institution, CAE will test enough students to yield statistically reliable results for the institution as a whole.

Thus, CAE has done for essays and complex performance tasks what ETS and IBM did for multiple choice tests half a century before—use technology to make test scoring cheap enough to make the test economically feasible for large numbers of colleges and universities.

The *U.S. News* rankings are partly based on student SAT and ACT scores, giving colleges and universities credit for how smart their students are when they arrive at college, not when they finish. The CLA, in contrast, compares the scores of seniors to those of freshmen and thus provides a "value-added" measure of performance, giving colleges credit for students' learning growth while they're actually enrolled at the institution. It also compares seniors' scores to the score statistically predicted by their performance on the SAT or ACT.

The circles on Figure 11.2 show CLA results for freshmen (in dark shade) and seniors (in light shade) at 45 institutions, plotted against students' ACT scores. The two measures are strongly correlated—as ACT scores rise, so do CLA scores. The light and dark blue lines show the statistically predicted relationship between the two. At some institutions, freshmen score *below* the predicted CLA score, but seniors score *above*, suggesting high value-added from the start of college to the finish. Other institutions have the opposite effect: freshmen start out ahead and finish behind. According to *U.S. News*, the highest-rated schools would all be on the right side of the chart, where ACT scores are highest. By the CLA's growth measure, some of the highest-rated colleges are on the *left* side of the chart, where ACT scores are *lowest*.

Figure 11.2 Freshman and Senior Scores on the Collegiate Learning Assessment (CLA) and the ACT at 45 Colleges and Universities

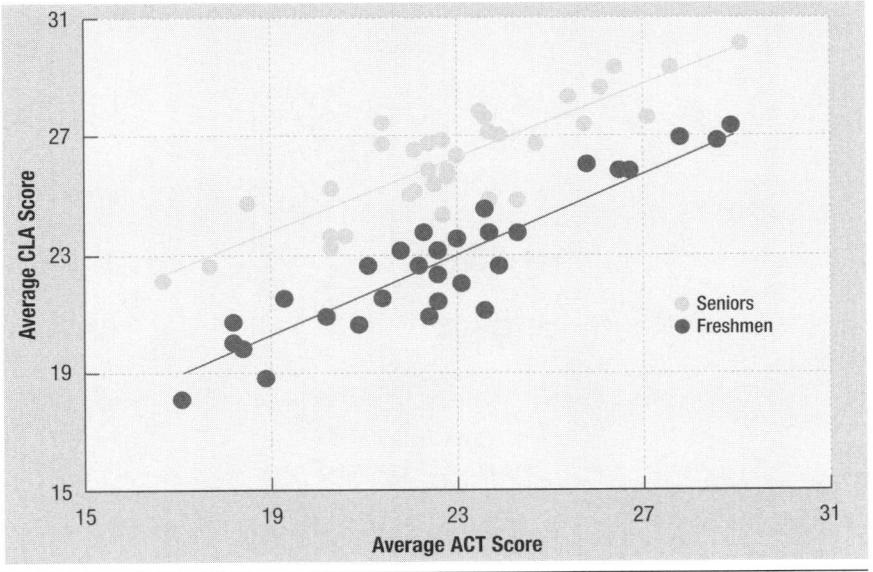

Source: Council on Aid to Education.

Most institutions haven't released their CLA results to the public—as with NSSE, they participate with a guarantee of confidentiality. The University of Texas system, however, has made its results known and they provide further evidence that traditional measures of higher education quality may be missing the mark.

Figure 11.3 shows the difference between senior scores on CLA performance tasks and their predicted score based on their ACT or SAT scores. The most highly ranked UT campus according to *U.S. News* is, by a wide margin, the flagship University of Texas at Austin. But UT–Austin is actually below average when it comes to senior scores on CLA performance tasks given where they were when they started college. The highest relative score was UT–San Antonio, ranked as a fourth (bottom) tier school by *U.S. News*. UT–Austin seniors did somewhat better on the CLA analytic writing task, but still fell below San Antonio, as well

Figure 11.3 Senior Scores Relative to "Expected" Scores on Collegiate Learning Assessment Performance Tasks at University of Texas Campuses

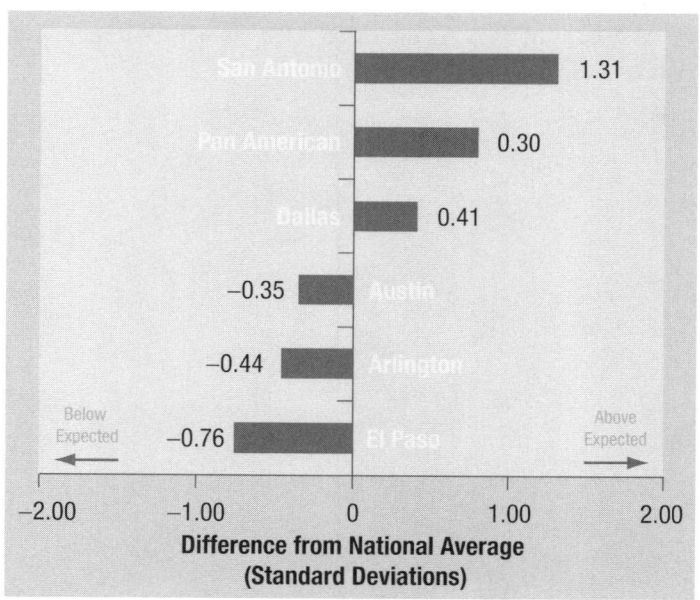

Source: The University of Texas System 2005–06 Accountability & Performance Report.

as UT–Pan American and UT–El Paso, also cellar-dwellers on the *U.S. News* list.

Figure 11.4 shows that the highest-scoring institution in terms of freshman-to-senior growth is UT–Permian Basin, which outscored all other UT campuses, as well as the large majority of tested institutions nationwide. Located in Odessa near the New Mexico border, UT–Permian Basin is an afterthought at best in the *U.S. News* rankings, tucked away on an alphabetical list of the fourth (bottom) tier of Master's-granting universities in the western United States. Ninety-five percent of applicants are accepted while only 2 percent of alumni donate money. The university's peer-determined "academic reputation" is 2.1 out of 5.0, one of the lowest of any college or university in the nation.

There is no chance of UT–Permian Basin ever distinguishing itself under the current rankings regime. But the CLA results suggest that if rankings and reputations were calculated in a different way—based on institutions'

Figure 11.4 Collegiate Learning Assessment Total "Value-Added" Difference Scores at University of Texas Campuses

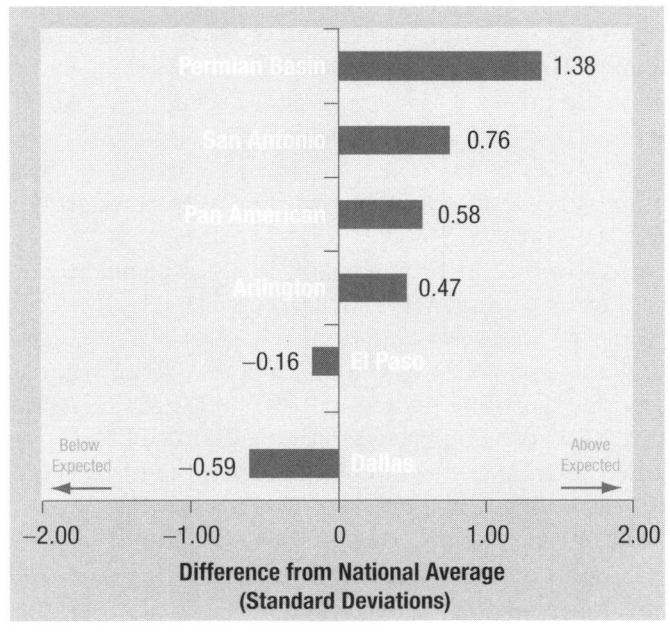

Source: The University of Texas System 2005–06 Accountability & Performance Report.

success in helping their students increase their knowledge and skills from their freshman to senior years—that could change.

ENGINEERING CHANGE

While the CLA measures the skills that are often most prized in the modern workforce, it doesn't test the advanced knowledge that college students are supposed to acquire as they specialize and major in specific fields. Fortunately, there are new developments in this area as well, in the form of "outcomes-based accreditation." Perhaps not surprisingly, the effort is being led by one of the more practical and quantitative of the academic disciplines: engineering.

Accreditation is intended to provide quality control for the public, ensuring that all colleges and academic programs adhere to certain minimum standards. But accreditation processes, like the *U.S. News* rankings, have historically been focused on measures of higher education inputs, such as curricular requirements and faculty credentials. By the late 1980s, many academic and industry leaders had concluded that the traditional process wasn't doing the job when it came to producing high-quality engineers.[7] New graduates had strong technical knowledge, but were lacking in areas that were becoming ever more important for modern corporations: creativity, design capacity, knowledge of manufacturing and quality processes, communication, and working in teams. The Accreditation Board for Engineering and Technology (ABET), moreover, was seen as a barrier to fixing this problem. ABET's evaluation criteria were lengthy and detailed, but mostly a matter of "bean counting" input measures. Innovative institutions were sanctioned instead of encouraged.

After criticism from the presidents of high profile institutions like the University of Michigan and MIT, ABET decided to change. With support from the National Science Foundation, it worked with representatives of industry and academia to develop a radically new set of criteria for judging engineering programs. Piloted in 1997 and made mandatory for all programs in 2001, the Engineering Criteria 2000 (EC2000) were much less concerned with input measures and much more focused on outcome measures of the skills and abilities of students.

Accredited programs assess their students' ability to apply math and science skills, solve problems, use modern engineering tools and work in teams. Some programs use "industry advisory councils" for this process, on the theory that the people with the best information about whether graduates have been prepared to succeed in the workforce are the employers who actually hire them. At Syracuse University, for example, companies told the program that their new engineers needed better writing and communication skills. As a result, the engineering school brought in a member of the university writing program to coinstruct the senior design course and provide students with a separate grade focused on their communication skills.[8]

Results from the first evaluation of EC2000, released in late 2005, found that students' self-evaluation of their skills increased significantly from 1994 (before the new process) to 2004.[9] When colleges and universities start to be evaluated based on student outcomes, student outcomes tend to improve.

Outcomes-based accreditation has also made inroads in teaching, led by the Teacher Education Accreditation Council (TEAC). Founded in 1997, TEAC-accredited programs gather concrete evidence about what their teacher candidates have actually learned. Programs rate themselves based on subject matter and pedagogy tests, licensure exam passage rates, hiring rates, surveys of alumni and employer satisfaction, and evidence of their graduates' success in the classroom. Some TEAC members have developed more novel measures, such as the extent to which local school superintendents waive interviews for recommended candidates from their program, or whether students in schools with higher densities of program graduates score better on state tests.[10]

ABET and TEAC show that gathering information about how well colleges teach advanced knowledge is more than possible; it's already being done. But like all accreditation processes, detailed results for individual programs aren't available to prospective students trying to choose a college. Most institutions choose to keep accreditation-based knowledge about how well they're educating their students, like NSSE and the CLA, to themselves.

STUDENTS' BEST WORK

A combination of CLA-type tests of higher-order thinking skills and ABET-type processes for gauging discipline-specific knowledge would be a huge leap forward in measuring college-student learning. But they still wouldn't measure everything. Some institutions use culminating senior theses and capstone projects to evaluate the sum of students' learning, their ability to combine research, analytic, and writing skills with a deep knowledge of particular subjects. This is widely regarded as a best practice in higher education.

Institutions can, at the very least, let the public know whether all students who attend will have the opportunity to have their work evaluated in this way. And some reformers believe colleges and universities could go further still. In a recent publication titled "Our Students' Best Work," the Association of American Colleges and Universities said:

> In the current climate it is not enough for an institution to assess its students in ways that are grounded in the curriculum; colleges and universities also must provide useful knowledge to the public about goals, standards, accountability practices, and the quality of student learning . . . Faculty members responsible for milestone and capstone assessments can be trained to judge the level of each student's achievement . . . A summary report to an accrediting body, a state official, or the general public can be prepared that aggregates the data across the institution . . . unlike tests based on quick responses to multiple-choice questions, these will be summaries of higher-order skills such as communication, analytic ability, and integration of knowledge, and will reflect meaningful education projects judged by professionals.

In other words, providing the public with the right kind of information about how well colleges educate students isn't impossible; it just has yet to be done.

LEARNING BY DEGREES

By 1989, Bill Bradley, the 6′5″ Basketball Hall of Famer and then-Democratic senator from New Jersey, had heard too many stories of big-time college sports programs racking up stellar win-loss records but abysmal graduation rates. So he spearheaded the "Student Right-To-Know Act," which required colleges and universities to report graduation rates, both for athletic programs and the student body as a whole. In doing so, Bradley created something that had never existed before: a standardized graduation rate measure for every college and university in the nation.

While the Act was passed in 1990, it took a while to bear fruit. Institutions asked for time to upgrade their data systems and get their procedures in place, so reporting wasn't made mandatory until 1996. Since institutions were given up to six years to graduate students, the rates couldn't be calculated until 2002. Some institutions reported late, and the statistics had to be cleaned up and verified, so the first complete data set wasn't released to the public until early 2004. Overall six-year rates had already been reported for many institutions by the NCAA, but this was the first time four-, five-, and six-year graduation rates were released for all institutions broken down by students' gender, race, and ethnicity.

Only 37 percent of students graduated in four years from the institution where they first enrolled. Extending the timeframe to six years brought the average up to 57 percent (typically another 8 to 10 percent transfer and graduate elsewhere). The new minority graduation rates were disturbing—the typical university had a 10 percentage-point gap between white and black students, and of the roughly 100,000 black students who started as first-time, full-time, degree-seeking freshmen at four-year institutions, only 6,400 enrolled at colleges with a six-year graduation rate for black students above 70 percent. Four times as many—more than 28,000—enrolled at colleges that gave them odds of graduating on-time of 30 percent or less.[11]

U.S. News places a lot of weight on graduation and freshman-to-sophomore retention rates, which together make up 20 percent of the rankings. This penalizes institutions that enroll large numbers of lower-income, nontraditional, and underprepared students who are statistically less likely to graduate. Harvard's national-best 98 percent graduation rate isn't solely a function of its educational greatness; it also has a lot to do with only admitting students who are most likely to succeed.

The Education Trust, a nonpartisan research and advocacy organization, recently used the new graduation rate data to compare rates at every four-year institution in the country to rates at other similar schools. It found that the highest performers by this "peer comparison" measure are often nowhere near the top of traditional lists of "best colleges."[12] Table 11.3 shows a group of universities ranked as "third tier" by *U.S. News,* each of which had 2004 six-year graduation rates much higher than most other institutions with a similar size, mission, funding level, and student body. *U.S. News* actually calculates a "predicted versus actual" graduation rate

Table 11.3 Unusually High Graduation Rates

Institution	U.S. News Ranking	Percentage-point Difference between 2004 Six-Year Graduation Rate and Median Rate of Peer Institutions*
Troy State	3rd tier	12.6
Bowling Green	3rd tier	9.1
South Carolina State	3rd tier	17.7
Fisk University	3rd tier	25.3
Westminster College (PA)	3rd tier	23.7

Source: http://www.collegeresults.org.

measure, which produces similar results. But it only makes up 5 percent of the rankings, not enough to move these institutions out of the lower echelons.

Like NSSE and the CLA, peer graduation rate comparisons give all institutions an opportunity to demonstrate their success in helping the students they enroll. The *U.S. News* rankings reward institutions for enrolling students that have already gathered the most momentum; these measures recognize institutions that do the most to help their students succeed.

THE PURSUIT OF HAPPINESS

Once teaching, learning, and graduating are finished, students move on to the rest of their lives. Well-educated people do more than pass tests and acquire credentials; they succeed in life as learners, workers, and citizens. The true test of students' higher education may not occur until years after they leave the institution.

That makes evaluation very difficult for the vast majority of colleges and universities, which don't have the resources to keep tabs on every one of their graduates (university development offices notwithstanding).

Advances in information technology, however, have created new ways to judge colleges and universities by how well their graduates succeed in further education and their careers. State governments gather data about earnings and field of employment for virtually every wage earner in the nation, so they can calculate unemployment insurance benefits for people who are laid off. This data can be matched with student records provided by colleges and universities.

That would give students and parents a huge amount of new detailed information about which colleges help their graduates get jobs in their field of study and earn a good living. Say you're a Latina high school senior who wants to design the next-generation space shuttle or send men to Mars. You'd want to know which universities nationwide graduate the most Latina engineers who get well-paying jobs in the aerospace industry. Linking education and employment data—information that already exists today—would give you the answer.

A handful of states have already made this connection. Florida is the best example, having developed what is generally regarded as the most advanced state education/employment information system in the nation. Florida's system has its genesis in the mid-1980s, when state policymakers wanted to increase the accuracy of student enrollment counts submitted by K–12 schools for the purpose of calculating state funding allocations. By assigning a unique identification number to each student, the state prevented double-counting and allowed enrollment counts to be adjusted for students who transferred from one district to another.

As this new K–12 data system was coming on line in the early 1990s, Florida was also improving its higher education data infrastructure by wiring the state's nine public universities together, allowing them to share information with each other and state agencies.[13] The universities serving as "nodes" in this network became points at which K–12 districts could upload their enrollment data to the state, well before the Internet made such data transfers easy for everyone.

Florida also has an unusually integrated higher education system. Both the community college and four-year university systems use unique student identifier numbers and common course numbers to facilitate transfer between institutions. By the late 1990s, Florida had all the pieces in place for a comprehensive data system—individual student records at both the K–12 and higher education level, an established system for moving data to a central location, and employment data from the unemployment insurance and job training system. All that was left to do was to put the pieces together.

That began in 2001, when the state constitution was amended to change the superintendent of public instruction from an elected to gubernatorially appointed position, and the legislature restructured the state's elementary, secondary, two-year, and four-year university systems into a single, integrated system. The legislature appropriated $6 million over the next few years to put all the information from those systems in one place: The Florida K–20 Education Data Warehouse, which currently stores over 1.5 terabytes of information on more than 10 million individual students from more than 16,000 education institutions.

Having the government build giant databases of information about people's education and work lives naturally raises the specter of Big Brother–type oversight and intrusion. That's why Congress passed the Family Education Rights and Privacy Act (FERPA) in 1974, which makes public disclosure of individual education records a felony. It's also why Florida keeps records containing Social Security numbers and other sensitive data at a separate physical location from the rest of the data warehouse, stored on computers that are not connected to the Internet or other electronic networks and are shielded from hackers.

Integrating education and employment information as Florida and a handful of other states have done opens up vast opportunities to create interesting, useful information about colleges and universities. For example, Florida publishes an annual profile of public university graduates living in state the fall after finishing college, detailing whether they went on to further education and/or entered the workforce, as well as the amount of money they earned and whether they received public assistance or were in jail. Table 11.4 shows data from the most recent report, along with each institution's ranking according to U.S. News.

Of Florida's nine biggest public universities, six rank relatively poorly, either falling in the fourth (bottom) tier of national research universities or below the top 50 Master's-granting universities in the South. But anyone expecting to find a correlation between those rankings and students' prospects for finding a well-paying job in state after college would be mistaken. In fact, the four institutions with the highest average earnings all fall among the six low-ranked universities. The school ranked highest by U.S. News—the University of Florida—ranks second to last on Table 11.4 in terms of the average earnings of graduates.[14] This is not a one-year anomaly; similar numbers were reported for 2003 and 2002.

Table 11.4 Outcomes for 2003–04 Florida Public University Graduates, Fall 2004

Institution	Average Earnings	U.S. News Ranking	Percentage of Graduates Employed in State	Percentage of Graduates Continuing Their Education in State	Percentage of Graduates Earning at Least $22,000
Florida International University	$34,756	4th Tier	70.0	17	75.4
Florida Atlantic University	$33,867	4th Tier	72.2	16	71.9
University of North Florida	$31,236	54th*	76.7	15	74.0
University of South Florida	$30,462	4th Tier	71.9	18	70.9
University of Central Florida	$29,278	3rd Tier	71.3	18	66.2
Florida A&M University	$27,383	58th*	53.5	18	61.7
Florida State University	$27,010	2nd Tier	60.4	18	62.2
University of Florida	$25,773	1st Tier	57.8	23	54.1
University of West Florida	$24,712	60th*	63.7	16	60.9

*Among Southern Masters-granting institutions.
Source: http://www.firn.edu/doe/fetpip/sus.htm.

There are many possible explanations for this. Perhaps more of the University of Florida graduates who took high-paying jobs left the state—although that would be cold comfort for state policymakers who invested taxpayer dollars in their flagship university. Perhaps more were younger or went on to earn sub-subsistence wages in graduate school—although the difference in the percentage of students who continued their education in state from the University of Florida—23 percent—and top-earning, low-ranked Florida International—17 percent—isn't all that large.

Or perhaps some low-ranked institutions do a much better job of preparing their students to succeed in life and their careers than their status in the *U.S. News* rankings would suggest.

Painting a complete picture of university success in preparing students to succeed in their careers requires a great deal more information than is found in Table 11.4. It would be important to have data for different kinds of students, in different majors and employment categories, over an extended timeframe. That hypothetical future Latina rocket scientist, for example, might be interested in earnings data specifically for students who majored in science, technology, engineering, and mathematics (STEM) disciplines. She might also want to see a profile of graduates six years after leaving college, to get a sense of whether a particular institution's students not only land jobs in their field but prosper once they get there.

Such information is available in Florida. Figure 11.5 shows exactly that information for the nine Florida public universities, tracking the 2002 earnings of students who graduated in 1996. University of Central Florida STEM graduates had the highest median earnings, more than $53,000, while the lowest earnings were found for non-STEM graduates from the University of West Florida, who earned only $25,000 on average. The University of Florida ranks somewhat higher than on Table 11.4, but remains behind some of its in-state peers.

Much more analysis is possible—the Florida data system can break all of these numbers down by students' gender, income, and race/ethnicity, as well as calculate placement and earnings in specific industry categories. The number of states that could calculate similar data is rising quickly—a recent survey found that 37 states are currently gathering individual student data in a way that could support Florida-type data systems, and others are planning to follow suit.[15]

But for all the rich new information Florida can provide about the success of its public universities, the impact of these reports on institutional reputations has been small. This is likely because the information is relatively new, limited to public institutions, and only based on graduates who stay in state to live and work. The fact that the data is nowhere to be found on the state's Web site for students choosing colleges probably doesn't help. In the long run, employment outcome data will only be useful to

Figure 11.5 Median Annual Earnings in 2002 for 1996 Florida Public University Graduates Living in-State

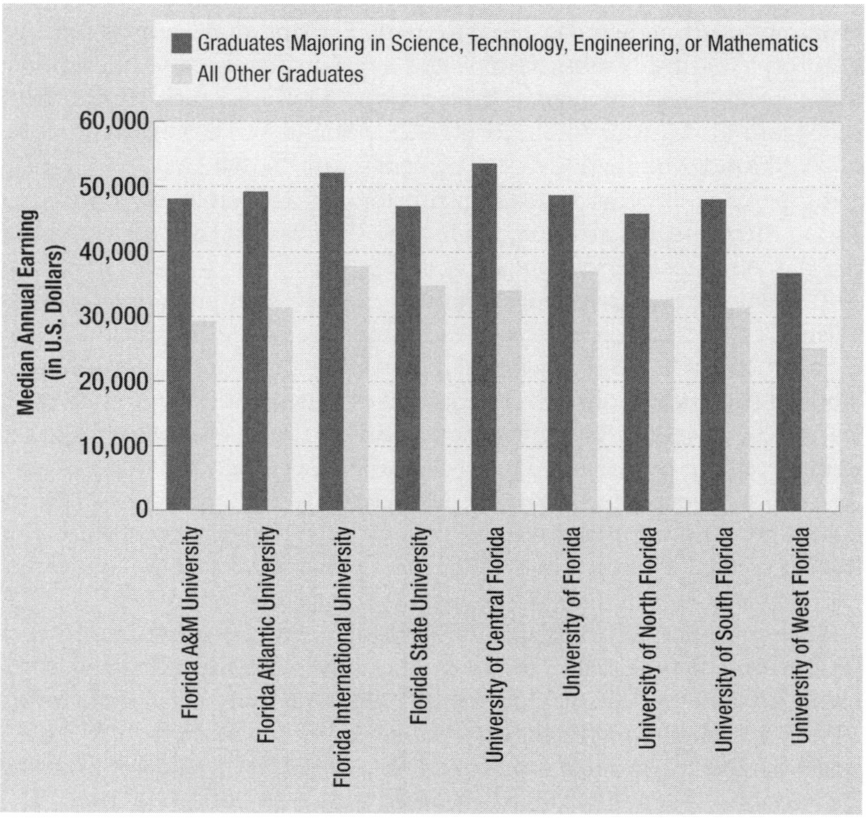

[Bar chart showing median annual earnings comparing "Graduates Majoring in Science, Technology, Engineering, or Mathematics" vs. "All Other Graduates" across Florida A&M University, Florida Atlantic University, Florida International University, Florida State University, University of Central Florida, University of Florida, University of North Florida, University of South Florida, and University of West Florida.]

Source: Florida Department of Education.

students choosing colleges—and thus, meaningful to institutions—when it becomes available for *all* colleges and universities nationwide.

BEYOND WORK

There's more to life than getting a job and making money, of course. Knowing if colleges prepare students to become lifelong learners and healthy, enlightened citizens is also valuable information for students and parents to have. Comprehensive alumni surveys are a way to get this information. While many institutions survey their alumni, the quality and type of survey varies greatly, making it impossible to compare alumni outcomes at one institution to another.

The Collegiate Results Survey (CRS) could help solve this problem. Piloted at 80 colleges and universities in 1999, the CRS surveyed more than 34,000 former students who graduated between 1991 and 1994, asking about their occupation, earnings, job skills, educational attainment, religion, physical fitness, civic engagement, and lifelong learning. It also explored their perceived competencies and deficiencies in communications, information gathering, and quantitative reasoning.

The CRS results reveal areas where most institutions have much room to improve. The results also show that some institutions do much better than others. Figure 11.6 shows that at the typical institution, between 30 and 50 percent of alumni display a "strong" commitment to arts and culture.[16] But at some institutions percentage was less than 20 percent, while at others it was greater than 70 percent.

The CRS was licensed to the for-profit *Peterson's* college guide, which uses the data and survey framework for a Web site designed to help students pick colleges.[17] But the process is opaque—while students answer a

Figure 11.6 Percentage of Alumni Who Displayed a "Strong" Commitment to Arts and Culture on the Collegiate Results Survey

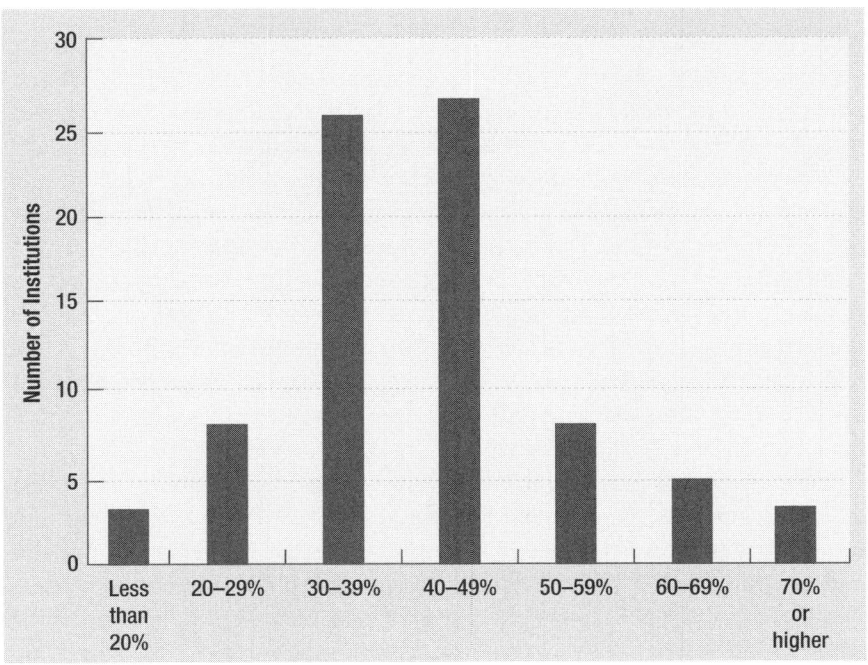

Source: "A Report to Stakeholders on the Condition and Effectiveness of Postsecondary Education, Part One: The Recent College Graduate," *Change,* May/June 2001.

range of questions and get a list of likely college matches, the actual results for individual institutions are not published. The results, moreover, aren't based on a representative sample of students, since the survey is only taken by students who self-select to log onto the *Peterson's* Web site.

Many colleges and universities commission alumni surveys for their individual use, but the results are generally kept from the public eye. Like a great deal of other useful information about America's colleges and universities, sophisticated alumni survey data exists, but it is not available to the prospective students who arguably need it most.

NEW COLLEGE RANKINGS

Higher education is a complex endeavor. A rankings system can only succeed if it can reflect that complexity accurately and fairly, by combining information from a variety of sources. With the advent of NSSE, the Collegiate Learning Assessment, outcomes-based accreditation, and new data about graduation, employment, and life outcomes, that critical mass of data now exists. There is now enough information to create sophisticated rankings of higher education quality to replace the wealth-exclusivity-fame paradigm of the *U.S. News* rankings.

Table 11.5 shows what a ranking system based on this new information would look like:

Twenty percent of the new rankings would be based on teaching. Instead of ranking universities based on faculty salaries and academic credentials — things that have nothing to do with how well faculty teach — or simplistic measures like class size, 4 percent of the rankings would be based on each of the five main NSSE categories. These student-based measures are much more detailed, sophisticated, and comprehensive than the current *U.S. News* measures, ranging from the degree of academic challenge, collaborative learning, and student/faculty interaction to the availability of enriching educational experiences and a supportive campus environment. NSSE also measures important aspects of college outside of academics, like community service and working with students from different economic, social, racial, and ethnic backgrounds.

Thirty percent of the new rankings would be based on learning. The Collegiate Learning Assessment would account for 15 percent, rating colleges and universities on their success in teaching students the higher-order thinking and communication skills they need to succeed in the modern workforce. While the current *U.S. News* rankings give institutions credit for how much students knew when they arrived at college, in the form of SAT scores, the CLA gauges how much students learn while they're *at* college, by measuring the value added from the freshman to senior years. Another 10 percent would be based on the results of outcomes-based accreditation processes, reflecting the deep knowledge students should acquire in specific fields. And 5 percent would be based on culminating projects that tie higher-order thinking skills and deep knowledge together into a cohesive whole.

Twenty percent of the new rankings would be based on retention and graduation. The *U.S. News* rankings include simple graduation and retention rates, penalizing institutions that enroll large numbers of students who have more barriers to college completion, such as first-generation students, nontraditional students, lower-income students, and students who were poorly prepared in high school. By ranking institutions according to the difference between their actual retention and graduation and their statistically *predicted* graduation rates—based on factors such as those listed above—institutions will be rewarded for exemplary graduation rates given their specific mission and student body.

Thirty percent of the new rankings would be based on success in life after college. The narrow, largely meaningless *U.S. News* measure of alumni donation rates would be jettisoned in favor of more concrete, detailed measures of students' success in their further education, their careers, and their lives. Five percent would be based on student success in going on to

Table 11.5 Components of the New Rankings

Measure	Percentage of Ranking	Measured Characteristic	Total
NSSE: Academic challenge	4%	Teaching	
NSSE: Active and collaborative learning	4%	Teaching	
NSSE: Student-faculty interaction	4%	Teaching	20%
NSSE: Enriching educational experiences	4%	Teaching	
NSSE: Supportive campus environment	4%	Teaching	
CLA: Value-added and freshmen–senior growth	15%	Learning	
Outcomes-based accreditation results	10%	Learning	30%
Culminating projects	5%	Learning	
Freshman retention rates: predicated versus actual	5%	Graduation	20%
Graduation rates: predicted versus actual	15%	Graduation	
Postgrad education: placement and success	5%	Success in life	
Employment results: earnings	10%	Success in life	30%
Employment results: placement/licensure	5%	Success in life	
Alumni surveys: satisfaction and success	10%	Success in life	

further education and succeeding there. Ten percent would be based on graduates' earnings 1, 5, and 10 years after graduation. These amounts would be compared to typical earnings in students' field of employment, so as to not penalize institutions that specialize in academic or vocational fields that are generally less well-paid than others.

Five percent would be tied to job placement, based on the percentage of students who obtain work in their field of study and success rates on professional licensure examinations. Ten percent would be based on alumni surveys like the Collegiate Results Survey, which can provide a full picture of the academic, vocational, artistic, and religious values that higher education represents and fulfills.

The Benefits for Students, Colleges, and Society

Replacing the current *U.S. News* ranking regime with this new system would have a number of important and long-lasting benefits.

Students and parents would have far more useful information for choosing colleges. Rather than relying on rankings that say virtually nothing about higher education quality, students would be able to find institutions that will actually teach them well and help them succeed in life. Most of the data that informs the new rankings can potentially be broken down by student characteristics like race, gender, and economic status, as well as by academic programs inside of institutions. This would further allow students to find the best college or university for them, given who they are and what they want to study.

The vast majority of colleges and universities would finally have fair terms under which to compete and excel. Instead of being forced to model themselves after a few elite institutions in a futile attempt to climb the greased pole that is the reigning status hierarchy in higher education, institutions could distinguish themselves for being good at what they were meant to be—educators of undergraduate students. Institutions that have focused their energies and ambitions on improving learning and success for students would finally get the recognition they deserve.

The higher education community would be armed with far better information to argue for more public resources. The percentage of public dollars devoted to higher education has declined in recent years, squeezed out by the demands of public safety, health care, and K–12 schools. Public officials are less receptive to investing vast sums of money in institutions that don't provide solid evidence of efficiency, effectiveness, and lasting benefits for the public. New evidence of improved teaching, greater learning, and better outcomes in the job market would help persuade policymakers to reinvest in higher education.

Institutions would have incentives to improve many of their practices. Instead of focusing on recruiting students with the highest SAT scores, institutions would focus on recruiting students with the greatest potential for academic growth. Instead of giving more financial aid to wealthy students—a practice that has become all too common in recent years—institutions would give more aid to low-income students to help them stay in school and graduate. Instead of focusing single-mindedly on raising and spending more money, institutions would focus on using money effectively to improve academic, career, and life outcomes for students. Colleges would have fewer incentives to be exclusive and more incentives to be inclusive, to admit students with a wider range of ability. The smartest, most effective, most well-managed institutions could expand and capture a greater share of the market without being penalized for diminished exclusivity.

Higher education abounds with examples of institutions and educators that have successfully implemented programs to help students learn and graduate. But many of these best practices have never been widely adopted because the current rankings and status hierarchy offer no incentives for institutions to seek them out. The lack of good ideas successfully implemented in higher education is not a problem of supply; it's a problem of demand.

Researchers, for example, have long known that impersonal lecture classes are a lousy way to teach. Students need more active, collaborative learning environments to succeed. But that costs money that most institutions don't have or aren't willing to spend. In recent years, however, researchers have found ways to use technology to change that equation. From 1999 to 2004, Dr. Carol Twigg of the National Center for Academic Transformation worked with 30 colleges and universities to improve their large introductory classes (50 percent of all enrollments at community colleges and 35 percent of enrollments at four-year schools are in just 25 introductory courses in foundational subjects like English and biology). Instead of passively absorbing information in a cavernous lecture hall, students worked in active learning environments where they had online access to tutorials, student discussion groups, and real-time, on-demand feedback and support. The technology also reduces the amount of time instructors need to prepare lectures, introduce content, and grade homework, lowering staff costs per student.

The result: more learning at a lower cost to the university. Scores in a redesigned biology course at the University of Massachusetts, for example, increased by 20 percent, while the cost to the university per student dropped by nearly 40 percent.[18]

But while Twigg's efforts are well known in some higher education circles, there has been no great rush to replicate them nationwide. That's because college administrators don't feel much pressure, for the sake of their careers or of the bottom line, to replicate educational best practices. Indeed, universities are notorious for basing hiring and tenure decisions on publishing and prestige, hardly indicators of the quality of teaching. The amount of time a professor devotes to publishing may be inversely related to the quality of undergraduate instruction. Improving educational quality is a fundamentally *optional* goal for colleges. That won't change until institutional reputations are primarily based on how well they educate students.

The new rankings would also help address the problem of rising college costs. Tuition and fees increase every year, raising barriers to access for low- and middle-income students. The *U.S. News* rankings exacerbate this problem. With 30 percent of the rankings based directly or indirectly on expenditures, colleges are *rewarded* for prying more money out of students and parents and then spending it, regardless of whether they spend it well. Institutions can raise prices with relative impunity, since demand is rising and it's very hard for new competitors to enter the market for traditional students. Colleges and universities today have few incentives to cut costs or become more efficient.

The new rankings would help shift the market dynamics from price to *value*. Value measures compare benefits to price. But students currently have little or no information about real benefits in terms of learning outcomes, and prices—particularly among private colleges that can charge what they like—tend to be about the same. The *U.S. News* college guide perfectly illustrates the current lack of real value measures in higher education. Under the heading of "Great Schools, Great Prices," *U.S. News* lists the top five "best values" among national universities as Cal Tech, Harvard, Princeton, Yale, and MIT—five of the top seven overall universities *absent* price. The top five "best value" liberal arts colleges are Williams, Amherst, Wellesley, Pomona, and Swarthmore—also five of the top seven on the main list.

Because the reputations of these institutions are basically set in stone, potential competitors have no opportunity to pursue an efficiency-centered strategy, offering customers the same benefits for less money, or more benefits for the same money. The new rankings would create a far larger, far more level playing field on which many more institutions could compete, making quality *and* efficiency necessary components of a successful long-term strategy.

The new rankings would also bring two-year institutions more fully into the mainstream conversation about higher education quality. *U.S.*

News doesn't publish a guide to "America's Best Community Colleges" because there's no market for it. People almost always choose two-year colleges that are close to home. As the Institute for Higher Education Policy recently noted, two-year colleges are also ill-served by state accountability systems.[19] This means the nearly half of all American college students who attend two-year institutions are denied the benefits of real accountability of any kind. Because the new rankings are primarily focused on value-added measures—learning growth and graduation rates given the students who enroll—as well as measures of quality teaching practices that any college could, and should, provide, they create an opportunity to compare and contrast two- and four-year institutions on common ground. NSSE has already successfully launched a community college survey of student engagement, the results of which (unlike those for four-year institutions) are made publicly available. There's a tacit assumption in higher education that any four-year institution is better than any two-year institution—the data in the new rankings could put that to the test.

Similarly, the new rankings would also open up the market to non-traditional providers, such as those who provide services primarily over the Internet. The current rankings rate institutions based on what they *are*—specifically, how much they resemble traditional, established, elite institutions. Any great deviancy in approach or strategy from that long-established model is penalized by definition, freezing out innovators from the opportunity to provide the high-value degrees students and society prize most. The new rankings primarily rate institutions on what they *do* and what they achieve for their students, opening the door to anyone who can prove that they offer superior teaching, learning, and chances for graduation and success in life.

OBSTACLES TO THE NEW RANKINGS

There is, however, one great obstacle to realizing these many benefits of the new rankings: higher education's unwillingness to make much of this new information available. NSSE, the CLA, alumni surveys, and accreditation results, which collectively provide more than half of the information for the new rankings, are for the most part held out of public view by colleges and universities. And some recent attempts to build new data systems that could support the rest of the ranking components, including postgraduation employment outcomes and more accurate graduation rate measures, are being fiercely opposed by factions within the higher education establishment.

The biggest obstacle to liberating higher education from the tyranny of the flawed *U.S. News* system is thus higher education itself. Some of the objections are grounded in reasonable—but addressable—concerns about the accuracy of information. Others go deeper, reflecting both a strong desire for autonomy and a basic instinct to preserve the status quo.

Making the Perfect the Enemy of the Good

Some people will object to the new rankings on the grounds that the measures driving them are not sufficiently accurate, reliable, or complete. Students responding to surveys like NSSE don't always evaluate their own educational experiences objectively. The Collegiate Learning Assessment is much better than a multiple-choice, fill-in-the-bubble test, but is still only an estimate of students' analytic and communication skills. Outcomes-based accreditation is easier to implement for more vocational disciplines like engineering and teaching than it is for philosophy or semiotics. State wage data doesn't include income earned from investments. Current federal graduation rate measures don't account for students who transfer from or to other schools.

All of these criticisms are accurate, and every effort should be made to increase the reliability of the data that drives the new rankings. Some solutions are there for the taking—a national data system like Florida's, for example, can solve the graduation-rate accuracy problem by tracking students who transfer from one institution to another. More resources should be devoted to researching new and better ways to measure teaching, learning, and success in life. None of the current measures are the be-all and end-all of higher education performance measurement—existing measures can be improved and new metrics can be developed.

But the possibility of improving the accuracy of the new class of higher education information is not a *prima facie* argument for preventing the public release of that information, nor, by extension, an argument against new, outcome-based rankings.

U.S. News rankings are based on largely accurate measures of factors that are disconnected from student learning. It is easy to be precise in measuring such things as spending per student. It is almost impossible to measure something as complex as student learning with the same exactness. But colleges and students would be far better off with rankings based on possibly less accurate measures of the right things, rather than very accurate measures of the wrong things. Currently available measures like NSSE, the CLA, and outcomes-based accreditation are more than accurate enough to be rich and meaningful—if they weren't, hundreds of institutions wouldn't be voluntarily paying for them every year. The benefits of waiting for even more accurate information, moreover, must be weighed against the cost of perpetuating today's flawed rankings.

Preserving Autonomy

Some higher education reformers support the idea of creating more public information about higher education outcomes, but object to using that information to create new rankings. Conversations about rankings in higher education frequently seem to imply that *U.S. News* might simply close up shop some day. In reality, college rankings are here to stay. The only issue to be debated is who will create them and whether they'll be based on the right information or the wrong information.

The National Association of State Universities and Land-Grant Colleges (NASULGC) embodies this more-information-but-not-for-rankings stance. The organization, whose member institutions educate 3.8 million students, recently published a draft white paper called "Elements of Accountability for Public Universities and Colleges." The proposal represents a good-faith commitment to providing more public information about teaching, learning, graduating, and succeeding in life. But it explicitly warns against using that information to give consumers what they want.

"We vigorously oppose creating any overall ranking scheme based on the bundle of accountability measures we recommend here," the organization argues. Elsewhere, NASULGC warns that colleges should only be compared against "their own past performance and with other universities with similar missions, academic programs and admissions practices." Moreover, "even comparable universities should be limited to individual accountability measures, not indices composed of multiple accountability measures."

These principles are quite reasonable when applied to the *U.S. News* rankings—comparing the public City University of New York to the private New York University based on SAT scores and graduation rates makes little sense. But many of the components of the new rankings are either relative measures—value-added on the CLA, graduation rates compared to peers—or represent goals like teaching well in the classroom, which any college or university accepting students for admission can and should be able to achieve. Understanding how very different institutions are more or less successful in producing results is the essence of informed consumer choice. Institutions may not like having multiple measures condensed into one ranking, but students choosing colleges can only choose one to attend—often at great expense.

As an alternative to new rankings, NASULGC advocates that data "be presented [for each] institution with the user of the data encouraged to place whatever weight on the individual data elements she/he prefers." The idea of prospective students creating their own rankings is appealing on the surface, but it falls short on two counts. First, students and parents need more than just raw data. They need and want someone to make *sense* of that information, someone to make informed judgments about which measures of quality are most important, in a way that facilitates the process of choosing a college.

Second, individualized rankings won't do what the *U.S. News* rankings do: change institutional behavior.

Colleges object to universal, highly public, well-understood rankings precisely because they're so influential. Rankings limit colleges' ability to control their image and the terms of their own success. Antipathy to rankings, as well as the consistent refusal of the higher education establishment to provide clear, detailed, public information about how well it serves students, is rooted in an intense desire for independence.

To be sure, diversity, freedom, and lack of burdensome and inefficient government regulation are among the principal virtues of the American higher education system. But that autonomy has come at a cost—nobody really knows what's going on inside the ivory tower. By comparison, private companies whose shares are traded on the stock market are models of openness and disclosure, filing detailed quarterly reports with the Securities and Exchange Commission outlining their financial performance. Many would probably rather avoid this kind of government-mandated transparency, particularly when results are bad.

But that's the price that must be paid for the public benefit of being traded on the market. It's universally acknowledged that while individual companies may have a selfish short-term interest in keeping certain kinds of information private, the public at large has a huge long-term interest in transparency and well-informed markets. Private companies also have a strong *collective* interest in transparency, because the competition it creates drives everyone to improve. It also gives people confidence when they invest their money, bringing more capital to the market.

Contrast this to the higher education sector, where behavior is distorted by an information-starved market, where institutional quality stagnates due to lack of competitive pressure to improve vital areas like teaching, where innovators are ignored at best and stifled at worst, where public investment is diminishing by the year due in significant part to a lack of information—and thus, confidence—in what the public receives in return.

Unfortunately, the best interests of most higher education institutions are being held hostage to the interests of a few, particularly elite, and private institutions. These highly esteemed universities occupy one of the most advantaged market positions imaginable. Despite sometimes-enormous wealth and administrative salaries on par with the corporate sector, they pay no income taxes. While demand for their product is consistently rising, opportunities for new competitors to enter the market and meet that demand are virtually nil, allowing them to raise prices with near-impunity every year. Their reputation as the world's best education institutions is virtually unquestioned by the general public, which sees them as both symbols of society's best values and portals to economic and social opportunity.

They are, in other words, institutions whose best interests lie in using whatever means necessary to prevent the release of any information that would upset the status quo or call their privileged position into question. That's why they're the least likely to participate in and release results from new measures like NSSE—when *U.S. News* asked institutions to voluntarily disclose some of their 2004 NSSE results, not a single one of the top 50 national research universities, and only three of the top 50 liberal arts colleges, complied. When the conventional wisdom says you're the best, you have no interest in proving otherwise.

The depth of private college opposition to new higher education information was recently made clear, when the U.S. Department of Education proposed making its higher education data system more like Florida's by using privacy-protected data about individual students. Public universities largely supported the new system. But lobbyists for private colleges put on a full-court press to block the proposal, pressing Congress to prohibit its creation and publicly denouncing it as "Orwellian" and "an assault on Americans' privacy and security in the shadow of the Fourth of July."[20]

A TIME FOR FEDERAL ACTION

Given this deep-seated opposition, there is no prospect that the higher education sector in its entirety will ever voluntarily agree to support a real system of rankings-based accountability. And that's what it would take—the only way to displace the reigning paradigm is to do what *U.S. News* does: consistently gather information from *every* college and university in the country, so students and parents can use a common measure to decide where to enroll.

This effectively gives veto power over the creation of new rankings that would ultimately benefit the sector as a whole to any institutional subsector of significant size. Some state governments have played a valuable role in creating new higher education data, and all states should work to promote more information and accountability for their colleges and universities. But the diversity of state policymakers and the strong political influence of universities in state legislatures means that it would take only a few holdout states to derail the entire system.

Therefore the only plausible path to a rankings-based accountability system that would be truly valuable to students and parents lies with federal action. The U.S. Congress should consider legislation to do the following:

1. Direct the U.S. Department of Education to create a "unit record," higher-education data system to provide more accurate information about all colleges and universities.
2. Direct the U.S. Department of Education to coordinate with states to connect the unit-record system to information from state unemployment insurance databases.
3. Increase the annual budget of the U.S. Department of Education's Fund for the Improvement of Post-Secondary Education (FIPSE) from $22 million to $100 million, end the practice of using FIPSE as a source of local higher education-related pork projects, and direct FIPSE to prioritize projects that would create new information about how institutions succeed or fail to teach students well and help them learn, graduate, and succeed in life.
4. Require all colleges and universities wishing to enroll students who pay their tuition with federal student aid (so-called "Title IV-eligible" institutions) to participate in the NSSE, CLA, selected alumni surveys, and other surveys and processes needed to understand institutional success. Appropriate sufficient funds to defray the costs of participation.
5. Require all Title IV-eligible institutions to disclose the results of accreditation review and other processes generating information about institutional success.
6. Direct the Secretary of Education to appoint a commission of persons from within and outside higher education to translate the results of those surveys, along with retention, graduation, and employment data derived from the unit record system and other available information into a new system of college rankings that rate all institutions on a common scale, the principal components of which are institutional success in teaching students and helping them learn, graduate, and succeed in life.
7. Require the commission to meet annually to consider adjustments to the rankings and the inclusion of new or more accurate information as it becomes available.
8. Direct the Secretary of Education to disclose the results of the new rankings to institutional leaders for three years on a confidential basis to give institutions the opportunity to understand how they are being evaluated and to begin efforts to improve.

9. After the three-year transitional period, direct the Secretary of Education to publish the new rankings and mail a copy to every student in the country enrolled in grades seven or higher, along with detailed information about the performance of local institutions.

Americans often declare with self-satisfaction that the nation's colleges and universities are the best in the world. But the reality is that colleges and universities do not have to teach undergraduates well in order to prosper. Higher education institutions do what all human institutions do: They respond to the incentives and values of the systems and markets in which they exist. They can't be regulated or threatened into improving their service to students. They have to *want* to change, not just vaguely or to a slight degree, but so much so that they're willing to spend the resources and endure the conflict that change inevitably brings.

The new rankings would provide those reasons. They would create fair terms of competition for everyone, giving educators and institutions that truly excel on behalf of their students the recognition and rewards they deserve. They would, in other words, make the values that govern higher education and the values that inspire it one and the same.

NOTES

1. www.pbs.org/merrow/podcast, from the PBS documentary "Declining by Degrees."

2. J. D. Baer, A. L. Cook, and S. Baldi, *The Literacy of America's College Students* (Washington, DC: American Institutes for Research, 2006).

3. Paul Boyer, *College Rankings Exposed: Getting beyond the Rankings Myth to Find Your Perfect College* (Lawrenceville, NJ: Peterson's Guides, 2004).

4. Kati Haycock, *Promise Abandoned: How Policy Choices and Institutional Practices Restrict College Opportunities* (Washington, DC: The Education Trust, 2006).

5. Amy Graham and Nicolas Thompson, "Broken Ranks," *The Washington Monthly*, September 2001, http://www.washingtonmonthly.com/features/2001/0109.graham.thompson.html.

6. Richard J. Shavelson and Leta Huang, *A Brief History of Assessing Undergraduates' Learning: Carnegie Foundation for the Advancement of Teachings' Heritage*, unpublished draft, Stanford University, 2006. This paper is the source of subsequent descriptions of the history of standardized testing in higher education.

7. John W. Prados, George D. Peterson, and Lisa R. Lattuca, "Quality Assurance of Engineering Education through Accreditation: The Impact of Engineering Criteria 2000 and Its Global Influence," *Journal of Engineering Education,* 94 (1), 165–84 (2005). This paper is the source of subsequent descriptions of the history of the engineering accreditation process.

8. Personal interview with Dr. Eric Spina, Interim Vice Chancellor and Provost, Syracuse University, July 25, 2006.

9. Lisa R. Lattuca, Patrick T. Terenzini, and J. Fredericks Volkwein, *Engineering Change: A Study of the Impact of EC2000* (State College: Center for the Study of Higher Education, Pennsylvania State University, 2005).

10. http://www.teac.org/membership/meetings/Novel%20Categories%20of%20Evide nce1.ppt#9.

11. Kevin Carey, *One Step from the Finish Line: Higher College Graduation Rates Are within Our Reach* (Washington, DC: The Education Trust, 2005).

12. Ibid.

13. This "Florida Information Resource Network" was originally put in place in the 1970s and 1980s.

14. Florida Education and Training Information and Placement Systems (FETPIP), http://www.firn.edu/doe/fetpip/sus.htm.

15. National Center for Educational Effectiveness, "2005 Survey of State Data Collection Issues Related to Longitudinal Analysis," (Austin, TX: University of Texas, 2005).

16. "A Report to Stakeholders on the Condition and Effectiveness of Postsecondary Education, Part One: The Recent College Graduate," *Change,* May/June 2001.

17. Peterson's. "Best College Picks." http://www.bestcollegepicks.com.

18. http://www.thencat.org/PCR/R2/UMA/UMA_Overview.htm.

19. Wendy Erisman and Lan Gao, *Making Accountability Work: Community Colleges and Statewide Higher Education Accountability Systems* (Washington, DC: Institute for Higher Education Policy, 2006).

20. http://www.naicu.edu/news/releases/Student_Privacy_Poll_Release.shtm.

About the Editors and Contributors

THE EDITORS

JOHN C. KNAPP is university professor and Mann Family Professor of Ethics and Leadership at Samford University, where directs the Frances Marlin Mann Center for Ethics and Leadership. A proponent of social responsibility in higher education, he has directed two international gatherings of university leaders: the 2005 Oxford Conclave on Global Ethics and the University Presidency and the 2008 Stellenbosch Seboka on Higher Education and Ethical Leadership. His books include *For the Common Good: The Ethics of Leadership in the 21st Century,* a collection of essays by internationally recognized thinkers, and *Leaders on Ethics: Real-World Perspectives on Today's Business Challenges*. He holds a PhD from the University of Wales.

DAVID J. SIEGEL is associate professor in the Department of Educational Leadership at East Carolina University. His research focuses on collective action by organizations to promote social change, with a particular emphasis on initiatives supporting diversity and inclusion. He is the author of *The Call for Diversity* (RoutledgeFalmer, 2003), *Organizing for Social Partnership* (to be published by Routledge in 2010), and journal articles exploring the dynamics of cross-sector collaboration. His essays have appeared in *Academe, Liberal Education, The Chronicle of Higher Education,* and *Diverse Issues in Higher Education*. He holds a PhD from the University of Michigan's Center for the Study of Higher and Postsecondary Education.

THE CONTRIBUTORS

LAUREL ANDREA BEESEMYER is a PhD student and Provost's Fellow in the Center for Higher Education Policy Analysis at the University of Southern California. Her research interests include governance, contingent faculty, and organizational change.

RONALD A. BOHLANDER is Principal Research Scientist in the Georgia Tech Research Institute at the Georgia Institute of Technology, where he currently directs the Commercial Product Realization Office. He has published widely on subjects including millimeter-wave systems, optical design, intelligent industrial automation, electronics manufacturing, and product realization. Prior to joining the Georgia Tech faculty in 1979, he served on the research staff of what is now the United Kingdom's Rutherford and Appleton Laboratory. He is a Fellow of the Society of Manufacturing Engineers, Fellow of the Georgia Tech Research Institute, and serves as Secretary of the Faculty of the Georgia Institute of Technology.

MARC BOUSQUET is an associate professor at Santa Clara University, where he teaches courses in radical U.S. culture, Internet studies, and writing with new media. His most recent book is *How the University Works: Higher Education and the Low-Wage Nation* (NYU, 2008). He is at work on a book about participatory culture in the United States, and serves on the national council of the American Association of University Professors (AAUP). He writes for the Chronicle of Higher Education's "Brainstorm" group weblog.

DANIEL M. CARCHIDI is Publication Director at MIT OpenCourseWare (http://ocw.mit.edu), where he is responsible for the overall schedule and quality of the OpenCourseWare publication, which includes over 1,880 courses from MIT's 33 academic departments as well as the Highlights for High School portal. Prior to joining MIT OCW, he held management positions at GE Corporate and GE Capital, where he developed knowledge systems and other e-learning applications. He holds a BA from the University of Connecticut, an MA from Teachers College, Columbia University, and a PhD from the University of Michigan's Center for the Study of Higher and Postsecondary Education.

KEVIN CAREY is the policy director of Education Sector, an independent think tank based in Washington, DC. In addition to managing Education Sector's policy team, he regularly contributes to the "Quick and the Ed" weblog and has published Education Sector reports on topics including a blueprint for a new system of college rankings, how states inflate educational progress under No Child Left Behind, and improving minority college graduation rates. He has published magazine articles and op-eds in publications including *Washington Monthly, The American Prospect, Phi Delta Kappan, Change, Education Week, Washington Post, Los Angeles Times, New York Daily News,* and *Christian Science Monitor.* He also writes a monthly column on higher education policy for *The Chronicle of Higher Education*.

CURTIS CARLSON is vice chancellor for University Relations at the University of Nebraska at Kearney, with responsibilities for media relations, marketing, community relations, state and federal relations, internal communications, and other areas. Previously he was vice president for public affairs at Emory University and held administrative and teaching positions at several other institutions. He is founder and former chair of Counselors to Higher Education (CHE), a national group formed in 1998 to provide a forum for public relations leadership in colleges and universities, and he served a three-year appointed term on the Commission on Communications and Marketing of the Council for the Advancement and Support of Education (CASE).

CYNTHIA C. DELUCA serves as the associate vice provost of Enrollment Management and Services (EMAS) at North Carolina State University. Her current research involves the development of strategic long-term partnerships between EMAS and schools, communities, and two-year institutions throughout the state of North Carolina, with the overarching goal of preparing students for postsecondary education. She also provides leadership to the Joyner Visitor Center and the University Summer Sessions. She has been at NC State for over 23 years. She received her bachelor's and master's degrees from North Carolina State University and her doctorate in Educational Leadership from East Carolina University.

HENRY ETZKOWITZ holds the chair in Management of Innovation, Creativity, and Enterprise and is Director of the Triple Helix Research Group, Newcastle University Business School, in the United Kingdom. He is also Visiting Research Professor, Department of Technology and Society, School of Engineering and Applied Sciences, Stony Brook University in New York.

RAYMOND B. FARROW III is the executive director of the Frank Hawkins Kenan Institute of Private Enterprise at the Kenan-Flagler

Business School of the University of North Carolina at Chapel Hill. In his role, he serves as the institute's chief operating officer and is responsible for helping to establish the strategic direction of the institute. He also serves as the associate director for administration of the Carolina Entrepreneurial Initiative. He is a Phi Beta Kappa graduate of Wake Forest University and received a Master of Arts in Law and Diplomacy (MALD) from the Fletcher School of Law and Diplomacy at Tufts University.

TRICIA BERTRAM GALLANT is the Academic Integrity Coordinator at the University of California, San Diego. Her most recent books include *Academic Integrity in the Twenty-First Century: A Teaching and Learning Imperative* (Jossey-Bass, 2008) and, to be published in 2009 by Wiley-Blackwell, a coauthored (with Steven Davis and Patrick Drinan) book on student cheating. She has published several book chapters and articles on academic integrity, organizational change, and leadership, appearing in *The Journal of Higher Education,* the *Review of Higher Education, NASPA Journal,* the *Canadian Journal of Higher Education,* and the *Journal of Library Administration.*

FRED GALLOWAY is currently associate professor in the School of Leadership and Education Sciences at the University of San Diego. Prior to joining the university faculty, he directed the national evaluation of the Direct Student Loan program at ORC/Macro International and served as director of federal policy analysis at the American Council on Education, where he represented the interests of the higher education community before the Executive and Legislative branches of the federal government. Dr. Galloway received his bachelor's and master's degrees from the University of California, San Diego, and his doctoral degree in the economics of education from Harvard University.

E. GORDON GEE is president of The Ohio State University. Previously he served as chancellor of Vanderbilt University and as president of Brown University, the University of Colorado, and West Virginia University. He also served in an earlier appointment as president of The Ohio State University. Earlier he was dean of the West Virginia University Law School, following a legal career that included serving as a judicial fellow and staff assistant to the U.S. Supreme Court, where he worked for Chief Justice Warren Burger on administrative and legal problems of the Court and federal judiciary. He holds JD and EdD degrees from Columbia University.

ERIC R. GILBERTSON has served as President of Saginaw Valley State University (Michigan) since 1988. He has authored numerous speeches and articles on subjects ranging from higher education to organizational leadership to constitutional law. He is active in several professional and community service organizations and was recently appointed to the Michigan Governor's Council for Labor and Economic Growth. Prior to joining SVSU, he served as Executive Assistant to the President of Ohio State University and as President of Johnson State College in Vermont.

MALCOLM GREAR has played a vital role in the field of visual communication design as both designer and educator for more than 45 years. He is professor emeritus at the Rhode Island School of Design, where he served for 28 years. Through his firm, Malcolm Grear Designers, he has done memorable identity and print design work for clients ranging from the Metropolitan Opera and the U.S. Department of Health & Human Services to *Scientific American* and a number of leading universities. He was lead designer for the 1996 Centennial Olympics in Atlanta, and is author of numerous publications including the book, *Inside/Outside: From the Basics to the Practice of Design*.

ERIC GOULD is Vice Provost for Internationalization and a professor of English at the University of Denver, Colorado. He is the author of several books, and his most recent, *The University in a Corporate Culture* (Yale, 2003) won the 2004 Frandson Prize for Literature.

KATHY HAGEDORN was vice president for human resources at Saint Louis University and chief human resources officer for 19 years prior to founding The Hagedorn Institute, a management and human resources consulting company. She received her BA and MS from Saint Louis University and also worked for the National Aeronautics and Space Administration (NASA) and the National Geospacial-Intelligence Agency (NGA).

MICHAEL S. HARRIS is an assistant professor of higher education in the Department of Educational Leadership, Policy, and Technology Studies at the University of Alabama. His research focuses on the policy and organizational implications of market forces on colleges and universities.

DANIEL J. HURLEY is Director of State Relations and Policy Analysis at the American Association of State Colleges and Universities (AASCU), a Washington, DC-based organization whose members consist of some 430 public college and university presidents, chancellors, and system heads. His research and advocacy work addresses issues pertaining to higher education access and affordability, finance, and the link between economic development and higher education. Prior to joining AASCU, he served as the Director of University Relations and Administrative Services for the President's Council, State Universities of Michigan and as an administrative assistant to the president at Ferris State University (Michigan).

KATHLEEN M. (KATE) IMMORDINO is the Manager of Organizational Research and Assessment for the Center for Organizational Development and Leadership at Rutgers, The State University of New Jersey. Prior to joining Rutgers in 2007, she was a career public administrator and Certified Public Manager. She served as a researcher for *Assessing the Impact of the Spellings Commission: The Message, the Messenger, and the Dynamics of Change in Higher Education* (National Association of College and University Business Officers, 2008).

ALBERT JOHNSON is a senior analyst in the Office of the Chief Technology Officer, Corning Incorporated, where he negotiates and manages research contracts, consortia, and other affiliations. Before joining Corning, he was a member of the technical staff of the Software Engineering Institute in Pittsburgh. He earned an MSIA (MBA) from the Tepper School of Business and a BS in management science, both from Carnegie Mellon University, as well as a certificate in management of research, development, and technology-based innovation from the Massachusetts Institute of Technology. He serves on the Board of Directors of the Industrial Research Institute.

JOHN D. KASARDA is the director of the Frank Hawkins Kenan Institute of Private Enterprise and Kenan Professor of Entrepreneurship at the Kenan-Flagler Business School at the University of North Carolina at Chapel Hill. He currently directs the Kauffman Foundation-funded Carolina Entrepreneurial Initiative (CEI) to foster entrepreneurship across the UNC campus. Kasarda has published more than 100 scholarly articles and nine books on entrepreneurship, aviation, and economic development, including co-editing (with Donald L. Sexton) *The State of Art of Entrepreneurship*. He is frequently quoted in *The Wall Street Journal, The New York Times,* and the national and international media on business and economic development issues. Kasarda received his BS and MBA (with distinction) from Cornell University and his PhD from the University of North Carolina at Chapel Hill.

ADRIANNA KEZAR is an associate professor at the University of Southern California. Her research focuses on leadership, change, governance, and organizational theory in higher education. Her most recent books include: *Higher Education for the Public Good* (2005) and *Rethinking the "L" Word in Higher Education: The Revolution of Research on Leadership* (2005). Her latest book, *Redesigning for Collaboration*, will be published by Jossey-Bass in 2009.

LARRY D. LAUER is vice chancellor for marketing and communication, and distinguished professor of strategic communication in the graduate program at the Schieffer School of Journalism, at Texas Christian University in Fort Worth, Texas. He was the founding chairman of The Council for the Advancement and Support of Education's (CASE) Advanced Seminar on Integrated Marketing in Higher Education, and is on the advisory board of the American Council on Education's (ACE) Solutions for America project. He is author of three books: *Communication Power*, a strategy and tactics guide for nonprofit executives, *Competing for Students, Money and Reputation: Marketing the Academy in the 21st Century*, and *Advancing Higher Education in Uncertain Times*.

VICENTE M. LECHUGA is assistant professor of Higher Education in the Department of Educational Administration & Human Resource Development at Texas A&M University. His current research agenda focuses on faculty motivation and work life issues, for-profit/proprietary institutions, and higher education policy. He is the author of *The Changing Landscape of the Academic Profession* (Routledge, 2006), which explores faculty culture at for-profit universities. In 2005, Vicente was awarded (with William G. Tierney) the Excellence in the Academy award from the National Educational Association for an article he coauthored on the changing nature of academic freedom within our current sociopolitical context.

TOM McMAIL has spent 13 years at Microsoft in a variety of roles at MSN and at Microsoft Research. In the External Research group, he focused on programs addressing declining enrollments, gender disparity, and software security. He introduced Tablet PCs to universities and drove experimentation to find best uses of technology to transform education. He was instrumental in introducing both gaming and robotics as change agents for reinvigorating curriculum in computer science, and later was involved in the search for breakthrough new academic research. Today, he manages External Research Programs for North America, and lives in the beautiful rural foothills of the Cascade Mountains.

KAZIMIERZ MUSIAL is assistant professor in the Department of Scandinavian Studies at the University of Gdansk, Poland. He graduated in Scandinavian Studies at Poznan University, Poland, and received his PhD in political science from Humboldt University in Berlin, Germany. His most recent research concerns higher education policy and management, with particular attention to northern Europe. His international research experience includes research scholarships in Denmark, Norway, and numerous shorter research visits in other Nordic countries, as well as work in Germany (research and teaching assistant at Humboldt University from 1997 to 2002 and a research fellowship at Greifswald Institute for Advanced Study from 2002 to 2004).

JUDY NAGY is an associate professor at the Deakin Business School in Australia. She is actively involved in research relating to macro and micro issues in higher education and leads numerous collaborative scholarship in teaching projects. Judy has been recognized for her contributions to teaching and learning with numerous faculty, university, and national teaching excellence awards.

CARY NELSON is Jubilee Professor of Liberal Arts and Sciences and Professor of English at the University of Illinois at Urbana-Champaign. He is also national president of the American Association of University Professors (AAUP). His work and career are the subject of a collection of essays by 20 contributors, *Cary Nelson and the Struggle for the University: Poetry, Politics, and the Profession* (SUNY Press, 2009). His 25 books include *Revolutionary Memory: Recovering the Poetry of the America Left* and *Academic Keywords: A Devil's Dictionary for Higher Education*. For representative essays on modern poetry and on the politics of higher education, a vita, and detailed biography see http://www.cary-nelson.org.

STEVEN D. OLSON is director of the Center for Ethics and Corporate Responsibility in the J. Mack Robinson College of Business at Georgia State University. A well-known consultant and leadership coach, his clients have global corporations, academic institutions, and governmental agencies. Earlier he was Director of Business and Professional Ethics at Emory University's Center for Ethics in Public Policy and the Professions and held appointments in the Goizueta Business School, the School of Medicine, and the Department of Environmental Studies. He holds a PhD from Emory University.

JAMES C. PALMER is professor of higher education at Illinois State University (ISU). Prior to joining the ISU faculty in 1992, he served as acting director of the Center for Community College Education at George Mason University, vice president for communications at the American Association for Community Colleges, and assistant director of the ERIC

Clearinghouse for Community Colleges at UCLA. In 2000, he assumed leadership of the *Grapevine* survey of state tax appropriations for higher education, which is conducted annually by Illinois State University's Center for the Study of Education Policy. *Grapevine* reports going back to fiscal year 1960–61 can be found at http://www.grapevine.ilstu.edu/.

JOSHUA B. POWERS is an associate professor of Higher Education Leadership at Indiana State University and chair of the Department of Educational Leadership, Administration, and Foundations. His research focuses on the commercialization of academic science and factors that explain technology transfer performance differences among universities as well as the ethical and financial implications of academic entrepreneurship. He has published in *The Journal of Business Venturing, Research Policy, The Journal of Higher Education, The Chronicle of Higher Education,* and *Health Affairs* among other outlets. Dr. Powers has also been a visiting faculty researcher at Harvard University/Massachusetts General Hospital and serves on the NSF Advisory Board for the revision of the Academic R&D Survey.

NEAL A. RAISMAN is a researcher, writer, and consultant on retention and academic customer service. He has worked with more than 260 colleges, universities, and career schools in the United States, Canada, and Europe. His books include *The Power of Retention* and *Embrace the Oxymoron,* a guide to customer service for education and related service industries. He served for 36 years as a faculty member, dean, associate provost, president, and chancellor of public, private, and for-profit colleges and universities.

ALAN ROBB is an adjunct professor at Saint Mary's University, Canada. He previously taught at the University of Canterbury, New Zealand, where he served two terms as Head of the Department of Accountancy, Finance & Information Systems and was an elected member of the University Council. Alan has written extensively on company and financial accounting, business ethics, co-operatives and mutuals, and has published in internationally refereed journals including *Abacus, Accounting and Business Research, Australian Economic History Review, Critical Perspectives on Accounting,* and *Higher Education Management*. He is currently on the editorial boards of three international journals. His weblog can be found at http://www.alanrobb.coop.

BRENT D. RUBEN is Professor II (Distinguished Professor) of Communication and Executive Director of the University Center for

Organizational Development and Leadership at Rutgers, The State University of New Jersey. He conducts research, teaches, publishes, and provides professional consultation nationally and internationally in the areas of communication and higher education leadership, assessment, planning, and continuous improvement. He is the author of 40 books and 200 book chapters and articles. His most recent books include *Assessing the Impact of the Spellings Commission: The Message, the Messenger, and the Dynamics of Change in Higher Education* (NACUBO, 2008) and *A Guide to Excellence in Higher Education 2007–08: An Integrated Approach to Assessment, Planning, and Improvement in Colleges and Universities* (NACUBO, 2007).

MARLENE SPRINGER is president emerita of College of Staten Island, The City University of New York. Prior to her appointment as president of CSI in 1994, she was vice chancellor for academic affairs at East Carolina University. Nationally recognized as an education administrator, she has served on the board of directors of the American Council on Education (ACE), chaired the Commission on the Role of Teacher Education of the Association of Teacher Educators, and chaired the College Consortium for International Studies (CCIS). A specialist in 19th-century British literature, she holds a PhD from Indiana University.

WILLIAM G. TIERNEY is a university professor and director of the Center for Higher Education Policy Analysis at the University of Southern California. His most recent work pertains to for-profit colleges and universities, globalization, and access to higher education for low-income youth. He writes frequently on the pressures surrounding academic freedom in the new economy.

J. DOUGLAS TOMA is an associate professor at the Institute of Higher Education at the University of Georgia and Dean of the Franklin Residential College. Toma writes primarily about strategy and management in higher education. His most recent book is *Building Organizational Capacity: Strategic Management and Systems Thinking for Higher Education* (Johns Hopkins, 2009). He is also the author of *Football U: Spectator Sports in the Life of the American University* (Michigan, 2003). Toma earned his PhD in higher education, his MS in history, and his J.D. from the University of Michigan. His BA in public policy and history, with honors, is from Michigan State University.

RACHEL TOOR (AB, Yale University) teaches creative writing in the MFA program of Eastern Washington University in Spokane. She was previously an acquisitions editor at Oxford and Duke University Presses, and worked in undergraduate admissions at Duke before earning an MFA from the University of Montana. She is the author of *Admissions Confidential: An Insider's Account of the Elite College Selection Process, The Pig and I,* and *Personal Record: A Love Affair with Running.* She writes a monthly column for the *Chronicle of Higher Education,* and is a senior writer at *Running Times.* She has published more than 100 essays; her work has appeared in *The LA Times, Inside Higher Ed, Glamour, Reader's Digest, JAMA,* and *Ploughshares.* Her Web site can be found at http://www.racheltoor.com.

SHERRIE TROMP is Associate Director of the University Center for Organizational Development and Leadership at Rutgers, The State University of New Jersey. She is coauthor (with Brent Ruben) of *Strategic Planning in Higher Education: A Guide for Leaders* (NACUBO, 2004) and primary author of *Process Improvement in Higher Education* (Dubuque, IA: Kendall-Hunt, 1997), *The Process Improvement Instructor's Guide,* and *Root Cause Analysis in Higher Education* (Dubuque, IA: Kendall-Hunt, 1997). She received her undergraduate degree in bilingual education from Arizona State University and her master's in cultural anthropology from Rutgers University. During her tenure at Rutgers she has also held the positions of Associate Director of Admissions and University Data Administrator.

SARAH VANSLETTE is assistant professor of Communications at John Carroll University in Cleveland, Ohio. She received her MS and PhD from Purdue University and her BA from Saint Louis University. Her research interests include rhetorical and critical approaches to public relations, employee relations, and international public relations.

ANDREW WESTMORELAND became the 18th president of Samford University on June 1, 2006. Samford University is Alabama's largest privately supported institution of higher learning. Dr. Westmoreland is a graduate of Ouachita Baptist University, having received a bachelor's degree in political science in 1979. He earned a master's degree in political science from the University of Arkansas at Fayetteville, and a doctorate in higher education administration from the University of Arkansas at Little Rock. Prior to coming to Samford, Westmoreland served 8 years as president of Ouachita Baptist University, and on the administrative staff for more than 19 years in various capacities, including Vice President for Development and Executive Vice President. In 2005, his book, *Leading by Design,* was published by Baxter Press.

ROBERT L. WILLIAMS is senior fellow with the Institute for Georgia Environmental Leadership at the University of Georgia. He also serves as lead faculty for the Academic Leadership Institute for the University of Missouri System, and as lead consultant for the National Institutes of Health "Public Trust" project. He consults regularly on leadership and organizational development for higher education, health professions, and national associations. He holds a PhD in Human and Organizational Development from the Fielding Institute, focusing on research of social advocates.

Index

Abstractions, 63
Academic attitude, 53
Academic customer service, 107–24; buying decisions and, 119–22; competition in, role of, 109–11; expectations of, 109, 111–14; factors in, 116–18; history of, 109; principles of, 124; student-centric approach to, 112, 114–19
Academic drift, 99
Academic enterprise, 95–97
Academic-MAPS, 111
Academic marketing, 50
Academic Progress Rate (APR), 204
Academic reputation, 224, 231
Academic support, 204
Academy, 25, 49
Accountability. *See also* Accountability, systems of: corporate, 13–14; hyper, 1; key components of, 13; leadership for, 11–16; stakeholder, 14–16; stakeholder-focused approach to, 11–16; system of, 5
Accountability, systems of, 2–11; for accrediting agencies, 5–6; for alumni/donors, 7–8; for federal/state government, 4–5; for news media, 8–9; for students/parents, 6–7
Accreditation, 5–6, 247–51
Accreditation Board for Engineering and Technology (ABET), 232, 233
Accrediting agencies, 5–6
ACT's, 138, 228
Adaptive thinking, 49
Adidas, 199
Admissions, college, 129–30, 134–37
Advancement, 25, 26–28
Affective return-on-investment, 114
Alexander, Lamar, 3

Allocated funds, 200
All-State Band Camps, 138
Alumni, 7–8
Alumni surveys, 240–42
American Alumni Council (AAC), 27
American Association for Higher Education, 222
American Association of College News Bureaus, 27
American Association of Colleges and Universities (AAC&U), 9, 10, 11
American Association of University Professors, 98, 202
American College Publicity Association, 27
American College Public Relations Association (ACPRA), 27
American Customer Satisfaction Index, 111
American Institutes for Research, 221
American Journalism Review (Stepp), 32
Andrew W. Mellon Foundation, 10
Apple, 60
Application Boot Camp, 134–35
Armed Forces Bowl, 198
Asia, 48
Associated Press, 203
Association of Alumni Secretaries, 27
Association of American Colleges and Universities, 234
Associative return-on-investment, 114
Astin, Alexander (Sandy), 222
Athletics, 10
Atlantic Journal Constitution, 191, 194
Authentic personality, 60

Bardo, John W., 6, 11
Barron's Guide to Colleges, 217, 224
Basic Grants, 162–63
Bates College, 63–64
Berry College, Georgia, 24, 34–35
Beschloss, Michael, 84
Big East, 191, 198
Big Ten, 189, 196, 198
The Big Test (Lemann), 131
Black Student Tours, 140
Boarding schools, 130, 136
Bonnet, William, 31
Bowen, Howard, 169
Bowl Championship Series, 188
Bowl Coalition Series (BCS), 182, 185, 187, 197, 200
Boyer, Ernest, 21–22
Bradley, Bill, 234
Branding, 36–38
Brands: defined, 51; development of, 51; institutional development of, 50–52; sub, 52
Braunstein, Alice, 115–16
Breed, Bobby, 80
Brennan, Joe, 39
Brewster, Kingman, 131
Bright Futures, 168
Bryant, James Conant, 131
Buying decisions, 119–22
Buyout, 203

Callahan, Bill, 202
Callahan, Harry, 64
Campus shootings, 78–79
Campus tours, 140–41
Canada, 225
Cape Cod, 140
Capital expenditures, 204
Capital One Bowl, 197, 198

Carey, Kevin, 3
Carnegie Foundation, 12, 21, 227
CBS, 196, 197
Celeste, Dick, 3
Center for College Affordability and Productivity, 8–9
Center for Creative Photography, 65
Center for Studies in Higher Education, 15
Chauncey, Henry, 131
Cheers (television series), 122–23
Cheers University, 122–24
Chickering, Arthur, 222
Cho, Seung-Hui, 78
The Chosen (Karabel), 131
Chronicle of Higher Education (Boyer/Pulley), 21, 24
Civil Rights Act of 1964, 10
Clark, "Inky," 131
Cliffs Notes, 133
Clinton, Bill, 166, 171
CNN, 81
Cohen, Katherine, 135–36, 137
Cold War, 160
College Board, 133
College Confidential, 142
College Cost Reduction and Access Act, 166–67
College Entrance Examination Board, 160
College Portrait, 11, 14
College preparation. *See* Pre-college preparation
College rankings, 217–53; accreditation and, 247–51; alumni surveys for, 240–42; college-student learning through, measuring, 233–34; employment data statistics and assessing, 236–40; magazine publishing's concerning, role of, 217–22; outcomes-based accreditation and, 232–33; rankings-based accountability through, 251–53; standardized graduation rates and, 234–36; systems for, new, 242–47; undergraduate education surveys for, 222–26
"College Student Experiences Questionnaire," 222
College-student learning assessment, 233–34
College Sustainability Report, 9
College Tours and Educational Trips, 140
College Visits, 140
Collegiate Learning Assessment (CLA), 226–32, 242–43
Collegiate Results Survey (CRS), 241
Columbia University, 130
Columbine High School, 77–78
Comcast Center, 199
Commercialization, 49
Commission on Higher Education, 157, 159–60
Commission on the Future of Higher Education, 2. *See also* Spellings Commission
Communication, 26, 30–31; graphic, 72; media/public, 80–81; signage, 70–71; visual, 57–58
Competition, 23–24, 109–11
Competitive years, 166–69
Concept development, 74–75
Conference USA, 197
Connecticut, 5
Consumerism: challenges of, 101; defined, 90; faculty, role of, 95–96; future of, 100–102; influences of, 90–93, 95–97;

paradigm of, 94; rise of, 97–100; student, 93–95
Contributions, 193–96
Corporate accountability, 13–14
Corporate culture, 22
Cost efficiency, 1
Cotton Bowl, 197
Council for Advancement and Support of Education (CASE), 26, 27–28, 30, 33–34
Council for Aid to Education (CAE), 227
Counseling, pre-college, 130–32, 142–46
Counselors to Higher Education (CHE), 31, 33, 39–40
Crean, Tom, 202
Crick, Francis, 73
Crises, coping with, 77–85; advancements in, 84–85; communication and, media/public, 80–81; learning from, 83–84
The Crisis Years (Beschloss), 84
Cuban Missile Crisis, 84–85
Customer service. *See* Academic customer service

Day schools, 130
Decision-making, 155–56
Deep Springs College, 138
Delta Project on Postsecondary Education Costs, Productivity, and Accountability, 6
Deresiewicz, William, 147
Development, 25
Digital media, 53
Direct institutional transfers, 200
Direct Loan Program, 166
Direct media, 52–53
Discipline, 41; hard, 41; hard advancement, 28; soft, 41

Disneyworld, 140
Disservice, 120
Distance education, 48
Distributions, 196–99
Diversity, 10
Donors, 7–8
Double helix, 73
Duke University, 128, 134

Early Decision, 144
Early years, 160–62
Eastern Michigan University (EMU), 186–87
Eastern Shore, 186
Edgerton, Russ, 222–23, 226
Edinboro University of Pennsylvania, 32
Edison, Thomas, 96
Educational Opportunity Grants, 161
Education Sector, 3
Education Trust, 235
Education Unlimited, 139
Effective Fund-Raising Management (Kelly), 29
Electronic signs, 72
Emory University, 25, 35, 37, 38, 63–64
Emory University Health Care System (EUHCS), 37
Emotional return-on-investment, 113–14
Employment, 9, 236–40
Endowment funds, 8
Endowment income, 200
Engineering Criteria 2000 (EC2000), 232–33
Enrollment management, 98–99
Enrollment officers, 26
Environmental blinders, 29
Episcopacy, 131

Equal Opportunity in Education Act, 10
Equity/efficiency tradeoff, 169–73
ESPN, 196, 197, 198–99
Essay Edge, 141–42
Essays, pre-college, 141–42
Ewell, Peter, 4, 14, 223
Expectations, 109
Expenditures, business, 201–4
External revenue, 200

Faculty, 95–96
Faith, 116–18
Family Education Rights and Privacy Act (FERPA), 237
Federal government, 4–5, 170–71; student aid from, 157, 161
Federalism, 3
Federal loans, 153, 165
Federal regulation, 3
Feigl, Chris, 79
Ferenz, Kirk, 202
Fiesta Bowl, 197
Final Four, 191
Financial aid. *See* Student aid
Financial return-on-investment, 112–13
First impression, 57
First Principles for Linking Funding to Goals and Performance report, 5
Fisher, James, 22
Fitzsimmons, William R., 130
Flattening planet, 2
Florida International, 200
Florida K-20 Education Data Warehouse, 237
Football Bowl Subdivision (FBS), 181–82, 185, 190, 193, 201
Football Championship Subdivision (FCS), 181–82, 185, 186, 192, 200, 201

Forbes magazine, 8, 183, 194, 195–96
Ford Foundation, 27
Formative years, 162–65
Fornell, Cales, 111
Fox News, 81
Franklin, Benjamin, 96
Freeman, R. Edward, 15
Full-time graduate equivalent (FGE), 111
Function, 65
Fund for the Improvement of Post-Secondary Education (FIPSE), 252
Fund-raising: advancement of, 28–29; defined, 29; development of, 25
Fund-raising encroachment, 29

Gaddie, George, 34
Generated revenue, 200
Georgia Tech, 200
G.I. Bill of Rights, 157, 159, 160, 170
Giamatti, Bart, 2
Globalization, 92
Global Reporting Initiative (GRI), 13
GMAC Bowl, 198
Goldberg Variations, 65
Golden, Dan, 142
Golden Gate University, 29–30
Google, 134
Gould, Glen, 65
Government, 48
Grants, 153
Grants-in-aid, 203
Graphic, defined, 57
Graphic communication, 72
Graphic design: effectiveness of, 59; key function of, 57; personality of, capturing,

59–61; problems/solutions concerning, 73–76; professional, 58; purpose of, 58; role of, 76; scope of, 57; signage for, creating, 70–73; visual presentation of, 57–58
Graphic identifiers, 75
Graphic identity system, 37
Graphic standards, 75
Great Depression, 158
Greenbrier Hotel, 27
Greenbrier Report, 27
Guaranteed loans, 164

Hale, Don, 40–41
Hard advancement discipline, 28
Hard discipline, 41
Harvard Admissions Office, 131
Harvard University, 114, 130–31, 135, 156, 189, 221
Harvard Yard, 131
Helicopter parents, 7
Hernandez, Michele, 134–35, 137
Higher Education Act, 4, 154, 161, 162, 170, 171
Higher Education Counts: Accountability Measures for the New Millennium report, 5
Higher Education Research Institute, 222
High Point University, 94
Homeschooling, 136
Hope Scholarship, 168
Hurricane Ivan, 84
Hyperaccountability, defined, 1. See also Accountability

IBM, 228
The Idea of a University (Newman), 21
Identifiers, 37

Illinois State University (ISU), 35, 36
Independent Educational Consultants Association, 136
India, 48
Indianapolis Star (newspaper), 182–83, 185, 194, 195, 199
Indiana University, 222
Information gathering, 74
Inman, Steve, 79–80
Institute of Higher Education, 206, 247
Institutional development of brands, 50–52
Institutional effectiveness, 1
Institutional goals, 25
Institutional identity, 35
Institutional need-based grants, 168
Institutions, 172; student aid from, 157–58
Integrated communication, 52–53
Integrated marketing, 27–28, 49–50
Interactive media, 52–53
Intercollegiate athletics, 179–206; business of, 180; expenditures from, 201–4; revenue-generating programs for, 182–85, 193–99; subsidized programs for, 185–92, 199–200
Internal funds, 200
International Business Machines, 227
International education, 48–49
International trends in marketing, 48–49
Internet, 48
Ivy League, 23, 141, 148, 189, 221

Jackson State University, 225
John Hancock Companies, 67
John Hopkins Center for Talented Youth (CTY), 138, 139, 180

Kabaservice, Geoffrey, 131
Kaplan, Stanley, 132–34
Kaplan Centers, 132
Kaplan Company, 133
Karabel, Jerome, 131
Katopes, Peter, 7
Katzman, John, 135
Keith Moore Associates, 34
Keller, George, 23
Kellogg Commission on the Future of State and Land Grant Universities, 15
Kelly, Kathleen, 29, 39
Kiffin, Monte, 201
Knight Commission, 188, 204
Koch, James, 22
Kramer II, Dennis, 206

Latham, Sarah, 80, 83
Leadership, 11–16, 50
Lemann, Nicholas, 131, 132
Lipman Hearne survey, 39
Lippincott, John, 33
Logos, 51
Logotype, 61–67; creating, 61; defined, 61; designing/redesigning, 62; function of, 61–62; goals of, 66; guidelines for, 66–67; visual identification and use of, importance of, 62–66
Long, Bridget Terry, 96

Maclean's magazine, 225
Madison, James, 185, 199–200
Magazine publishing's, 217–22
Major League Baseball, 184

Malcolm Grear Designers, 60, 62, 69, 74
Management, 29
Management culture, 50
Market forces, 32
Marketing. *See also* Marketing, business practice of: academic, 50; adaptive thinking in, way of, 49; barriers to, 53–55; brands in, 50–52; integrated, 49–50; integrated communication in, 52–53; international trends in, 48–49
Marketing, business practice of, 21–43. *See also* Public relations (PR); advancement of, 26–28; ascendance of, 34–36; branding in, role of, 36–38; competition of, 23–24; debates concerning, 39–41; development of, 28, 31–32; influences of, 24–25; professional development options within, rise of, 33–34; public relations and, decline of, 29–31; rise of, 40; university culture within, importance of, 25–26; *U.S. News* and, role of, 38–39
Marketing first idea, 41
Marketing Higher Education (Topor), 35
Marketing task force, 54
Market trends, 49
Marlins, 184
Mason, George, 191
McDonald's, 133
A Measure of Equity: Women's Progress in Higher Education report, 10
Media communication, 80–81
Media relations specialist, 26

Medical expenses, 204
Messages, 72–73
Meyer, Urban, 202
Mid-American Conference (MAC), 186, 189, 190, 202
Middle East, 48
Middle Income Student Assistance Act, 164
Miles College, 225
Mission creep, 99
Mobile Bowl, 198
Model Admission Essay Development, 141–42
Morrill Act, 157

National Association for College Admission Counseling (NACAC), 28
National Association of Intercollegiate Athletics (NAIA), 182
National Association of State Universities and Land-Grant Colleges (NASULGC), 11, 249
National Basketball Association (NBA), 185
National Center for Academic Transformation, 245
National Center for Higher Education Management Systems, 223
National Center for Public Policy and Higher Education, 4, 6
National Collegiate Athletic Association (NCAA), 10
National Commission on Accountability in Higher Education (NCAHE), 10–11
National Defense Education Act, 160, 161, 171
National Football League (NFL), 185, 202

National Survey of Student Engagement (NSSE), 222–25
NBC, 196
NCAA, 197
Need-based grants, 164–65
New American College, 21–22
Newman, John Henry, 21, 23
New Mexico, 5
News bureau director, 26
News media, 8–9
New York State Regents, 132
New York Times (magazine), 129, 135, 137, 191, 202
New York University, 249
Nike, 199
Noah's Ark, 148
Non-need-based state aid, 168
North Carolina Governor's School, 138
Nunn, Lucien, 138

Obama, Barack, 100
Ohio State University (OSU), 27, 183, 204
Operational principles, 30–31
Orange Bowl, 197
Organizations: first impression of, 57; personality of, capturing (*See* Graphic design); signage for, creating (*See* Graphic design); visual identity of, 68–69
Orlando Sentinel, 197
Outback Bowl, 197, 198
Outcomes-based accreditation, 232–33
Oxbridge Academic Programs, 139

Palmetto Fellows, 168
Papa John's Cardinal Stadium, 199

Parents, 6–7
Partial scholarships, 192
Participatory process, 53–54
Partnerships, 48
Pauling, Linus, 73
PayScale, Inc., 148
Pearl, Bruce, 202, 203
Peer comparison, 235
Pell Grants, 162–63, 167, 170
Pepsi, 199
Perry, Rick, 5
Personality, 59–61; authentic, 60; graphic design and capturing, 59–61; symbolizing (*See* Logotype)
Peterson's guide, 217, 241–42
Pew Charitable Trusts, 222
Peyronel, Anthony C., 32
Pickens, T. Boone, 195
Pittman, Randy, 80, 83
Policy for Accountable Post-Secondary Education, 5
Poole, Philip, 80–81
Pre-college preparation: admissions testing for, 129–30, 134–37; advantages/disadvantages of, 147–50; counseling for, 130–32, 142–46; summer programs for, 137–40
Prepared mind, 73
Prep for Prep, 140, 147
Presbyterian Church USA, 62–63
Presentation, 74–75
Presidential Commission, 160
Princeton Review, 8, 133–34, 142, 217
Princeton University, 8
Private universities, 159
Proactive transparency, 14–15
Production preparation, 75
Production supervision, 75

Productivity, 1
Professional graphic design, 58
Proposals, 74–76
Public affairs, 26, 33
Public Affairs Plan, 25
Public Agenda, 6, 12
Public communication, 80–81
Public funding, 31–32
Public information officer, 26
Publicity, 25
Public relations (PR). *See also* Marketing, business practice of: advancement within, 26–28; components of, 29; conceptualization of, 29; decline of, 29–31; demise of, 40; development of, 28; goals of, 25; public funding and, 31–32
Public Relations Plan, 25
Public relations practice, 27
Public Relations Society of America (PRSA), 29, 31, 33–34
Pulley, John L., 24
Pythagorean Theorem, 227

RAND Corporation, 227
Randolph College, 8
Randsell, Gary, 218
Rankings-based accountability, 251–53
Rapid Revision, 141
RateMyProfessors.com, 9
Rave system, 79–80
Rave Wireless, Inc., 79
Recession, 90–91
Recruitment officers, 26
Remembering Denny (Trillin), 132
Reports of Institutional Effectiveness, 5
Republicans, 164

Responsible Endowments Coalition, 8
Retention, 108, 111
Return-on-investment (ROI), 111–14; affective, 114; associative, 114; defined, 112; emotional, 113–14; financial, 112–13; financial formula for, 112; types of, 112–14
Revenue-generating programs, 182–85, 193–99; sponsorship/royalties, 199; television/distributions, 196–99; tickets/contributions, 193–96
Riesman, David, 96
Rockefeller Institute of Government, 3
Rose Bowl, 197
Royalties, 199

Saban, Nick, 202
Sachs, Goldman, 8
Sales manager, 26
Samford University, 77, 79–84
Sarbanes-Oxley Act, 13
SAT's, 132–34
School shootings, 78–79
Science, technology, engineering, and mathematics (STEM), 239
Self-regulation, 14
Senate, 164, 171
Servicemen's Readjustment Act, 159, 170–71
Shain, William M., 130
Shared governance, 101–2
Shuffling, 120
Shula, Mike, 202
Signage, 70–73
Silos, 52
Smith, John L., 202
Social Security, 237
Soft discipline, 41

Sokolove, Michael, 191
Southern Adventist University, 26
Soviet Union, 160
Spellings Commission, 2–3, 5, 10
Sponsorship, 199
Stakeholder accountability, 14–16
Stakeholder-focused approach, 11–16
Standardized graduation rate, 234–36
Stanford University, 188–89
State Council on Higher Education, 5
State government, 4–5, 171; student aid, role of, 158
State University of New York, 39
Stepp, C. S., 32
Steppingstone Foundation, 140
Stoops, Bob, 202, 203
Strategic dialogue, 15–16
Strategic integration, 15
Strategic stakeholder management, 13
Student aid, 153–75; business/economic models for, importance of, 155–56; education prior to, history of, 156–60; equity/efficiency tradeoff perspectives of, 169–73; federal government and, role of, 157, 161; institutions and, role of, 157–58; private universities and, role of, 159; provisions of, 160–69; state government and, role of, 158
Student consumerism, 93–94; satisfying, 94–95
Student grants. See Student aid
Student loans. See Student aid
Student Right-To-Know Act, 234
Students, 6–7

Sub brands, 52
Sub-entities, 63
Subsidized programs, 185–92, 199–200
Sugar Bowl, 197
Sullivan, William M., 12
Summer programs, 137–40
Summers, John, 147
Summer Search, 140
Sun Belt, 197, 202
Sun Sports, 196
Sustainability, 9
Swift, Jonathan, 142
Symbols. *See* Logotype
Syracuse University, 232–33

Taber, Jane, 29
Talent Identification Program (TIP), 138–39
Tax credits/deductions, 153
Taylor, William H., 26
TCF Bank Stadium, 199
Teacher Education Accreditation Council (TEAC), 233
Television, 196–99
Texas, 4–5
Texas Charter of Higher Education, 5
Texas Higher Education Coordinating Board, 4
Thompson-Boling Arena, 203
Tickets, 193–96
The Times (magazine), 130
Title IX, 10
Top-down authority, 22
Topor, Bob, 35
Transfers, 200
Trillin, Bud, 131–32
Trillin, Calvin, 148
Trust, 116–18
Tuition, 91
Tulane University, 8

Turfing, 120–21
Tutoring, 203–4
Twentieth century corporation, 2
Twigg, Carol, 245–46

Undergraduate education surveys, 222–26
USA Today magazine, 202
U.S. Department of Education, 5, 78, 251, 252
U.S. News, 38–39, 217–21
U.S. News & World Reports magazine, 8, 23, 91, 217, 219–20
U.S. Supreme Court, 10
University culture, 25–26
University grapevine, 81–83
University leadership strategy, 14–16
University of Alabama, 10
University of Alabama at Birmingham (UAB), 191
University of Arizona, 65
University of California, 181
University of Central Florida, 239
University of Chicago, 228
University of Florida, 199, 238–39
University of Kentucky, 190
University of Maryland, 186
University of Massachusetts, 245
University of Michigan, 10, 114, 180, 232
University of Mississippi, 203
University of Montana, 149
University of Montana-Missoula, 94
University of Nebraska at Kearney (UNK), 22, 23, 25, 36
University of Notre Dame, 182, 183–84
University of Oregon, 189

University of Tennessee, 202
University of Texas, 40, 77, 180, 199, 230
University of Wisconsin, 181
University of Wyoming, 181
University relations, 26
Upward Bound and Talent Search program, 161

Value, 246
Vanderbilt University, 69
Virginia, 5
Virginia Tech, 180; massacre, 77–79
Visual communication, 57–58
Visual devices, 60
Visual identification, 62–66
Visual identity, 67–68
Visual presentation, 57–58
Viswanathan, Kaavya, 135–36
Voluntary System of Accountability, 11

Wall Street Journal, 148
Watson, James D., 73
Western Carolina University, 6
Western Kentucky University (WKU), 190, 218
White House, 164
Whitman, Charles, 77
William Morris Agency, 136
Williams College, 27
Wolf Trap Foundation for the Performing Arts, 67
Wordmarks, 36, 64
Work study, 153
World Wide Web (WWW), 12

Yale Alumni, 131
Yale University, 130, 132, 221
Yankees, 184
Yankelovich, Daniel, 15–16

Zemsky, Robert, 97